THE NATURE OF WHITENESS

RACE, ANIMALS, AND NATION IN ZIMBABWE

YUKA SUZUKI

UNIVERSITY OF
WASHINGTON PRESS
Seattle and London

21   20   19   18   17   5   4   3   2   1

UNIVERSITY OF WASHINGTON PRESS
www.washington.edu/uwpress

LIBRARY OF CONGRESS CATALOGING-IN-PUBLICATION DATA
Names: Suzuki, Yuka, author.
Title: The nature of whiteness : race, animals, and nation in Zimbabwe / Yuka Suzuki.
Description: Seattle : University of Washington Press, 2017. |
    Series: Culture, place, and nature
Identifiers: LCCN 2016035956 | ISBN 9780295999531 (hardcover : alk. paper) |
    ISBN 9780295999548 (pbk. : alk. paper)
Subjects: LCSH: Whites—Race identity—Zimbabwe. | Nature conservation—Zimbabwe. |
    Wildlife management—Zimbabwe. | Zimbabwe—Race relations.
Classification: LCC DT2913.E87 .S89 2017 | DDC 305.80906891—dc23
LC record available at https://lccn.loc.gov/2016035956

CONTENTS

FOREWORD

A small but growing body of scholarship across fields such as social or medical history, anthropology of body and ethnicity, and the politics of citizenship has grappled with the cultural politics of race, specifically the idea of whiteness and its community of belonging in locations where white settlement occurred after 1492. To this emergent scholarship Yuka Suzuki offers a powerful and well-crafted addition that approaches the topic through concern with terrain, wild animals, and inhabitation.

A little over a decade ago, Donald Moore, Jake Kosek, and Anand Pandian described what they called landscapes of affect, where "race and nature gain their tangible presence . . . through the play of passionate desires, fears, and faiths."[1] Yuka Suzuki delivers a monograph about such landscapes of affect in Zimbabwe, where race and nature collide as white and back inhabitants reimagine and enact their relations to each other and the wild animals caught between them.

Visible whiteness is the creative analytical category that Suzuki develops and deploys to unpack the logic of white settler relations to land and black Zimbabweans in her brave and lucid study of whiteness, nature conservation, and contested belonging in twenty-first-century southern Africa. How white settlers imagined themselves into a landscape they had only recently entered, through conquest and displacement of natives, is a topic that has received some attention in the Americas and occasionally in antipodean settings such as Australia or New Zealand. Histories of land and struggles around it in Africa have less often paid close attention to the sentiments and attachments of white settlers, who have more easily been rendered as the rulers and expropriators, with a more instrumental and exploitative relation to the land—incapable of ideas of stewardship or care in these foreign territories.

Especially across eastern and southern Africa, transitions following the end of colonial rule included redefining vast areas earlier marked as game reserves and protected forests or wildlife sanctuaries. Intense pressure on land for

African farmers and pastoralists, pushed aside or confined in earlier times, made the transitions explosive. Land invasions, decimation of wild animals, and attacks on settler lifestyles that had been expansive and exclusive in their use of land and forest scarred the land as well as settler-native relations. Settlers asserted their claims and attachments to their land by displaying their intimate familiarity with nature, wildness, and conservation ideas. Beleaguered settlers worked hard, after Zimbabwean independence, to articulate a lived and worked landscape on which they remained—no longer as cattle ranchers, but increasingly as custodians of the wild animals that, like them, faced extinction, as they became objects of fear or desire, identified as bearers of unbridled wild power that was out of place and order in a majority-ruled nation.

Suzuki's sensitive ethnography unveils the predicament of the white settlers without buying into their exculpatory accounts about land that was still very unevenly distributed between them and native Africans in Zimbabwe. Along the way, she provides a fascinating account of human-animal relations and the interplay between the categories of race and nature through which interpersonal relations forged in this embattled landscape are sustained or break down.

As the study of human-animal relations moves more predictably into the purview of multispecies ethnography, Suzuki reminds us of all that remains to be learned by inspecting the natural history of race relations via human relations with wild animals—as food, spectacle, farm companions, and indices of civility and belonging—at times of dramatic social upheaval.

K. Sivaramakrishnan
Yale University

ACKNOWLEDGMENTS

This book would not have been possible without the generosity and kindness of the farmers of Mlilo. I owe my greatest debt to Jon and Marie Van den Akker, whom I can only refer to by pseudonym, but whose encouragement, fiery spirit, and humor sustained me throughout my research in Zimbabwe.

The scholars I met at the University of Zimbabwe offered input that helped shape this project in significant ways. I extend my gratitude to Vupenyu Dzingirai, Elias Madzudzo, Isaac Malasha, Phanuel Mugabe, James Murombedzi, Marshall Murphree, and Nontokozo Nabane for sharing their knowledge and ideas. The Centre for Applied Social Sciences at the University of Zimbabwe, where I was affiliated as a research associate, provided me with institutional support during my fieldwork. The research on which this book is based was funded by the Wenner-Gren Foundation, the Social Science Research Council, the Program in Agrarian Studies at Yale University, and the Yale Center for International and Area Studies.

Over the years, many people have provided commentary on chapters or entire drafts of this book. Others have influenced its development through ongoing conversations and exchanges. I thank Megan Callaghan, Rebecca Cassidy, Jean Comaroff, Carole Crumley, Bill Derman, Michèle Dominy, Omri Elisha, Abou Farman, James Ferguson, Harold Forsythe, Amanda Hammar, Donna Haraway, Rebecca Hardin, Jeff Jurgens, Yoonhee Kang, Jake Kosek, Cory McCruden, Pamela McElwee, Donald Moore, Molly Mullin, Juno Parreñas, Hugh Raffles, Josh Rubin, Blair Rutherford, Jesse Shipley, Anna Tsing, Katja Uusihakala, and Vron Ware.

I am profoundly grateful to Eric Worby, whose work in Zimbabwe and South Africa has been deeply inspiring, and whose brilliant insights and generosity have been absolutely formative in my own thinking and writing. Bill Kelly offered exceptional depth and clarity in broadening my knowledge of the discipline, as well as guidance in my development as an anthropologist. I owe a particular debt to Luise White, whose innovative work on Rhodesian history was eye-opening and made me think about the politics of whiteness in new ways. David Hughes has been an invaluable interlocutor in understanding the dynamics of race and environment in Zimbabwe. My deepest appreciation goes to K. (Shivi) Sivaramakrishnan, whose scholarship was one of the reasons I became a political ecologist, and whose encouragement made the completion of this project possible. Jim Scott and Shivi maintained the vibrant intellectual community in the Program in Agrarian Studies at Yale University that I was fortunate enough to be part of in 2009–10. During that year, Ponciano del Pino, Matt Garcia, Annu Jalais, and Kay Mansfield became close colleagues and co-conspirators on the second floor of 230 Prospect Street.

At the University of Washington Press, I am grateful to the two anonymous readers who provided richly detailed feedback on this manuscript. Their sharp observations and critiques helped me refine and clarify large portions of this book. I especially thank Lorri Hagman, who has been unfailingly supportive throughout this process, and whose expert guidance and kindness have been immeasurable. Sue Carter's superb copyediting also benefited this work significantly.

Excerpts from chapter 4 of this book were originally published in the *Journal of Agrarian Change* and have been reproduced here with permission from John Wiley and Sons. Sections of chapter 5 appeared in the volume *Where the Wild Things Are Now: Domestication Reconsidered*, edited by Molly Mullin and Rebecca Cassidy and published by Berg Press, and have been included with permission from Bloomsbury Publishing Plc. My sincere thanks to Chaz Maviyane-Davies for allowing me to reproduce his beautiful graphic commentaries in this book.

I am fortunate to be surrounded by wonderful colleagues at Bard College. I am particularly indebted to Laura Kunreuther, who read entire drafts of this book multiple times, and whose friendship and wisdom have been my anchor throughout the time we've worked together. Mario Bick, Diana Brown, and Sophia Stamatopoulou-Robbins have all offered rich and constructive insights in relation to my work, and through their warmth and generosity have made the anthropology department a joy to be part of. I am grateful to Myra Armstead, Christian Crouch, Rob Culp, Tabetha Ewing, Drew Thompson, and Wendy Urban-Mead for their collaboration and support, and for impressing upon me the importance of historical thinking.

Last but not least, I owe much to Stephanie Rupp, who has been a steadfast champion since we first met, and whose energy and spirit always give me courage. I dedicate this book to my family: to both of my parents and my younger brother, who have allowed me to follow my own path, even when it took me halfway across the world. To Keizo, who inspires me with his inexhaustible curiosity about animals. And finally, to Vincent, who has been with me on this journey since the very beginning; your constant encouragement has made this project possible.

ABBREVIATIONS

BSAC	British South Africa Company
Campfire	Communal Areas Management Programme for Indigenous Resources
CBNRM	Community-Based Natural Resource Management
CCJPZ	Catholic Commission for Justice and Peace in Zimbabwe
CFU	Commercial Farmers Union
CITES	Convention on International Trade in Endangered Species
DNPWLM	Department of National Parks and Wild Life Management
GKG	Gaza-Kruger-Gonarezhou
GPA	Global Political Agreement
ICA	Intensive Conservation Association
Kaza TFCA	Kavango Zambezi Transfrontier Conservation Area
MDC	Movement for Democratic Change
NGO	Nongovernmental organization
PAC	Problem Animal Control
RF	Rhodesian Front
SPCA	Society for the Prevention of Cruelty to Animals
SVC	Save Valley Conservancy
TTL	Tribal Trust Land
UDI	Unilateral Declaration of Independence
UNWTO	United Nations World Trade Organization
WINDFALL	Wildlife Industries New Developments for All
WPA	Wildlife Producers Association
ZANLA	Zimbabwe African National Liberation Army
ZANU	Zimbabwe African National Union
ZANU-PF	Zimbabwe African National Union–Patriotic Front
ZAPU	Zimbabwe African People's Union
ZIPRA	Zimbabwe People's Revolutionary Army
ZISCO	Zimbabwe Iron and Steel Company
ZNSPCA	Zimbabwean National Society for the Prevention of Cruelty to Animals

THE NATURE
OF WHITENESS

1.1 This image, created by Zimbabwean artist Chaz Maviyane-Davies, was circulated by the opposition party, the Movement for Democratic Change (MDC). The traditional Ndebele proverb in this context serves as a critique of ZANU-PF's racially divisive policies.

1

THE LEOPARD'S BLACK
AND WHITE SPOTS

Ingwe ikhotha amabala ayo amhlophe lamnyama.
The leopard licks all its spots, black and white.

—Ndebele proverb

J N. Pelling, who authored several textbooks and dictionaries for the Ndebele language in the 1970s, classifies the leopard proverb as "behavior which is commendable." According to Pelling, the observation that leopards lick all of their spots, regardless of color, upholds the idea that there should be no favoritism on the basis of race. The idiom gained broad currency in 2000 when it appeared in a collection of images and expressions circulated by Zimbabwe's opposition party, the Movement for Democratic Change (MDC). Through an array of media, MDC activists highlighted the state's many failures, including widespread corruption, the obliteration of a once prosperous economy, and the siphoning of wealth to the ruling party elite at the expense of increasingly impoverished Zimbabweans. They forged dialogue in urban spaces already humming with deep disillusionment: the fiction of democratic nationhood had long since evaporated, and state claims to legitimacy no longer held any validity. At the same time, threats of violence from ruling party supporters were very real. As a result, veiled metaphors and double entendres figured prominently in the opposition campaign. It was in this context that the leopard surfaced as one image of the ideal nation, where favoritism does not exist and basic rights are guaranteed to all, regardless of race, ethnicity, or political affiliation.

To imagine an absence of favoritism in contemporary Zimbabwe is no easy task. When Zimbabwe won its independence in 1980, the newly elected prime minister, Robert Mugabe, appealed for a "new amity between the races, of forgiving and forgetting the past, and building a new nation together."[1] The proposal shocked the country, and white Rhodesians who had seen Mugabe as the devil incarnate until that very morning began to believe that he of all people might represent the best hope for restoring peace and stability to the country.[2] The newly formed government instituted a ten-year period during which the security of white property would be guaranteed by law. Top-ranking ex-combatants were then dispatched across the country to visit white farmers and convince them that they would be genuinely welcome in the new Zimbabwe. The logic for national reconciliation clearly lay in economic necessity, but was framed in terms of moral idealism and cross-racial, cross-ethnic collaboration.

By the 1990s, the official rhetoric had changed. A brilliant orator and strategist, Mugabe transformed his bid to retain power into a war over race. Deftly conjuring specters of colonialism, he labeled white Zimbabweans as "enemies of the state," accused the United Kingdom of neoimperialism, and denounced Morgan Tsvangirai, the opposition party leader, as Tony Blair's "tea boy." The most spectacular outcome of this shift occurred in 2000, as liberation "war veterans" occupied thousands of white commercial farms across the country over the course of a few months.[3] Despite repeated court rulings declaring the invasions constitutionally illegal, they continued to escalate until all but two hundred of the nation's forty-five hundred white commercial farms were occupied. This marked a calculated gamble on the part of the ruling party, the Zimbabwe African National Union–Patriotic Front (ZANU-PF), which was widely understood to be the orchestrator of these invasions. By restoring land to the spotlight, the ruling party deployed the most powerful weapon in its artillery; land ownership, symbolizing centuries of racial domination, offered the most direct and incriminating evidence of disproportionate white privilege. The invasions, according to Mugabe, represented "the last round of the liberation struggle, and the final chance to rid the country of all vestiges of colonialism."[4] A majority of Zimbabweans recognized the land invasions as a ploy to divert attention from the country's real problems, rooted in an economy on the verge of collapse. Nonetheless, the stakes for white farmers were high. Nearly all lost their properties, and dozens were killed through beatings, shootings, and live torchings.

Faced with the extinguishment of a way of life, farmers have fought to retain their place in the country, to assert their individual histories, and to claim the rights of citizenship they feel entitled to after generations of settlement in Africa. This project is by no means a recent undertaking, but one that these Zimbabweans have been consumed by in the three decades since independence. In the context of a rapidly vanishing population, they have drawn on increasingly creative ways through which to redefine and reassert their claims to belonging. The challenge is considerable, for how *does* one make such claims as a former settler bearing the stigma of history? How does one defend a way of life based on visible inequalities in wealth? And finally, what forms of ideological work are necessary to keep intact a worldview that has become increasingly indefensible?

VISIBLE WHITENESS

To many in southern Africa, white farmers represent an archetype of rural conservatism, resolutely loyal to a pre-independence past and stubbornly persevering in the post-independence present. They are objects of suspicion but also romanticization, subject to intense scrutiny while kept at a distance. As the most publicly recognizable white figures, farmers have been seen as representative of entire white populations in southern Africa, collapsing a diversity of subjectivities and experiences. And while farmers themselves are taken as iconic, relatively few studies until recently have explored their worlds from the point of view of the individuals who inhabit them. Much is assumed about farmers as a category, and it is also often assumed that anything more about them is not worth knowing. This book attempts to complicate such assumptions by exploring the inner workings of rural white worlds in Zimbabwe.

In the global context, images of the "white settler" circulate as a series of stereotypes, including monstrous perpetrators of racial oppression, big game hunters, hefty rugby players, or landowners presiding over vast estates catered to by multitudes of servants. The reality, however, is far more complex. Settlers of European descent have long histories in southern Africa, bearing the mark of some of the most brutal forms of domination the world has ever seen. At the same time, this region was the site of tremendous aspiration, promising settlers fortunes and status impossible to attain elsewhere. For most of the immigrants, these dreams and experiments in social engineering were tied to the color of their skin, which they believed entitled them to superior positions in their new society. At the heart of this reinvention, the stakes of being white took on a new urgency and significance. Whiteness became the very basis on which privilege was conferred, and thus its boundaries were carefully policed, and the meaning of whiteness itself took on unequaled weight and power.

Unlike the vast majority of situations where whiteness is "unmarked," white privilege in Africa is glaringly conspicuous.[5] In a setting where whiteness is out of place—both visually and politically, following independence—

racial formations must be attended to explicitly, utilizing conscious, rather than subconscious, forms of articulation. Forced out of its usual concealment, whiteness becomes a matter of visible ideology as opposed to invisible hegemony. People must work hard to keep their identities intact, as well as convince themselves and others of their correctness. Such experiences of whiteness are useful to examine precisely because they bring to the surface processes that are usually hidden. Under a close lens, we can examine how whiteness is constructed and maintained, and its associated privileges justified. Making implicit ideas about racial identity explicit allows us to understand how discourses of whiteness work more generally. At the same time, a close exploration reveals important differences from experiences of whiteness in other parts of the world with distinctive histories, political economies, and social contexts. In both its universalities and specificities, whiteness in Zimbabwe is instructive to think with, particularly when compared with racial dynamics elsewhere.

Race is always fluid, but the rapidly changing postcolonial landscape has a way of telescoping racial transformations in Zimbabwe. Before independence, the distinction between black and white signaled the stark difference between a life of guaranteed comfort and privilege on the one hand, and a life of limited access to inferior education, land, housing, and employment on the other. Not surprisingly, the absolutism of these categories left an indelible mark, as racial constructs after independence continued to be shaped by previous constellations of symbol and meaning. Such effects were perpetuated by the continued presence of whites in the country, who often carried on as if very little had changed at independence. From cashier transactions at the supermarket to the lunch crowd in the tearoom at Meikles, Harare's oldest department store, much of the visible inequality remained unaltered. In this respect, Zimbabwe was by no means exceptional; many postcolonial countries have had to deal with the conundrum of how to deal with non-native settlers after liberation. What did make Zimbabwe unusual, however, was its staggered transition: the initial ten-year period of national reconciliation, offering the protection of white business and property, followed by a gradual intensification of racially charged discourse and policies working against white interests. The terms of reconciliation were dramatically reversed, and white Zimbabweans found themselves scrambling to justify and retain the privileges they once took for granted, even after independence. For whites, the sudden shift of the ground they stood on spelled certain disaster unless they could quickly and persuasively argue their claims to belonging within the country. The particularities of the country's transition accelerated and deepened transformations in racial experience, making whiteness in Zimbabwe an especially interesting case to explore.

Over the course of the past sixteen years, what began as a crisis for the nation with the farm invasions has settled into an impasse, with no long-term resolution in sight. However, the Global Political Agreement (GPA) of Zimbabwe, which established a power-sharing arrangement between the ZANU-PF ruling party and the MDC in 2008, did succeed in introducing greater plurality in political arenas.[6] White politicians now occupy key ministerial positions and parliamentary seats within the government and form part of the top leadership in the opposition party. Many white Zimbabweans have moved away from the label of "white European" in favor of "white African," a term that they would have rejected outright in the years immediately following independence. The public meaning of whiteness in Zimbabwe has shifted perceptibly: although their presence continues to be an uneasy one at best, whites have won a degree of inclusion in the national imaginary in recent years. Thus, the stigma of whiteness is no longer as categorically negative as it was ten years ago.

Yet the issue of race remains an explosive one, always close to the surface. *Black* and *white*, with their contrasting meanings, still remain inseparable from the experience of everyday life in Zimbabwe, and race is a constant raw nerve, exposing the nation's deepest vulnerabilities. These dynamics have transnational reverberations as well. When Julius Malema, former president of the South African National Congress Youth League, popularized the Zulu struggle song "Dubula Ibhunu" (Shoot the Boer) in 2010, he ignited deep racial tensions, inviting both intense support and critique in South Africa.[7] The South African courts subsequently banned the song as a form of hate speech, but Malema was unrepentant and resumed his trademark performance upon his arrival in Zimbabwe on an official visit with Robert Mugabe. This move was meant to signal alliance with a president infamous for mobilizing race as a dividing practice. For Malema, Zimbabwe presented an opportunity in which the state would not only ignore such explicit threats of violence to Afrikaners, but might in fact welcome them. While referencing the anti-apartheid struggle in South Africa, the song registered its intended effect in Zimbabwe. By assigning accountability exclusively to whites, the song obscures the complex dynamics that give rise to the country's situation today. Race serves as a powerful tool, and understanding whiteness as a site of cultural politics is key to understanding nationhood itself in southern Africa.

NATURE AND WHITENESS

Whiteness in Zimbabwe has many dimensions; this work specifically engages the ways in which whiteness is articulated in relation to nature. Both nature and environment play a prominent role in white Zimbabwean identity more broadly, based on founding mythologies of the pioneers who settled the country as well as long-standing traditions of leisure activity outdoors. For white farmers whose livelihoods and identities are embedded within rurality, this engagement with nature runs especially deep. In this account, I focus on such connections by exploring the uses of nature in a small white farming community in western Zimbabwe. I refer to this community by the pseudonym "Mlilo" throughout my work to help conceal its identity. My informants' names and some of their biographical details have been changed as well. Nature has particular significance in this setting because farmers' economic success has always been tied to the environment—whether in battling its forces or aiding in the proliferation of its flora and fauna. For the greater part of the twentieth century, Mlilo was comprised of vast properties of land devoted to cattle ranching. In the late 1970s, however, Mlilo became one of the first sites in the country where farmers pioneered the concept of wildlife "production." Throughout the 1980s, they experimented and refined its practice, achieving a complete transformation through which wildlife came to eclipse cattle as the central form of property and medium of accumulation. Despite this shift, the one constant for farmers remained the environment around which their livelihoods revolved. Saturating both their physical and ideological worlds, nature became the currency through which farmers established their places in the world. The value of this currency only grew as wildlife tourism became the second highest foreign income–generating industry in the country in the 1990s. By the end of the twentieth century, when the political tide turned against them, nature had become the most expedient and powerful resource they had at their disposal.

Based on ethnographic fieldwork in Mlilo, this book argues that projects of whiteness are aligned with projects of nature. This connection has been highlighted by scholars working in other contexts, including adventure economies that revolve around "encountering nature," where identities other than whiteness are not sanctioned (Braun 2003); and "nature loving" students in Indonesia, who position themselves as cosmopolitan, westernized subjects by engaging in environmental conservation efforts (Tsing 2005). This alignment replicates older logics such as those embedded within colonial scientific expeditions, where the act of discovering, hunting, identifying, and naming new species extended the work of empire and reinforced imperial authority over the colonies (Haraway 1989). For individuals like Henry Walter Bates of the Amazon, acquiring a reputation as an intrepid explorer, naturalist, and collector of specimens also secured upward social mobility (Raffles 2003).

Articulations of whiteness in Mlilo thus emerged from long and deep histories of engagements with nature. In contemporary contexts, the most successfully commodified forms of identity linked to the environment are those that make simultaneous claims to indigeneity.[8] The ties between whiteness and nature, on the other hand, are less legible because of the ontological distinction between indigenous people who live *within* nature and those who live outside of it.[9] In Mlilo, however, nature was a continual presence in everyday life, as well as a perpetual counterpoint in everyday discourse. The daily rhythm of farmwork revolved around tracking wildlife species and numbers, maintaining boreholes and water pans, organizing photographic and hunting safaris for clients, and importing new species of animals. Because of its pervasiveness in the physical landscape, moreover, nature also operated as metaphor—as in the example of the leopard proverb referenced at the beginning of this chapter. At other historical moments, nature was equated with adversarial wilderness, against which stories of heroic achievement unfolded. White farmers in Mlilo thus have routinely called upon the environment to naturalize and legitimize their claims to belonging.

In sum, nature has served as an essential vehicle and medium for constructions of whiteness. This work specifically addresses four key sites of practice where this connection has been consistently forged: the metaphorical uses of nature in discourses concerning racial difference, the transformation from cattle to wildlife ranching and the development of the safari industry, conservation as a depoliticizing tool in refiguring white identity, and the reinforcement of social hierarchies through animal-based practices and meanings. Within nature more broadly, wildlife has carried particular significance in Mlilo due to the emphasis that the Zimbabwean state has historically placed on conservation policies, as well as existing global political economies of wildlife tourism. The aforementioned dynamics are specific to Mlilo, and one might argue that articulations of whiteness in this context are distinctly contingent upon place. At the same time, they reflect much larger valences of meaning that fuse white identity, nature knowledge, and environmental consciousness. These ties are clearly amplified in Mlilo, but they make sense only because they capitalize on ideas that already have long-standing cultural resonance.

ENCOUNTERING MLILO

In July 1997, at the very first Rural District Council meeting that I attended, I spied a single white person sitting in the room, surrounded by a sea of black figures. Occupying one end of a table that he shared with two district councilors, he was in his early thirties and wore a jacket with a tear in the back seam that was visible even from a distance. I wondered at first whether he was a development worker, but over the course of the meeting, I came to realize that he was in fact a white district councilor. Up until that point, it had not occurred to me that white Zimbabweans continued to be involved in politics after independence. As recognition dawned, I began to read arrogance in his voice, his language, his gestures, and even the disproportionate amount of speaking time he claimed at the meeting. At one point, he turned around in his seat and smiled at me. Caught off guard, I didn't return his smile, but met his eyes briefly before looking away. At the time, I never would have guessed that this very same person would become a close friend a few years later.

When I think back to my reactions to Riann during our very first encounter, I know that they were informed by a set of assumptions on my part about which "side" I should be positioned on, as well as my lack of basic understanding about the social and political workings of the country. And yet my response was also a direct product of the ways in which most Western scholars have approached the question of white settlers in Africa. As lingering and distasteful reminders of colonialism, settlers constitute the exotic Other, but one not entitled, at least until recently, to serious consideration. Thus, the idea of focusing on white farmers had never crossed my mind when I began working in Zimbabwe. My first trip to the country during the summer of 1997 was as an environmental anthropologist-in-training, and emerged from a desire to see the country that had pioneered sustainable utilization through the Communal Areas Management Programme for Indigenous Resources (Campfire), one of the most renowned Community-Based Natural Resource Management (CBNRM) programs in the world. By the mid-1990s, critiques of the program and its failures were already beginning to appear in publications, but attitudes in general were still full of hope and promise. Campfire was crowned as the definitive solution to community-conservation conflicts, and the instances of failure were understood to be exceptions caused by isolated local circumstances.[10]

After a four-week visit to Hwange National Park, the country's oldest and largest national park, I returned to Harare and the University of Zimbabwe's Centre for Applied Social Sciences, an institute devoted to the study of CBNRM. There, I met a researcher who, upon hearing about my project, declared that there were already too many people working on Campfire. What would be far more interesting, he challenged, would be to study one of the wildlife conservancies that seemed to be cropping up everywhere in the country. He could point them out on a map, but knew nothing about them. Access to these communities was limited because they were privately owned white commercial lands, and this created a significant gap in the knowledge about changing landscapes of conservation in the country. With a mischievous look in his eye, he proposed that because I was neither black nor white, I might have success gaining entry into these conservancies and working with communities on both sides of the fence.

At first, I was taken by surprise, but the idea intrigued me. In particular, I was drawn to the idea of studying the movement of wildlife between commercial and communal areas, as well as the practice of poaching as a "resource crime" with symbolic and material dimensions (Neumann 1998).[11] This was how I found myself, sixteen months later, making the nine-hour drive from Harare to Mlilo, which I knew in name only as a private conservancy that shared boundaries with Hwange National Park. I had in hand the contact details of a prominent family in the community that had been given to me by the director of the Wildlife Producers Association in Harare. As I drove into the Van den Akkers's dirt driveway in a swirl of dust, setting off a profusion of barking dogs, I saw four men in mechanics' jumpsuits bent over the engine of a truck. They unfolded themselves from their work and stood up at the sight of my approaching vehicle. They did not look particularly welcoming as I opened the door and climbed down from my truck. To make matters worse, one of the men looked vaguely familiar, and it dawned on me that he was same person I had pointedly ignored during the council meeting two years earlier. The same realization seemed to hit him at the same moment.

"I remember you. You were at that council meeting last year." Despite my embarrassment, he smiled at me once again. "Well. So you've come back, have you?" The expression on his face was warm, and he did not appear to hold the memory of our first encounter against me.

Riann turned out to be one of three sons in the family, all of whom lived on their father's property; all three were helping him repair the truck engine the first day I turned up in their driveway.[12] Jon and Marie Van den Akker looked doubtful as I sat on their verandah and explained why I wanted to live in the valley. "If you want to study anthropology," Jon suggested helpfully, "you should go down into the communal areas there, and take a look at the real traditional culture. Those are nice people, hey?" He spoke with genuine enthusiasm. His assertion that "real" culture existed elsewhere came from the authority of his own racial positioning, in which whites did the studying, and were never objects of study themselves. Nonetheless, within a half hour of my meeting them for the first time, with astonishing graciousness, Marie and Jon invited me to come and live with them for as long as I planned to stay in the valley.

This was the beginning of my residence in the Mlilo community. Years before, Jon and Marie had constructed a small building beside their main house with two rooms and a bathroom, where they could accommodate clients who came from abroad to hunt with Jon in his days as a professional hunter. Since then, they had built an upscale hunting lodge, which was run at the time by Riann and his wife, and the two rooms to the side of the house were used only for family guests. Marie invited me to stay in one of them, and it was there that I spent the subsequent thirteen months, followed by a two-month visit the next year, living with the family, sharing meals with them, watching the evening news with them, going to monthly church services, and above all, listening to their stories.[13] The household that I became part of was a busy one—Marie and Jon knew many people from different worlds—and there was a constant flow of guests stopping by, grandchildren being dropped off and picked up, family relatives from South Africa who came for monthlong visits, missionaries, biologists, and Peace Corps volunteers who passed through regularly for dinner and a hot shower. Well known for their hospitality, Marie and Jon enjoyed the company, and this in turn opened up a new world for me of people brought together by the intersection of conservation, development, and rural livelihoods.

My research in Mlilo spanned a period of fifteen months, from November 1998 to December 1999, and from July to August of 2001. For the first four months of my fieldwork, I spent extended periods of time in the neighboring communal area of Mfula, which was heavily involved with Campfire. As I continued research in both places, I ran into conflict with the local district councilor, who had been newly elected to the position the previous year. Even though she had grown up in Mfula, where ruling party loyalties were typically not strong, she had spent the past two decades in Harare, and was therefore a staunch member of ZANU-PF. Although my conversations with people focused largely on wildlife policy, she became suspicious of the questions I was asking and began actively discouraging people from talking to me. As I discovered later on, she was also at political odds with the traditional chief, with whom people had come to associate me because of my friendship with his daughter. Thus, my attempt to understand how wildlife worked as a resource for both black and white communities proved trickier than I had anticipated.

Feeling more cautious after extricating myself from this situation, I gradually shifted my focus toward a primary emphasis on wildlife resources within the white farming community. As I spent more time with white farmers, it became evident that the concepts and practices involved in wildlife production were in fact inextricable from ideas about race, identity, and difference. People made continual references to nature based on the assumption that the ability to manage the environment was constitutive of whiteness itself. With this realization, I began listening more closely to farmers' stories to understand how nature was utilized not only physically, but also metaphorically, in establishing belonging.

During my fifteen months in Mlilo, I became acquainted with the two dozen families who lived in the small community and interviewed twenty-two women and twenty-five men, often over the course of multiple conversations. These discussions usually took place over extended lunches or afternoon tea on shady verandahs. Because of the sheer distance between properties in the valley, in some instances I was invited to stay overnight with the families I visited, which gave me a glimpse into the daily workings of their households. I attended monthly gatherings by the local chapters of the Commercial Farmers Union (CFU) and the Intensive Conservation Association (ICA), as well as meetings called by the Department of National Parks and Wild Life Management (DNPWLM) for "stakeholders" in the wildlife industry.[14] Because they were key actors in the tourism industry, I also became acquainted with the wildlife guides, lodge proprietors, safari operators, and administrative staff who worked closely with the farmers in the valley.

Finally, perhaps it is important to note that my own identity often became a subject of interest within these encounters. Most of my informants had a difficult time situating me at the outset; although all of them had encountered Japanese visitors before, I never fit the prototypical image of the Japanese tourist outfitted with high-tech cameras and plenty of cash to spend. My presence was also a constant one, rather than temporary, and people had to contend with my liminality in a context that was usually stratified according to a black and white racial dichotomy. The fact that I had an American accent, however, allowed me to win partial inclusion among farmers in a way that might not otherwise have been possible.

Much has happened since then. When the land invasions first began in February 2000, Mlilo's geographic remoteness, as well as its poor soil, insulated the valley for a limited time from events that were sweeping across the rest of the country. But by the beginning of 2001, groups of war veterans had arrived and laid claim to certain areas; in most cases, farmers were still able to carry on with their lives as long as they kept their distance from the occupied sections of their farms. This tense coexistence continued until the end of October 2002, when, despite mobilizing every legal resource at their disposal, the farmers in the valley were arrested and forcibly evicted from their properties under police surveillance. The outcome was the disbanding of a community that many had called home for over a century. The former population of Mlilo is now dispersed across the world, in Botswana and Tanzania, South Africa and Mozambique, the United States, United Kingdom, and Australia. The Mlilo depicted here is the community I came to know during the main period of my fieldwork: at the very height of its success in the wildlife industry, just before the land invasions changed this landscape forever.

DANGER, WILD ANIMALS

Mlilo lies between Bulawayo and Victoria Falls, along a road that divides the western part of Zimbabwe in half. The landscape extends toward each horizon in an unbroken yellow ocher, with the exception of several weeks each November when the first rains begin to fall, and everything is washed in green. From the 1980s to the early 2000s, hundreds of visitors, including tourists, hunters, and volunteer wild dog researchers, journeyed to this destination each year, drawn to an economy that revolved principally around wildlife. Mlilo presented an isolated haven, where signs painted with "Strictly No Walking; Danger, Wild Animals" heightened the perception of "authentic" wilderness. The local residents who ran the lodges and hunting tours actively cultivated this representation because it fulfilled a certain fantasy of what it means to vacation in Africa. And yet the reality was quite different. Mlilo was deeply embedded in a larger political economy encompassing the area, one that involved the four black communal land areas that shared its borders, and the national park that lay adjacent to its western boundary. Commuter buses stopped by hourly en route to Victoria Falls, and people walked freely back and forth in the "bush" between their communal area homes and the lodges and farmhouses at which they worked. Lion attacks were known to happen, but only rarely, and always as the exception.

1.2 The Mlilo landscape during the winter season. Photograph by author.

The geography of Mlilo is centered around the Bulawayo–Victoria Falls Road as its main artery, from which dozens of rough dirt roads branch off on both sides into individual properties. In width, Mlilo covered an expanse of 80 km ranging from north to south, while lengthwise, the area's 20 km distance was marked on its eastern and western boundaries by veterinary grids.[15] Aside from these grid markers, very little on the surface distinguished the area from its adjacent regions, with one place blending seamlessly into the next. In the neighboring communal areas, this outward continuity quickly melted away to reveal dense land settlements just a couple of kilometers in from the main road. In Mlilo, on the other hand, one had to negotiate 15 to 20 km of rough roads often accessible only by 4x4 vehicles to reach the first house. The properties themselves were startlingly vast, typically ranging from thirty to sixty thousand acres in surface area, a scale difficult to imagine unless one has seen it firsthand.

On these properties, slender trees reigned over the landscape, punctuated by occasional water pans, vleis, and stretches of grassland.[16] The tranquility was broken only by fleeting glimpses of zebra, sable antelope, and giraffes, and this illusion of emptiness made wildlife ranching particularly vulnerable to being deemed a less legitimate form of land use in the 1990s.[17] Farmers who surveyed their properties on a daily basis measured water levels in the pans religiously, checked on the growth of buffalo grass, and deciphered spoor to determine amounts of wildlife traffic on different sections of their farms. Their lands spanned across such immense spaces that it was often impossible, even by vehicle, to cover a whole property in a single day. Taking me to a hilly outcrop on one boundary of his property, one farmer declared, "Everything from here to that river belongs to me," accompanied by a generous sweep of his arm across the landscape. Such statements, which were not uncommon, always revealed a comfortable entitlement and conveyed belief in the right of ownership, without reference to the stark contrast between these lands and the crowded communal areas that surrounded them.

The success of Mlilo's economy revolved around wildlife, and its appeal as a destination relied upon a particular fantasy of "wild Africa." In the nineteenth century, images of the continent as the world's last wilderness, branded in the Western imagination by the works of Mungo Park, Richard Burton, and David Livingstone, among others, offered the promise of escape from industrial disenchantment.[18] The longing for a lost Eden propelled an age of African exploration and fused the dream of a place of untouched and exquisite yet savage beauty, with the idea of a land resplendent with material resources.[19] This "Edenic myth complex" (Neumann 1998:18), moreover, continues to cast its spell in the present, taking contemporary form as "the darkest desires of the tourist imaginary" (Bruner 2001:886). In his discussion of the relationship between colonial taxidermy and recent practices of photography, James Ryan suggests that "hunting with a camera," just like hunting with a rifle, is "implicated in broader movements to create and preserve a vision of African nature as a timeless domain for white European and American 'men'" (2000:218).[20] As in other areas of the world where species tourism has blossomed, the success of the wildlife industry in Mlilo depended on the ability to re-create this vision to convincing effect.

By the 1990s, the tourism economy consisted of two dimensions: photographic safaris and hunting safaris. The luxury bush camps and lodges in Mlilo catered to foreign tourists drawn to the prospect of rustic accommodation, often in tents or small rondavels with no electricity. Armed with guidebooks, video cameras, and binoculars, these visitors spent their days on "game drives" within Hwange National Park and the Mlilo Conservancy.[21] These camps charged exorbitant rates that placed them firmly beyond the budgets of many Americans and Europeans; however, the main source of profit in Mlilo came from the hunting side of the industry.[22] Safari companies owned and operated by farmers serviced an extremely wealthy clientele from the United States, Australia, Germany, India, and Japan, among many other countries. Clients were required to have advanced experience in shooting as well as the physical endurance to withstand hunts ranging from ten days to three weeks. During this time, people typically paid a flat rate of US$1,500 or more per day for the hunt, which included the services of trackers, 4x4 vehicles, a professional hunter, and sometimes a videographer. When a client successfully shot an animal, trophy fees ranged from US$800 for smaller species, such as impala and warthogs, to US$20,000 or more for elephants, leopards, and lions.[23] The two types of safaris—photographic and hunting—occasionally came into conflict, for the last thing an individual on a game drive wanted to see was an animal fleeing from hunters in pursuit. Despite the subtle parallels between hunting and photographic tourism, the two forms of engagement remained distinct and oppositional in the minds of their participants, who approached nature consumption from very different perspectives. The properties of Mlilo, however, were usually large enough to avoid direct confrontations as long as hunters and wildlife guides coordinated beforehand to avoid overlap between their respective parties.

In recent years, similar wildlife industries have developed in places such as Texas, where ranches import exotic species from Asia and Africa for the purpose of sport hunting. Most of the clients are doctors, lawyers, and businessmen who lack the time, and sometimes the necessary skill, to go on a "true" safari (Bilger 2001). In Texas, they can fly in for a single day or weekend and depart with just the trophy heads, while the game meat is donated to organizations such as "Hunters for the Hungry." The appeal here clearly lies in the expediency of hunting exotic animals in convenient places. In contrast, the thick, glossy brochures of safari companies in Mlilo drew heavily on the mythology of legendary "Great White Hunters" (Cartmill 1993), invoking expeditions undertaken by Frederick Courteney Selous in the very same locations and liberally quoting from passages of his diary that extol the region's beauty.[24] In short, these companies sold a packaged fantasy of "*in situ* species tourism" (Desmond 1999) that remains impossible to replicate anywhere else in the world. The prosperity of Mlilo's economy depended on the ability to convince tourists of the unassailable authenticity of its natural wild setting.

In similar ways, the social landscape of Mlilo mirrored the experience of stepping back into time. At first, the dynamics of the community were difficult to pin down simply because people literally were hard to find. With most families living in the center of their properties rather than along boundaries adjacent to the main road, people bumped into each other infrequently, and social gatherings were rare. Days and weeks went by when people saw only family members who lived on the same ranch; farmers were generally located at least forty-five minutes away from the community's tiny post office, and would come in only once a week to collect their mail. When asked the approximate population of Mlilo, farmers typically replied, "About one hundred, more or less." The question was received, however, with the implicit assumption that one was referring to whites, when in reality, the black workers and their families who also lived on these properties easily doubled the total population of the community.[25] Their residence remained more tenuous as old workers left and others were hired according to the seasonality of farmwork.

The creation of new lodges and safari outfits always spurred a flurry of employment, drawing from the outlying communal areas as ready sources of inexpensive, nonskilled labor. In the domestic household, each family typically had at least two workers who took orders from the "madam" of the family and did the cooking, cleaning, laundry, and child care.[26] Along equally gendered lines, the male head of the family, or *baas*, was usually surrounded by an entourage of four or five male workers who assisted him in the workshop repairing vehicles and engines and accompanied him on routine rounds on the property for the maintenance of boreholes and fences.[27] In addition, each family also employed a number of individuals who formed anti-poaching units that returned to the "main house" once or twice a month to report their findings.[28] Workers therefore had a pervasive presence in Mlilo, but in the eyes of the people who employed them, they were publicly invisible as formal members of the community. After spending time in this community, however, I found it difficult to imagine white farmers' lives without these workers in constant attendance.[29]

In the 1990s, what was envisioned as the core community of Mlilo revolved around the two dozen white Zimbabwean families who owned land in the area. While a few were relative newcomers to the region, most of these families had resided in Mlilo for over fifty years, some dating from as far back as the early 1900s.[30] In addition to these landowners, a surprising number of white individuals had moved into the area since its turn to a wildlife-based economy. These included entrepreneurs who leased land from farmers and set up their own lodges and bush camps; professional hunters who purchased hunting concessions and brought their clients in search of trophy animals; and young people who relocated from as far away as South Africa to work in various capacities in the wildlife business.[31] Some of these new residents were urbanites who professed a love for the bush, and others came simply to tap into the latest cash gold mine, represented by the tourism industry.[32]

In the majority of contexts, the public face of Mlilo revolved around men, with women operating primarily in the domestic realm, reflective of the conservativism of rural white Zimbabwean society. The political domain, consisting of monthly meetings of the Commercial Farmers Union (CFU) and the Intensive Conservation Association (ICA), was administered almost exclusively by men, who sat through long meetings while smoking incessantly. Women focused their energies on serving as unofficial secretaries for family-run businesses, homeschooling younger children, and driving older children to and from boarding schools in Bulawayo. As was true in Jon and Marie's family, the majority of children chose to remain on the farm after completing their educations, building separate houses and dividing up the businesses established by their parents, which often led to tensions within the family.[33] Surprisingly, many people met their spouses abroad in countries such as South Africa, Britain, and Australia, and brought them back to Mlilo to create new lives there. Aside from bypassing the problem of an ever diminishing pool of single white Zimbabweans, this represented a strategic move for people who hoped to retain open doors in friendlier countries given the political instability in Zimbabwe since 1990. During the crisis of land invasions and illegal occupations, the first step in evacuation for many families was for women to move back to their home countries with their young children, leaving their husbands behind to defend their farms. When the final round of evictions occurred in 2002, the remaining residents were almost all men and women in their sixties, seventies, and eighties, for whom the idea of voluntarily leaving their lands was unthinkable.

RETHINKING WHITENESS

In academic circles, whiteness became an object of inquiry later than other racial identities, as the unmarked center against which other "peripheral" identities were measured. It was only in the 1990s that the field began to expand significantly, focusing first on the United States and Europe, and gradually moving into transnational, diasporic contexts. While studies of whiteness have diverged along a number of different trajectories, they return to a set of consistent themes and questions. Some scholars have explored the symbolic meanings of whiteness and how these meanings shape relations of power both nationally and globally. Others have focused on ontological questions of "being white" in societies where everyday experiences and conditions are lived through race (Rasmussen et al. 2001:3). At the same time, much effort has been devoted to understanding historical processes and emergent forms of racial stratification, and how such hierarchies are maintained and reinforced through practice.

Consequently, whiteness has been explored in an assortment of contexts, ranging from indigenous dispossession and the making of whiteness in Australia (Moreton-Robinson et al. 2008), to the workings of identity in an urban minority white high school in California (Perry 2003), to ideas about European femininity and morality in the Dutch Indies (Stoler 2002), and to the phenomenon of young Japanese women who fetishize white men and seek out transnational romances (Kelsky 2001).[34] All of these works suggest that definitions of whiteness are fluid and context specific. Because experiences of whiteness differ substantially according to place, close analysis of "localized whitenesses" (Frankenberg 1999) becomes key to understanding differences in meaning and practice. Given the importance of how race is experienced locally, my work is particularly inspired by studies of whiteness that emphasize the narrative form. Scholars such as Kathleen Blee (1991), who interviewed women active in the Ku Klux Klan in the 1920s and '30s, have been helpful in elucidating how supremacist identities are articulated and internalized by members of a society. Other works privilege individual voices while experimenting with expository techniques, such as *Heart of Whiteness*, in which Goodwin and Schiff (1995) present lengthy transcripts of conversations between Afrikaners debating the role of tradition and history within their culture. In his examination of racial dynamics in Detroit, John Hartigan (1999) focuses on what he terms the "cultural poetics of race" to trace how whites come to be categorized as "hillbillies," "racists," and "gentrifiers" according to socioeconomic class. In each of the studies above, narrative constitutes a key analytic tool, providing insight into experiences of race as both an individualized and collective process.

In southern Africa, the number of autobiographies and memoirs written by individuals of European descent has expanded exponentially over the past fifteen years, especially after the popular success of authors such as Alexandra Fuller and Peter Godwin.[35] Saturated with vivid first-person narrative, these works capture the uniqueness of childhood in southern Africa, as well as the authors' struggles to reconcile their inherited worldviews with the transitions that accompanied independence. In the academic literature, the number of works addressing white citizenship, affect, and belonging in contemporary southern Africa has increased markedly in parallel with the proliferation of memoirs. Melissa Steyn (2001), for example, focuses on how white South Africans construct new senses of self within a nation that is now redefining itself as African, challenging many of the underpinnings of white identity in the process. She draws our attention to the fragmentation of whiteness, as different narratives of "what it means to be white [vie] for legitimation in the hearts and minds of white South Africans" (xxxi).

Richard Schroeder (2012) examines the effects of the fall of apartheid on the rest of the continent, tracing the movement of white South Africans who chose to leave their country and migrate northward to Tanzania. Acting primarily as investors and entrepreneurs, whites dramatically altered the social and economic landscapes in their newly adopted country, causing a "whiteness crisis" as Tanzania became reluctant host to the very group of people whose rule they had actively opposed under the apartheid regime. Focusing on a different set of dynamics within the diaspora, Katja Uusihakala (2008) explores how Rhodesian settlers who immigrated to South Africa after independence formed a "community of memory" through collective reminiscences about Rhodesia as homeland. Constructing a "home away from home" entailed constant reflection upon the place of belonging as well as ritual commemorations of the past, as in the centennial celebration of the Pioneer Column's flag raising in Salisbury.

Within much of this literature, the "land," the "wilderness," and the "bush" recur as pervasive themes. Jessica Dubow (2009) takes a visual, phenomenological approach in resituating the experiences of colonial settlers in South Africa who saw an entirely unfamiliar, foreign space and created a position for themselves within this landscape through perception and representation. With a similar emphasis on aesthetics, Jeremy Foster (2008) looks closely at how imaginative appropriations of landscape helped mediate the construction of South African cultural identity. He suggests that cultural interpretations of the terrain enabled the formation of nationhood during the first three decades of the twentieth century, producing representations that were infused with both anxiety and desire. Examining more recent transformations in Zimbabwe, David Hughes's work (2010) focuses on the uses of landscape in the "imaginative project of colonization," illustrating how white farmers engineered the construction of dams and lakes on their properties in what he calls a "hydrology of hope." These physical alterations to the geography were magnified by other practices, such as literary writing, which became an indispensable technique in the "art of belonging." Hughes also describes how certain individuals were able to negotiate terms with war veterans and local politicians for continued residence on their farms even after they were taken over in the land occupations. While his informants are depicted at a particularly vulnerable moment, this book engages whites farmers' reinventions vis-à-vis nature at the height of their success. In western Zimbabwe, moreover, wildlife, rather than water, was the tool of transformation.

WHITES AS CULTURAL OTHER

Until recently, Western scholars have regarded white Zimbabweans as anachronistic and distasteful reminders of colonialism—a burden that had to be tolerated even in the liberational context of independence. With the exception of a few individual white scholars, publishers, and activists, the majority of whites have been summarily ignored or dismissed, even as many foreign academics depended on them in their research. White Zimbabweans therefore constitute what Susan Harding (2000) has termed the "repugnant cultural Other," and as such are perceived as unsympathetic figures. The description of her interviews with Christian fundamentalist preachers resonates with my own experiences among white farmers. As Harding recounts, "I just gripped my chair, and took [Reverend Campbell's] words in straight. I was willfully uncritical as well in the sense that I wanted to understand, as best I could, his words from his point of view, to assume his position, to make his speech mine" (2000:56–57). The phrase "willfully uncritical" captures the position I attempted to adopt, although not always with success.

Not surprisingly, the aspect of white farmers' worldviews that required the most effort in this respect lay in ideas about race and difference. Long after independence, many individuals continued to hold on to the conviction that whites were superior to blacks, as well as all other racial categories. In Mlilo, *munts*—from *umuntu*, meaning "person" in Ndebele, and a common reference used in relation to black Zimbabweans by white farmers—were often cited as thieves who should not be trusted. This belief in black inferiority was manifested through various spheres of practice, including the assumption that black people should always sit in the flatbeds of pickup trucks, even when seats in the passenger cab were empty. In another example of racism in a startling form, one woman in Mlilo who drove a Toyota Land Cruiser—and thus did not have a convenient flatbed on the outside of her vehicle—was known to spray workers up and down with air freshener before she would allow them to get into her car. In this case, the air freshener became the symbolic boundary that made black presence inside her car less "dangerous."

One might then ask, does the desire to know these social worlds, to understand them through native eyes, come to equal a legitimizing of their worldviews? We might find it troubling, or even outright objectionable, to find coherence and logic within such ideas. Narratives by white farmers minimize—and most often occlude altogether—the realities of deep structural inequalities based on race, both past and present. As such, they appear to rest on a fundamentally distorted representation of the world, and their credibility may seem implausible. At the same time, a society that fails to naturalize its own belief systems is virtually unheard of—it is only when we see gross abuses of power built on such worldviews that alarm bells sound. Accentuating this disquietude, moreover, may be the assumption that as people who look familiar and in many ways lead lives similar to our own, white Zimbabweans ought to know better. Understanding how power and privilege are constituted, and how they were reproduced for so long and with such conviction, however, is crucial. The act of writing culture under these circumstances, while inherently fraught, emerges from this intention.

Along similar lines, one might raise the question of complicity in my choice to remain "willfully uncritical" during my fieldwork. Hughes describes his efforts to engage white Zimbabweans as "objects of both criticism and charity" (2010:141), recounting multiple occasions when he voiced his dissent with farmers in individual conversations as well as public gatherings. In contrast, in his ethnography of a small Afrikaner community in South Africa during the 1980s, Vincent Crapanzano describes the inward tension that he experienced as a "moral claustrophobia" in which he was forced to bracket off his outrage and sadness for the sake of objectivity (1985:25). While experiencing similar emotions, I made a conscious decision to refrain from expressing my own viewpoints on race unless explicitly engaged. This was a position that I struggled with throughout my research, but ultimately weighed against the probability that vocalizing my critiques would do little to change the way farmers thought about race and difference. Instead, I chose to set aside my moral judgments on the surface, which, over the long run, allowed moments of admission of uncertainty and contradiction by farmers that might otherwise have been impossible.

This goes to the very heart of the question of what we do as ethnographers. Rather than attempting to change or challenge the way people thought, I chose to search for places where the seamlessness of ideology unraveled, where the things people insisted they did diverged from what they did in practice. This was how I came to realize that white farmers could also be possessed of kindness, generosity, loyalty, and affection for black Zimbabweans. Putting this statement side by side with the examples of racism noted above might seem like an altogether absurd proposition. And yet, ideas about race in this setting were never singular, but always pluralistic, and consistently threaded through with *in*consistency and individual interpretation. This work therefore engages race as an uneven topography of ideology and practice, holding that white farmers cannot be summarily dismissed as simple racists or victims of false consciousness. Instead, their multiple modes of discourse and practice are highlighted, along with the complexities and contradictions that continually surfaced in their articulations of identity, entitlement, and belonging.

Such articulations invoked farmers' positionings vis-à-vis the environment with striking regularity. These entanglements between nature and whiteness were woven through farmers' engagements with wildlife ranching, conservation, animals, and metaphorical language. People used nature to naturalize cultural assumptions about race and highlighted symbolic distinctions by claiming exclusive authority in particular spheres of practice. Moreover, farmers in Mlilo idealized a pre-independence past as opposed to a post-independence catastrophic present at every opportunity. Narratives invoked individual hardship and perseverance to demonstrate that economic wealth was based on merit, rather than privilege derived from racial status. Finally, challenging institutionally racialized postcolonial mythology, blacks and whites in this region were often allied in sentiment and were collusive in their opposition to the state.

It is essential to remember, moreover, that these articulations took shape against the historical backdrop of transition from cattle to wildlife regimes in Mlilo. While wildlife production has been considered one of the most desirable paradigms of land use until recently, its unique configuration also gives rise to tensions within the community, exacerbating old fracture lines and creating new ones. In order to succeed, wildlife ranching relies on a conceptualization of animals as fluid, communal property, which in turn poses conflicts with deeply ingrained ideas of private ownership. Despite this inherent contradiction, this work argues that wildlife production became the predominant form of production in Mlilo in part because it enabled farmers to reinvent their identities. It created the opportunity for people to engage with the global arena through the morally charged field of conservation, and as a result, they were temporarily successful in recrafting themselves as public brokers of environmentalism.

With the turn to wildlife production, animals came to play an ever more visible role in the cultural politics of Mlilo and were routinely called on to mirror and reinforce human social hierarchies. Lions iconicized masculinity and the conquest of nature, and the meaning of African wild dogs was reinvented from detestable vermin to darlings of the conservation movement, paralleling transformations in farmers' own identities. Certain animals were appropriated as political symbols in discourses of nationhood, and other species were criminalized as they transgressed human boundaries and created tensions between black and white farming communities.

The book concludes with an examination of the changes that Zimbabwe has undergone in the past fifteen years, precipitated by the controversial occupation of white commercial farms. These land invasions brought a new dimension to the crisis when thousands of animals in wildlife conservancies were massacred by liberation war vets. In defiance against international protests, President Robert Mugabe's regime turned a blind eye to these events, choosing to disavow conservation as synonymous with Western imperialism. I explore the use of wildlife in this context, examining how its destruction became the physical manifestation of erasing the social and moral universe that white settlers had inscribed in this landscape over the past century.

Faced with the dissolution of their worlds following independence, farmers in Zimbabwe had to contend with their whiteness as a liability and find ways to transcend the stigma of race. This work explores the multiple strategies that farmers employed, principally through their engagements with nature. Through this study, moreover, my aim is to show how cultural worldviews are vigorously defended and reproduced long after the height of their utility, however untenable they may appear from the outside. The challenges of ethnography are heightened when the people we study are implicated at the core of political controversy. Whether called on to validate a group's right to stay, or to align with dominant national narratives and critique a group's history, writing constitutes a form of power, remaking reality through particular modes of representation. What does it mean to take part in the production of white farmers at this particular moment? And what does it mean to write about a community that no longer exists? These questions have lingered with me throughout the time I have spent thinking about white farmers. Anthropology's engagements with the world, typically complex, become much more nebulous under such circumstances. And yet, to see how culture is produced in the most unlikely places, and under the most precarious conditions, is to understand both the possibilities and limits of our imaginations as world-making subjects.

Annexing nature as both adversary and ally, white farmers created a culture riddled with impossible contradictions over the course of the twentieth century, until the land invasions at the beginning of the millennium brought their way of life to an abrupt end. Although they have long since vanished from my fieldsite, the farmers of Mlilo continue to instruct me in projects of nature and whiteness everywhere.

2

A SHORT SETTLER HISTORY

MILILO'S demise in 2002 was one dramatic moment within a far longer history of tumultuous conflict in Zimbabwe. Because it was one of the few places in Africa charted for permanent settlement by the British, the country has been branded with the mark of brutalities that far surpassed normative applications of colonialism. Symbolic and physical boundaries required more maintenance, extractive enterprises demanded ruthless efficiency to support the settler economy, and superior fictions were invented to rationalize colonial rule. This chapter presents a brief history of white settlers, with an emphasis on Matabeleland in western Zimbabwe. From the very first European expeditions into this region, explorers were fascinated with the Ndebele people, establishing a preference that shaped colonial and settler state policy into the twentieth century. Today, white Zimbabweans often express admiration for Ndebele people at the expense of the Shona, who constitute the nation's ethnic majority. During the 1980s, when ethnic genocide swept Matabeleland, many farmers stood by their workers when they were under siege. Memories of this time continue to reverberate and are crucial to understanding the position of white farmers at the end of the millennium.

THE COLONIAL ENCOUNTER

Mzilikazi, the first ruler of the Ndebele nation, entered the colonial imagination in the early nineteenth century, when tales of the absolute authority he commanded over his people achieved fabled proportions.[1] The biographical details of his life became an object of great curiosity for many colonial authors. By the age of twenty-seven, Mzilikazi was a high-ranking general in charge of twenty thousand soldiers unified under the Zulu kingdom, which spanned along the Indian Ocean coast between the Tugela and Pongola Rivers. When his military career with Shaka, the legendary warrior king, came to an abrupt end in 1817 over charges of treason, Mzilikazi and his headmen fled

Zulu territory, taking three hundred of their closest followers with them (Hole 1995). The name "Amandebele" was given to the group by the Sotho local people at this time, a term that can be translated as "outsider," "a person who does not speak the Sesotho language," "those who hide behind their big shields," or "men of the long shields" (Posselt 1935).[2] Over the next two decades, repeated skirmishes with Zulu armies and Boer militias gradually drove Mzilikazi out of the Transvaal and into the north, even as Mzilikazi's own regiments conquered and incorporated large groups of people, increasing the number of his followers to six thousand (Bhebhe 1977). In 1838, the first wave of Ndebele immigrants settled in what subsequently became the province of Matabeleland, followed closely by a second group of settlers in 1840.

It was to this newly appropriated territory that Mzilikazi invited Robert Moffat, whose missionary work in the northern Cape of South Africa had sparked the king's curiosity. Moffat's reports depicted Ndebele society as a world in which violence was pervasive and people were subject to an uncompromisingly despotic regime. His journal entries, on the other hand, complicated this picture by revealing his uneasiness with the powerful influence he seemed to wield over Mzilikazi, who altered many of the practices of his rule under the missionary's urging.[3] Other colonial records were just as inconsistent in their representations of Mzilikazi, expressing grudging admiration for his intrepid leadership along with abhorrence for his totalitarian rule. What was deemed a shockingly draconian system of governance became an indictment against Africans overall: Mzilikazi "was heir to the failings of his race; avarice, duplicity and indifference to human suffering marked his dealings with Natives. . . . It would be unjust to expect his rule to be more enlightened than that of his compeers" (Posselt 1935:191).[4]

When Mzilikazi died in 1868, his successor, Lobengula, strengthened his political standing by creating strategic alliances with whites that allowed missionaries to preach among his people and by granting exploration rights to British prospecting expeditions in search of gold.[5] During this period, the enterprises that Europeans ventured into—whether religious, commercial, taxonomic, or otherwise—relied heavily on the region's rich wildlife resources. The most noticeable profits came from the extraction of ivory, but big game hunting supported imperial advances in less visible yet equally significant ways. Missionaries financed the building of churches by hiring labor in exchange for game meat; similarly, they acquired converts by rewarding their supporters with regular supplies of hippopotamus, buffalo, and antelope meat. Thus, in order to be a successful missionary, one also had to be a successful hunter

(MacKenzie 1988). Both Mzilikazi and Lobengula monitored the movements of white hunters in the region with varying degrees of success; they charged license fees per gun and attempted to confine European routes of entry to the peripheries of their kingdom.[6]

While earlier representations of the Ndebele emphasized elements of "barbarism" and cruelty within the society, paving the way for the spread of Christianity framed as a moral imperative, the second half of the nineteenth century brought a set of contradictory views among explorers, hunters, traders, and scouts, who chose to focus on other aspects of the Ndebele state. In the late 1880s, reports of the British South Africa Company (BSAC) highlighted the majesty of Lobengula and expressed the company's willingness to supply him with large quantities of arms in payment for coveted mining concessions. Such policies did not betray any sense of anxiety over Lobengula's military ambitions or his society's supposed propensity for violence (Summers 1994).

Other commentators raised the critical issue of Ndebele sovereignty in the region rather than focusing on social organization within the nation itself. Frederick Courteney Selous, one of the renowned "Great White Hunters" of the era, traveled extensively in Matabeleland in the mid-1880s and remarked on the constantly shifting landscape of conquest and resistance between the Ndebele and neighboring ethnic groups. Viewing the Shona primarily through their relationship with the Ndebele, Selous's memoirs depict them as a timid, "unremarkable" people living in constant terror of attack by the Ndebele, who were notorious for plundering their villages and stealing their cattle (1894).[7] Despite the strength of conviction behind these statements, the scope of Ndebele sovereignty over their neighbors was clearly overstated.[8] Robin Palmer (1977) speculates that the boundaries of the Ndebele state stretched to the Zambezi River in the northwest, the Hunyani River in the northeast, and the Mtilikwe River in the southeast, instead of the Save, as Europeans and the Ndebele themselves often claimed. Outside of this area, the Ndebele held no political sway; many independent Shona chiefdoms in northern and eastern Mashonaland had in fact never even witnessed a Ndebele raid, much less entered the kingdom's tributary network (Beach 1984).[9]

European visitors to the area, however, clearly found something distinctive and remarkable about the Ndebele that compelled them to identify these people as the region's dominant ethnic group.[10] Echoing colonial policies in other parts of the continent, British administrators in later decades often conferred certain privileges upon ethnic groups whose appearances they considered more appealing (Malkki 1995). In this case, what they perceived to be the tall and slender stature of the Ndebele proved to be more arresting to white observers than the shorter, stockier physiques of their neighbors. Added to this disquieting assessment were the simpler logistics of geography, which dictated that the first European travelers trekking northward from South Africa would have to cross the border into Matabeleland. Once there, the Ndebele more or less controlled their access to the rest of the country.[11] The aura of far-reaching influence thus was not a difficult one to sustain.

The legal fiction of absolute Ndebele sovereignty, moreover, had clearly served the interests of the BSAC. From the British vantage point, any concessions that could be wrested from Lobengula would cover as large an area as possible (Palmer 1977). And equally importantly, the colonial state could lay eventual claim to authority over a vast population once Ndebele rulers had been installed in its administrative structures (Worby 1994). This particular "reality" had in fact become so essential to British schemes that Cecil Rhodes of the BSAC, upon hearing that Selous was about to publicly correct his earlier misapprehensions and reveal the truth about Mashonaland's independence, silenced him with a "gift" of £2,000.[12]

The pragmatism of Rhodes's vision became self-evident in 1888, when Lobengula was persuaded, through the skilled duplicity of BSAC emissaries, to sign a concession that surrendered the right to all metal and mineral resources in his kingdom. Although he repudiated the agreement soon afterward, the damage had been done. On October 29, 1889, the imperial government granted a royal charter to the BSAC that empowered the company to make treaties, promulgate laws, and exploit the territory at its own risk. The Pioneer Column, comprised of farmers, tradesmen, and sons of politically influential families in the Cape Colony, set off toward Mashonaland in June 1890, fortified by steam-powered searchlights to ward off night attacks by the Ndebele (Kennedy 1987; Phimister 1988). In September, they reached their destination and raised an encampment that marked the foundation of Salisbury—later to become Harare. No sooner had this been accomplished than the column disbanded, and its members scattered across the countryside to seek the "Second Rand."[13]

The enchantment of the gold rush in Mashonaland had faded, however, by 1892, by which time the BSAC had exhausted nearly all of its capital, and pioneers were trekking back to South Africa, penniless and defeated.[14] Desperate to raise the value of company stock on the London market, Rhodes turned his hopes to Matabeleland and the new fiction that the country's true riches lay in the west. Very deliberately, he set out to engineer a war: by building on hostilities from a conflict that arose between prospectors and a Ndebele scouting party near Fort Victoria, Rhodes instigated a series of border incidents to appease imperial consciences and lobbied for swift military action against the Ndebele (Phimister 1988). It was through this course of events that the European invasion of Matabeleland began in October 1893. Gaining a critical advantage by virtue of the fact that the majority of the Ndebele army was stationed far away in the north, the BSAC won a sweeping and dramatic victory.[15] The company occupied Bulawayo on November 4, and Lobengula retreated to surrender and death in the Zambezi Valley. His quarter-century reign and the era of the powerful Ndebele state had come to an end.

DREAMS ON THE FRONTIER

The British occupation of Southern Rhodesia was exceptional for the number of Europeans that flocked to the territory during the first decade of colonization.[16] The perception that the region's "pacification" had been achieved by settlers, rather than administrators, created a conviction among pioneers that they had conquered and established rights to the country with a legitimacy that was unparalleled in other parts of the continent. In his analysis of colonial practices of ethnicity in Gokwe, Eric Worby (1994) identifies the use of history and ethnography as "discrete rhetorical resources" in settler discourse. History was invoked to argue that Europeans had rightfully displaced the Ndebele by virtue of conquest in the *same way* that the Ndebele had displaced the Shona five decades before. This argument was employed "to justify settler entitlement to sovereignty according to rules they presumed to share with natives" (Worby 1994:373). A myth was born that white Rhodesians in later decades would work tirelessly to maintain.

The sacrifice of common bloodshed among settlers, moreover, played an essential role in intensifying what they felt was the *unassailability* of their claims to the colony. In March 1896, in protest against the heavy burden of forced labor and taxation, as well as cattle quarantines mandated after an outbreak of rinderpest, the Ndebele mobilized an attack against the British. Shona groups in the north and east followed suit three months later, taking most of the region's white population by surprise.[17] Because company troops had been deployed to crush resistance in Matabeleland, Mashonaland residents were left with no defense and abandoned their farms and stores in a desperate attempt to reach the protection of Salisbury.[18] A total of 372 Europeans died during this period, along with 129 injured, constituting one-tenth of the white population at the time (Palmer 1977). Responding to the crisis, the British government sent a force of eight hundred men to suppress the rebels, and European authority was reestablished in 1897.[19] These uprisings, also called "Chimurenga"—meaning "fight" or "struggle" in Shona—were "the most violent, sustained and highly organized instance of resistance to colonial rule anywhere in Africa" (Palmer 1977:55). For imperial ambitions in the colony, this uprising represented a devastating setback with lingering effects. Histories of Chimurenga—both remembered and popularly imagined—would return to animate the liberation movement seventy years later, fueling an emergent nationalism among blacks.

By the first decade of the twentieth century, the once bright hopes for gold in the region had largely been extinguished. Images of the colony began to shift at this point, highlighting the potential of the vast, "unoccupied" lands themselves rather than minerals that might lie underneath. The promise of an agrarian frontier drew colonists of a very different sort from the fortune hunters that arrived with the Pioneer Column. The new settlers were rural South Africans, in most cases Afrikaners, whose hunger for land propelled them northward with their families, household possessions, and livestock in tow. Martinus Jacobus Martin, a member of Parliament in the Orange Free State, coordinated a trek of 104 Afrikaners in 1894, but only after securing assurances from Rhodes that their cultural differences would be respected (Kennedy 1987).[20] The new communities had very few resources and lived off the land as they struggled to grow maize, and bartered with local villages for food when their crops failed. They lived in poverty, as well as a geographical and social isolation that was reinforced by their adherence to a separate language, religion, and cultural tradition.[21] Tolerated because of their color, these early Afrikaners nonetheless lived in ethnic exile and became the "invisible white men of Rhodesia" (Kennedy 1987:21).

The BSAC grew more deliberate in its promotion of agrarian settlement in 1905 with the creation of the Land Settlement Committee.[22] Company officials traveled far in search of skilled farmers, wooing potential settlers from Sweden, Finland, Italy, the United States, and India; operating emigration offices in London and Glasgow; passing out promotional literature at agricultural events; and offering reduced prices on ship and rail tickets to Southern Rhodesia. Special efforts were devoted, moreover, to the immigration of women in order to counterbalance the predominance of men in frontier society. As wives and mothers, women would bring domesticating and civilizing influences to the frontier, ensuring the reproduction of national culture far from home (Wilson 2003). Propaganda articles advertised fantastic matrimonial prospects: "A girl of very homely appearance will loom a veritable beauty before the excited imagination of the up-country colonist, whilst a girl comely in look and figure will have the male population at her feet."[23] Immigrating as nannies, governesses, maids, and nurses, single women married soon after their arrival and became key actors in establishing a permanent settler colony (Schmidt 1992). In contrast, the government targeted as ideal *male* immigrants small-scale agriculturalists from Britain who would allay the fear that Southern Rhodesia was being overridden by poor white Afrikaner immigrants.[24] Despite its desire to restrict the latter demographic group, the government was virtually powerless to regulate its incoming movement, as many Afrikaner families trekked across the Transvaal and quietly slipped across the country's southern border. Accordingly, the white population multiplied at an unprecedented rate during the first two decades of the twentieth century, expanding from 11,100 in 1901 to 33,800 in 1921 (Palmer 1977).

Throughout this period, Southern Rhodesia cast its spell over poor, unskilled, uneducated whites with the promise of elevated status and wealth. Short in both symbolic and material capital, these settlers felt deeply threatened by African competition and opposed missionary education on the grounds that it would make Africans useless for "pick and shovel work" (Schmidt 1992:9). Although fewer in number, British-born professionals, public school graduates, and younger sons of landed gentry also made their way to Rhodesia to test their fortunes. There, as doctors, teachers, lawyers, engineers, military officers, and colonial administrators, they attained a level of social standing that would have been unimaginable at home: they became the ruling elite of the country. Thus, even in the absence of mineral gold deposits, other forms of wealth—in land, in climate, in inexpensive African labor—lay waiting, untapped. In colonial dreams, Rhodesia beckoned with her beautiful, dark red soil, promising further riches.

RACE AND SEGREGATION

In 1922, the Colonial Office announced that the British government would not be renewing the BSAC's charter; instead, a referendum would be held for the white electorate to choose between joining the Union of South Africa as its fifth province or becoming a self-governing colony. The majority voted for the latter option, effecting a transference of political power into the hands of the white settlers. Concurrent with the consolidation of settler society, this period was characterized—not coincidentally—by the intensification of contradictions within the colonial system that could no longer be ignored. Central among these concerns was the question of African social mobility. Debates originated from a law passed in 1894 proclaiming that "a native may acquire, hold, encumber and dispose of land on the same conditions as a person who is not a native" (Palmer 1977).[25] European farmers abhorred the emergence of a new African landowning class: they objected to the idea of Africans as neighbors, which cut deeply across their racial prejudices, and even more importantly, they feared African competition within commercial markets. These white farmers constituted the most outspoken driving force behind the campaign for segregation.

The term *segregation* was useful precisely because it signified different things to different people (Palmer 1977).[26] Missionaries, for example, supported the movement because they recognized that an open land market would only increase racial animosities toward Africans.[27] Similarly, native commissioners, who had previously encouraged African settlement on commercial farms as a progressive step, now found themselves espousing segregation for what they believed to be the natives' own protection. The confluence of these different logics led to the appointment of the Morris Carter Land Commission in 1925 and the issuance of the Land Apportionment Act in 1930. Under this act, white farming areas were set aside as "European Areas," claiming 49.1 million acres of the best land in the country; the African Reserves were left intact,[28] totaling 21.6 million acres; and another 7.4 million acres was divided into new "Native Purchase Areas" where Africans could buy land.[29] The Land Apportionment Act managed to defuse a highly polarized debate in the settler community: white farmers congratulated themselves for securing zones that were exclusively white, and critics speaking on behalf of African interests were placated with the assurance that blacks were acquiring 7.4 million acres to which they would otherwise have not had access, an area much larger than the allotment to blacks in South Africa (Phimister 1988).[30]

For the whites of Southern Rhodesia, the Land Apportionment Act came to represent "a *Magna Carta*, guaranteeing the preservation of their way of life against encroachment from the black hordes" (Palmer 1977:178). To black Rhodesians, on the other hand, this act was blatantly discriminatory and unjust. In the years that followed, the segregation of land ownership was extended to legitimize social segregation in other arenas. When the Great Depression reduced many white farmers to the verge of bankruptcy in the 1930s, they once again raised the specter of African competition as lying at the heart of their economic problems. They demanded that the government take action to ensure that their lifestyles would be restored to "civilized standards" (Murray 1970). As a result, the government instituted new measures such as the Cattle Levy Act and the Natives Registration Act, which heightened levels of state regulation and intervention in agrarian production.[31] The most politically explosive bill of protective legislation was the Maize Control Act of 1931, which implemented a two-tiered system weighted in favor of European producers.[32] Each of these laws bolstered European production at the direct expense of African farmers, who responded with ingenious countermoves at every turn, but found their options systematically quashed by the government. The events of this period incited growing antagonisms between black farmers, white farmers, and the state, which would only deepen in the decades to follow.

In contrast to the 1930s, the 1940s and '50s marked a time of significant expansion for the Southern Rhodesian economy. Exports of chrome and asbestos increased dramatically during World War II, and the demand for Rhodesian raw materials continued during the postwar boom. White farmers quite happily remained beneficiaries of a government system that sought to guarantee them extraordinarily high living standards.[33] A new infusion of white migration to the country occurred at this time, and the European population more than doubled, from 69,000 in 1941 to 158,000 in 1954 (Herbst 1990). To capture a larger regional market, Southern Rhodesia combined forces with Northern Rhodesia and Nyasaland to form the Central African Federation in 1953. When the latter two countries won their independence in the early 1960s, and became Zambia and Malawi, the federation dissolved, throwing white Rhodesians into a panic. Exacerbating their dilemma was Great Britain's declaration that it would not grant the colony formal independence unless the government expressed willingness to entertain the idea of majority rule. Refusing this proposal outright, the white electorate placed its government in the hands of the Rhodesian Front (RF), and, led by Ian Smith, the nation issued the Unilateral Declaration of Independence (UDI) in 1965.

Rhodesia's defiance brought swift and heavy punishment in the form of global sanctions imposed by the United Nations. Yet the country not only survived during this period, but actually *thrived*. By means of manufacturing domestic substitutes and trading illegally with countries throughout Africa, the Middle East, and Asia, the national economy grew even stronger. This success, however, was shadowed by the feeling among white citizens that their "cowboy government" had invited disaster by mobilizing black nationalists and precipitating a war that the country had little chance of winning (L. White 2003). Black political opposition confronted many obstacles at the beginning of the Smith regime, including restrictions against open meetings in Tribal Trust Lands and a rather passive stance on the part of the general black population, which trusted that the sanctions would eventually bring the minority government to its knees. When the futility of such hopes became clear, the Zimbabwe African People's Union (ZAPU) and the Zimbabwe African National Union (ZANU)[34] began mobilizing military operations based in Zambia and Mozambique.[35] By the early 1970s, ZAPU and ZANU resistance armies had established sophisticated underground networks inside Rhodesia, and the Second Chimurenga swept the country.[36]

By the end of the 1970s, the fourteen-year liberation war, dwindling economic resources, and a mass exodus of whites had taken their toll, leaving the government with no choice but to enter into settlement negotiations with black nationalist leaders.[37] A new constitution, dubbed the Lancaster House Agreement, was drafted in 1979, which mandated transition to black majority rule but also included provisions against the seizure of white property and the assurance that 20 percent of the seats in Parliament would be reserved for white representation (Herbst 1990). In February 1980, as the country held its breath, the interim government tabulated the results of the first national elections: Robert Mugabe was the new prime minister of a newly independent Zimbabwe.

WHITE LIES

In the years preceding independence, one of the most vivid images projected by the country both internally and to the rest of the world was that of a "white Rhodesia." The phrase evoked a series of rigidly defined sentiments and shared understandings, and thus necessarily presupposed the existence of a relatively monolithic community. While perhaps not as differentiated as the white communities of regions such as Canada, Australia, and South Africa, Rhodesian society by the 1970s was by no means ethnically or socially homogeneous. Only a minority of the population could lay claim to a heritage of three generations or more within Rhodesia, and the great majority constituted recent migrants or members of families who had settled in the country only after World War II. Fracture lines remained particularly deep between settlers of English and Afrikaner descent, as a lingering legacy of the Anglo-Boer War in South Africa at the turn of the century. From the collective population, in which diverse interests and backgrounds provided little incentive or basis for a unified community, there emerged an increasing need for the invention of a national loyalty, particularly following UDI.[38] Once the foundations for a collective identification had been laid, it was assumed that other loyalties to specific ethnic, religious, and class categories would no longer take precedence. The obvious bond, of course, was race, and the idea of "Rhodesian-ness" began to take shape.

The ideological basis of Rhodesian-ness was assembled from popularized imaginings of a "Rhodesian way of life" and the construction of myths concerning the national community. These ideas were numerous and diverse in content. They suggested, for example, that Rhodesia never lost the war for independence but was "defeated" at the conference table by high-handed British politicians.[39] An equally strong conviction held that Rhodesia had the most superior race relations in the world, and any racial tension or conflict, like the war itself, was the work of communist-inspired agitators who incited the ignorant, apolitical black population.[40] In addition, by invoking parallels with the glorified Voortrekker experience in South Africa, members of the Rhodesian community constructed themselves as rugged individualists who continued to carry the adventurous spirit of the Pioneer Column. In 1973, the song "Rhodesians Never Die" achieved the status of an unofficial national anthem due to its overwhelming popularity (Godwin and Hancock 1993).[41]

Another element that served to unite white Rhodesian sentiment lay in the strategic labeling of guerrilla movements during the war as "terrorist." The graphic power of the word has given it many political uses in the United States since the events of 9/11. In much the same way, by simple use of the term *terrorist*, Rhodesians were able to summon vivid and frightening images of communists, malcontents, and violent murderers: in short, a dehumanized evil requiring complete annihilation.[42] Guerrilla activities were thus attributed to agitators who made cowardly attacks on local villages and white farmers' wives and children without ever directly confronting the Rhodesian Security Forces. The myth maintained, moreover, that guerrillas worked solely for the sake of personal power or to advance the agendas of Soviet and Chinese communism. Opposition to terrorism could unite all except a handful of Rhodesians, whereas racially based national policies had the potential danger of dividing people into opposed camps.

Through these dynamics, white Rhodesians invented an identity and a tradition just in time for both to become irrelevant. In this case, however, political inviability did not lead to the extinguishment of an ideology; members of the community within both Zimbabwe and its global diaspora continued to cling to the myth of Rhodesia with determination. Reunions assembled to lament the tragic loss of the country and relive past glories. In 1990, for instance, the Rhodesia Association of South Africa commemorated the centennial of the Salisbury flag-raising with a week of celebrations at a resort near the Zimbabwean border. The association named the resort "Rhodesianaland," published a newspaper in honor of the occasion, and gave each road a street name from Salisbury and Bulawayo (Uusihakala 2008).

In the context of the country's rapidly unraveling economy and severe political crisis at the turn of the millennium, the one certainty held by white Zimbabweans was that they should not feel any guilt for the past. Instead, they continued to reinscribe the historical transcript, reenacting their parts as proud defenders of their country against "terrorism" and external economic sanctions. Their consolation lay in the belief that Rhodesians will "never die." Thus, in exploring Rhodesian-ness, we see the power of the social imagination in fusing together diverse groups of people and the haunting grip narratives of group identity continue to have even when their original purpose has long since faded.[43]

RECONCILIATION AND RUPTURE

The end of the fifteen-year liberation war in 1980 brought the moment of greatest challenge to the country yet, when disparate parties assembled for the first time on equal terms and sought to establish common ground for dialogue. It was in this context that the term *reconciliation* appeared everywhere, defined in different ways by different groups. In heated discussions revolving around the politics of national tribute and commemoration, Nathan Shamuyarira, who was appointed minister of information and chairman of the National Monuments Committee, interpreted reconciliation as a means for reconciling Africans to their past, present, and future. In marked contrast, the Rhodesian Front Party asserted that reconciliation required the new government to legitimize the colonial past and let its monuments and statues stand (Kriger 1991). Ruth Weiss (1994) suggests, moreover, that reconciliation applied in many cases to resolution of black-black conflict and resulted in a large number of intermarriages between Shona and Ndebele men and women. Government policies attempted to bridge the old with the new, as in the acceptance of traditional healers (called *n'anga* in Shona) as integral components of the newly created health services system. At the most fundamental level, then, the construction of nationhood in postcolonial Zimbabwe involved a shared vocabulary of interreferential terms such as *reconciliation*. Feeling profoundly unsettled by new voices that emerged at the cost of their own marginalization, many whites referred to peace and reconciliation as "piss and reconciliation." Thus, the very plasticity of these ideas was what made them effective as potential tools of recrimination, instruments of placation, and in the larger sense, a new lens through which to understand the postcolonial nation.

In the months following independence, Zimbabwe's black elite sought to strengthen its political legitimacy and the idea of a shared identity through the public destruction of colonial symbols, followed by replacement with their own heroes as national symbols. In the absence of a common cultural foundation, the state drew on the liberation war as a counterpoint for collective memory in the hope that these symbols would capture the popular imagination. With the highly emotional controversy that ensued, however, the politics of choosing heroes exposed the stark contrast between the rhetoric of "equity, participation, and unity" (Kriger 1991:140) on the one hand and the realities of top-down decision making by the government on the other.

In response to the public outcry by the Rhodesian community at the removal of statues and monuments sacred to the colonial past, the government declared that the memorials were strongly tied to an oppressive history and thus were offensive to African people. Similarly, Rhodesians were prevented from erecting memorials to those of their own community who had died in the war. As political scientist Norma Kriger argues, "To leave all colonial monuments alone or to promote monuments that did not differentiate between those who died fighting for the survival of colonialism and those who fought for liberation would strike at the heart of the new African nation's quest for political legitimacy and a national, African identity" (1992:144).

At the same time, there was a striking lack of consensus on the African side as well. The opposition party, the Zimbabwe African People's Union (ZAPU), consistently sought to undermine ZANU's legitimacy by pointing to the partisan bias in choosing national heroes, and eventually turned its back on the project altogether. This move by the chief opposition group regionally and ethnically based in Matabeleland, the stronghold of the Ndebele people, exposed all at once the untenability of national unity. Fundamentally, the key issue in creating new national symbols lay in debates over who should control the process of establishing a national mythology, what exactly that mythology should be, and whose interests the agendas of elite actors were serving.

While nonviolent contests for nationhood exist in multiple forms, as in the example of national symbols and commemoration, the state at times resorts to the "systematic application of pain" to preserve its vision (Mbembe 2001:103). This application took a particularly extreme form in Matabeleland during the early 1980s, when a regime of terror inflicted profound physical, psychological, and material destruction. The Zimbabwean government's position concerning this period of violence has been largely to withhold knowledge of incidents in the area from both national and global audiences. Great measures were undertaken to censor information; public exposure in the local media was silenced, and the government went so far as to stage a press tour of Matabeleland for foreign journalists to refute international allegations of genocide. As a consequence, any accounts that managed to come to light for over a decade thereafter proved widely divergent and unsubstantiated in their figures and descriptions.[44]

An explanation of the political violence that erupted in Matabeleland requires contextualization of the two main revolutionary parties that opposed the Rhodesian Front during the liberation war. The Zimbabwe African People's Union (ZAPU) split off from the Zimbabwe African National Union (ZANU) in 1963, and the two groups developed very different political cultures. The military wings of these movements called themselves the Zimbabwe People's Revolutionary Army (ZIPRA) and the Zimbabwe National Liberation Army (ZANLA), respectively. ZIPRA was trained by Chinese allies, and ZANLA was trained by Russian military experts. ZANLA used recruitment tactics that involved *pungwe* (community political meetings), with song, dance, and political education, while ZIPRA drew members through its superior arms supplies and intelligence networks. Perhaps the most important distinction, however, lay in each group's geographical associations, with ZANLA relying heavily on Mashonaland for support and ZIPRA basing itself in Matabeleland. While Shona speakers and Ndebele speakers could initially be found in both groups, regional recruitment tactics combined with mutual antagonism between the parties increasingly led to a growing identification between ZAPU and Ndebele speakers.

Once the cease-fire was negotiated in 1979, leaders of both ZANU and ZAPU ordered their guerrilla fighters to turn themselves in to Assembly Points throughout the country, from which they would then be demobilized. This proved difficult, however, as party members who had long led underground political lives feared treachery and refused to come forth (Alexander and McGregor 1996). For those who did turn themselves in, a daunting task awaited—the integration of three armies: ZANLA, ZIPRA, and the Rhodesian Defense Forces, which had fought to defend white supremacy. These groups held deeply entrenched animosities toward one another, and due to their common confinement in close quarters, violent conflicts between these factions arose and led to mass defections of ZIPRA members from the Assembly Points. These fugitives joined the estimated two hundred or so guerrillas who had remained in hiding and formed the first ranks of what the government came to label as "dissidents." Rather than acting on the basis of any strong political motivations, ZIPRA soldiers seemed to feel that they had become the objects of persecution and discrimination by ZANU, which had ascended to ruling status within Zimbabwe's fledgling state.

Those who defected took their weapons with them, and random acts of armed banditry increased in the Matabeleland countryside. These arbitrary acts of violence were at least initially overlooked by much of the rural peasantry, among whom dissidents' status as ex-guerrillas often earned them tacit and sometimes substantial support (Kriger 1992). In February 1982, the government staged the "discovery" of large arms caches within former ZAPU territory, with the ultimate aim of discrediting Joshua Nkomo, the party's leader. ZANU leadership now openly accused ZAPU of planning an armed revolt and proceeded to arrest key figures in the ZIPRA command structure. Immediately upon hearing of these drastic measures, thousands of ZIPRA soldiers who had remained at the Assembly Points fled to join their comrades. During this time, anti-ZAPU and anti-ZIPRA rhetoric within the government escalated, and a shift in semantics took place wherein all armed robberies in Matabeleland were identified as the work of "bandits" or "dissidents" (CCJPZ 1997).

The rapid dissolution of any working relationship between ZANU and ZAPU was accelerated by the South African destabilization policy of the period (Dzimba 1998). Perceiving other southern African countries that began gaining independence in 1975 as an imminent threat to its own regime of white supremacy, South Africa embarked on an increasingly coherent policy to destabilize their internal workings. Within Zimbabwe, South African agents systematically supplied misinformation to the government and orchestrated military attacks that were designed to appear as if members of ZAPU were responsible. To incite further strife, South Africa also backed the creation of Super ZAPU, an elite group of dissidents who were trained in a covert project known as Operation Drama. Supplied with ammunition by South Africa, Super ZAPU was directly responsible for many deaths, including the execution of thirty-three white farmers in southern Matabeleland.

The murders among the Ndebele for which Super ZAPU was responsible often verged on the sensational, employing particularly gruesome methods. In Matobo, an area where dissidents were responsible for the deaths of sixteen missionaries, certain dissidents achieved notorious status and were greatly feared and despised, as many of their given names, such as "Fidel Castro" and "Idi Amin," attest. Within the larger region, any sympathy expressed by local people for dissidents quickly dissipated as these outsiders destroyed property and demanded luxuries such as bread, tea, and meat, as well as free reign with young women. Dissidents as a collective group came to be known as *ozitshwala*, referring to the staple maize porridge, or *Silambe over* (meaning "we are extremely hungry") (Alexander and McGregor 1996:10).

Despite this genuine lack of support for dissidents by civilians in Matabeleland, the government insisted that anyone who provided food for these fugitives, even at gunpoint, would be arrested and detained. To further enable extreme measures on the part of the state, the government enacted the Emergency Powers (Security Forces Indemnity) Regulations, which granted freedom from prosecution for officials supposedly acting in the national interest. This policy effectively denied citizens protection from violence and retaliation by members of security forces (Hodder-Williams 1983). Mugabe then commissioned the creation of the Fifth Brigade, trained under North Korean supervision and comprised exclusively of soldiers drawn from ex-ZANLA ranks. This operation was dubbed "Gukurahundi," a Shona term signifying "the rain which washes away the chaff before the spring rains" (CCJPZ 1997).

The Fifth Brigade rapidly achieved status as the most controversial military unit formed in Zimbabwean history. Within six weeks of its initial deployment, over two thousand civilians had died at the hands of the Fifth Brigade, and many thousands more had been severely injured. While the state continually denied that such atrocities were taking place, the evidence indicates that the Fifth Brigade was trained to target civilians in systematic fashion. The tactics employed defy imagination in their scope of brutality; villagers frequently reported, for example, "being forced to sing songs praising ZANU while dancing on the mass graves of their families and fellow villagers, killed and buried minutes earlier" (CCJPZ 1997:19). In most areas, the Fifth Brigade prevented individuals who were badly injured by their beatings from seeking medical attention; in some places, the brigade went so far as to return the following day in order to execute those in the worst condition.

The Fifth Brigade thus constituted a regime of extreme terror and violence in which innocent local populations were trapped in the middle and suffered brutalities from both sides of the conflict (MacBruce 1992). Mugabe's administration attempted to counter public commentary concerning these horrific measures, even while denying knowledge of them, with the charge that ZAPU, along with the whole Ndebele nation, was guilty of organizing, directing, and supporting the armed dissidents. After nearly five years of sustained violence among the different parties involved, Mugabe and Nkomo reached an agreement over the 1987 Unity Accord, which united ZANU and ZAPU for the first time in over a decade under the single title of the Zimbabwe African National Union–Patriotic Front (ZANU-PF). Four months later, Mugabe announced an amnesty for all dissidents, and Nkomo called for ex-ZIPRA soldiers to lay down their arms. The remaining individuals surrendered almost immediately, but the long years of violence left people distrustful of any possibilities for peace. Moreover, the reign of oppression left a lasting fear of speaking out, as well as a reluctance toward cooperation with the government that endures in the region even today.

Through the course of this prolonged conflict, local people came to see state violence against ZAPU as synonymous with attacks against Ndebele people as a collectivity. The violence of the Fifth Brigade in particular was interpreted through a specifically "tribalist" framework. For example, while rapes committed by dissidents might be understood simply as the abuse of power, rapes on the part of the Fifth Brigade were seen as "a systematic attempt to create a generation of Shona infants" (Alexander and McGregor 1996). In addition, the state had certain vested interests in alluding to past injustices inflicted by the Ndebele in the nineteenth century and "remembered" by the Shona today; this served as a mechanism for justifying Ndebele persecution in the contemporary context.

Most scholars agree that the issues leading to this tragic period lay not in an irreconcilable conflict between the two ethnic groups, but rather in what the state considered to be more fundamentally pressing questions key to its own viability: that is, "Who controls the dissidents?" and "How do you create a single party in Zimbabwe?" These two problems were in fact inextricably intertwined, and Mugabe saw the solution to both dilemmas as lying in the dual stroke of destroying ZAPU and its leader. Ironically, however, this calculated move against the party led to almost entirely counterproductive results because it had the effect of "consolidating a divided province into a sullen antagonism to the dominant party and the majority tribe associated with it" (Hodder-Williams 1983:20). This tension remains deeply embedded today, with the palpable feeling among residents of Matabeleland that they have been shortchanged by Mashonaland, a region they refer to as "Bamba Zonke," or "Takes All." With the dual stroke of dismissing Nkomo and arresting ex-ZIPRA leaders, the government unwittingly created a degree of unified sentiment in Matabeleland that had never existed before.

The three decades since the deployment of the Fifth Brigade have witnessed a radical alteration in the politics of nationhood, as the state appears to have shifted its public focus from ethnicity to the even more volatile domain of race. According to this viewpoint, whites were seen as threatening the nation's purity, and old scores would finally be settled. Thus, through Mugabe's deft political rhetoric, Zimbabwe would emerge as a true champion of postcolonial decolonization among African nations. In contrast to what was understood to be Mugabe's use of the "race card," some observers have questioned the extent to which he was actually in control of the state when the farm occupations began in 2000, speculating instead that they may have been initiated by the war veterans working with security forces. Many others, including the majority of white Zimbabweans, identified the invasions as a political smokescreen engineered by the state to conceal the deeply embedded economic problems that had plagued the country for the preceding two decades. According to this interpretation, by bringing the racial question to the center of debate, the state attempted to unify an increasingly disaggregated and disillusioned black Zimbabwean population. As we see from history, such strategies are not new, but surface time and again in the making of nationhood. The next chapter moves into a closer exploration of how individual white farmers responded to these intensifying pressures through their use of nature, narrative, and nostalgia.

3

BLACK BABOONS AND WHITE RUBBISH TREES

DURING the course of my fieldwork, the most interesting conversations I had with women often occurred at the breakfast table, after the men had hurried off to attend to the farm's latest mechanical problems, and women had a chance to sit back and pour themselves a second cup of tea. White women in rural areas, particularly of the older generation, adopt a deferential position in relation to their husbands, and thus there was a dramatic difference in the way they opened up when men were absent. On one particular morning, Marie Van den Akker, mother of five children and grandmother of twelve, sat across the table from me and sipped her *rooibos* tea meditatively. Her brother and sister-in-law had left that morning after a five-day visit. She expressed regret at their departure, but more than that, she was eager to discuss the real reason for their sudden arrival over the past weekend. Their only son, a forty-year-old man who would soon take over their large dairy business back home in Darwendale, had just announced his love for a younger black woman who worked as an assistant for a neighboring white farmer. She had already moved into his house, bringing her two illegitimate children, and they intended to get married as soon as possible. It was, for all intents and purposes, a fait accompli.

His parents were shocked, and far worse, it quickly became clear that many in the community had known about their son's clandestine liaison, which had been ongoing for the past three years. Feeling disgraced, they fled to the comfort of family members nine hours away, spending the entire duration of their visit at the Van den Akker house engaged in murmured, tearful conferences with Marie and Jon.

Once they left, Marie, who loved any hint of gossip, couldn't wait to relay the cause of her brother and sister-in-law's distress. Time and again she had warned them, she now told me with a certain amount of relish, that they needed to arrange for their son to see more women, with the color white here of course implied. Farming communities were small and isolated, and opportunities to meet "suitable" young women miniscule; the son himself was a shy, rather awkward man who had never had much romantic success. It was the responsibility of parents to ensure that their children's chances of meeting appropriate partners were improved in the face of such odds. No wonder, then, that her middle-aged nephew had turned to the arms of a black woman, who he claimed understood him and made him feel comfortable and at ease as no woman had before. As if sexuality and the objects of one's desires had to be imprinted at an early age before tastes could run dangerously aberrant, Marie blamed her brother and sister-in-law for this unfortunate state of affairs.

Fascinated, I listened to the story despite the all-too-familiar plot distinguishing socially acceptable from unacceptable forms of love. At the time, it had been only a month since I had moved into the household, and the project of educating me in the significance of racial difference was still very much an ongoing one in which the whole family took part. Consequently, this story, too, ended in a moral lesson about race and the careful policing of boundaries. On this occasion, Marie chose a metaphor as her mechanism of explanation. "Just look outside," she gestured toward the window that overlooked the vast expanse of bush beyond the house. "The wildebeest don't mate with the zebra, even though sometimes they graze in the same place. Animals stick to their own kind. That's the way nature is, and that's what nature intended for people, too. Black and white mustn't mix because it's not natural." She placed her hands at opposite ends of the table, drawing attention to the blank expanse in between.

The analogy was one that I had not heard before, and it intrigued me. Marie had invoked a distinctly apolitical metaphor from nature to naturalize her ideas about race, in the process removing agency and culpability from the equation, and neatly sanitizing the racial ideology that formed her worldview. Moreover, she had used animal species that one might imagine as being roughly equal, both herbivores of similar size, thus avoiding an allusion to hierarchy. Wildebeest and zebra keep separate circles not because one is superior and the other inferior, but simply because they are distinct species.[1] The logic of nature neatly reproduces the logic of Marie's social world, resonating with her belief in the fundamental correctness of its rules.

The intertwining of race and nature in this context acts as a strategy of persuasion. While most of us would rightfully question the validity of Marie's conclusions, the seductiveness of such pure and simple, natural, reasoning engenders a moment's hesitation. Through the use of nature, Marie's argument wins a fleeting credibility that would have been categorically denied had she presented her ideological and cultural reasons for segregation. In this way, discourses of race and nature are often mapped onto each other in the exercise of power; the two invoke each other, build on each other, and speak through each other (Moore et al. 2003) to disguise the symbolic and material forces at work. As social theorist Stuart Hall suggests, the "hope of every ideology is to naturalize itself out of History into Nature, and thus to become invisible" (1988:8). Social constructions of race, woven into the basic fabric of ideology, depend on representational strategies of naturalization to achieve their seamlessness. Marie skillfully employed her intuitive understanding of such processes to accredit her worldview with a logic seemingly removed from politics and culture.

The distinctiveness of the wildebeest and zebra metaphor, which I had never heard urban white Zimbabweans use, led me to think about the question of how race is constituted according to local specificity, in the actual microcosms where racial identities are articulated and reproduced. In his study of urban whites living below the poverty line in Detroit, a city that is over 80 percent black, John Hartigan (1999) draws attention to what he calls "the localness of race" in a setting where blackness, rather than whiteness, is dominant. Racial identities in this city, he suggests, are constituted through a distinct "cultural poetics" composed from local stories, concerns, events, and remembered histories. These cultural poetics as they shaped local discourses of race in Mlilo form the focus of this chapter. Collected and polished over generations, the repertoires from which white farmers drew their highly chromatic language, emotions, morals, and humor surrounding the meaning of race seemed inexhaustible.

The following sections explore some of the more common themes and motifs that lend constitutive force to racial identifications in everyday life. The role of narrative takes center stage in this chapter, for there is something distinctive and vital about the stylized way in which farmers tell stories. Within this framework, I examine the question of how whiteness is negotiated in Mlilo, paying particular attention to how distinctions between black and white are drawn, what kinds of "boundary work" are required in dangerous zones of intimacy, and under what conditions transgressions become permissible.[2] The emphasis placed on local cultural poetics does not imply that ideas about race take shape in isolation from discourses and representations occurring at the national and global levels; the following section considers how whiteness has been articulated more broadly across space and time in Zimbabwe.

POST-INDEPENDENCE CHAOS

The narration of chaos always requires as its counterpoint an identifiable state of order, or a sense of how things once were. The myth of "Beautiful Rhodesia" was a common point of beginning for those who told the story of the spiraling descent into decline after Zimbabwe's independence. "Rhodesia was the best country in the world," many of my older informants reminisced. "They [i.e., blacks] had this country handed to them on a silver platter . . . things worked better here than they did anywhere else, and in twenty years, they've taken the country apart, piece by bloody piece." Others assured me that "Rhodesia was a wonderful country—the best in the world. There were no politics, no problems, everyone cooperated with each other. It was day and night when you compare the past with the country today. If you love this country now, you would have loved it much more when it was Rhodesia."

White Rhodesian history is a comparatively brief one, and at any given moment marked by migration into and out of the nation. Many contemporary whites immigrated to the country—whether from South Africa, Britain, or other parts of Europe—to make their fortunes. People who remained in Zimbabwe explained ruefully that the strongest and the weakest left the country following independence: the ones who were smartest had the professional skills to succeed abroad, and at the opposite end of the spectrum were the cowards who abandoned the country, driven by fear.[3] The people who chose to remain admitted that they themselves were foolishly naive; they were the ones who decided to "wait and see," a theme that has characterized their entire existence in the postcolonial decades. But they were also the *brave* ones, and this has been reconfigured to signify people who were truly loyal to Rhodesia and cared enough about what happened to the country to stay put after the tides turned to black majority rule.

The people who remained became consummate narrators of the story of decline into chaos. These stories were driven by incredulity and moral outrage in equal parts, fueled by a force and passion that seemed undiminished by repetition time after time. A dilemma emerged for me as the ethnographer: how could I relate these stories with a sense of balance, remaining aware of the artistic license that the narrative form allowed, while also preserving its integrity as a tool of self-description for the narrator? As anthropologist Vincent Crapanzano observes in the context of South Africa in the early 1980s,

> White South Africans seem always to be talking about their country, its
> problems, and its image abroad. It is their subject. Few, if any, of the "new"

countries of the world have produced as large a self-descriptive language. Self-description is, like rugby, a national pastime. As it occurs among South African whites, it is repetitive, mythic, closed in on itself—a series of variations on a single theme or a small group of related themes. It is morally and politically charged. It gives a frozen and ultimately unrealistic picture of social reality that requires confirmation and reconfirmation through endless repetition. (1985:27)

The same held true for white Zimbabweans twenty years later. The feeling that they were misunderstood by the outside world was universal, and the desire to present counternarratives ran deep—and deeper still as they became ever more vulnerable in the political landscape. These narratives were sophisticated and eloquent works of oratory, and constitute one of the most powerful forms of currency available to white Zimbabweans to this day. At times it was difficult not to fall completely under their spell; on several occasions I witnessed white farmers hold development workers, tourists, and missionaries in thrall, as expressions of polite disbelief among listeners shifted to skepticism, and eventually, reluctant head-nodding as if against their wills. Thus, a well-executed story had the potential to transform its narrator into a forceful contemporary authority, rather than a lingering curiosity from the past.

Like the South Africans Crapanzano describes, white Zimbabweans were constantly engaged in the art of self-description, not only for the benefit of outsiders but also to reaffirm and maintain their own worlds from within. The work of keeping intact a fragile worldview is never-ending, and white Zimbabweans tended to it religiously, for the sake of self-preservation. With physical markers of racial identity quickly disappearing from the national landscape, identity was increasingly lived through an imagined past—the golden age of Rhodesia—and articulated in diametrical contrast to the morally corrupt contemporary state.[4] Stories exposing the government's conspiracies and incompetence were proffered as gleaming jewels of truth and became an important form of currency traded among white Zimbabweans. These stories were exchanged, consumed, and reworked, the best ones destined to enter into white mythology, where they became collective property. The story of a (white) woman who checked into a state hospital in Bulawayo for a routine procedure, only to be dropped on her head by a negligent (black) nurse and end up in a coma, was relayed to me in at least three different versions by individuals who had no personal connections to the patient. People offered such stories with an intensity that I often found exhausting.

"Yuka," Marie's husband, Jon, had a habit of announcing as he settled into his favorite chair on the verandah, "I want to tell you a story." And one story would become four or five stories, one after another, as Jon fiddled with engine parts in need of repair, fingers stained with oil, glancing up occasionally from his work to make sure I was still listening. Within these narratives, many of which I initially would have dismissed outright, I gradually came to find an overpowering persuasion. They had a moral force that somehow managed to eclipse the knowledge that they served a specific agenda. Over time, I found myself increasingly conflicted about how to interpret them. Despite the deconstruction of ethnographic authority that revolutionized the discipline nearly two decades ago, many anthropologists continue to feel pressured to extrapolate the "truth" from the stories that people tell about themselves. Crapanzano (1985) cautions us that people's stories must always be accepted with a grain of salt. Unfortunately, in his case, he may have extrapolated and revealed too much, rendering the return of any anthropologist to the area difficult.[5]

Scholars to whom I presented my work after returning to the United States sometimes asked how white farmers' voices could further our understanding of the role of false consciousness in relation to culture. We can certainly identify a level of false consciousness that operates within these self-descriptions, which work methodically to erase the histories and structures that enable white privilege and entitlement. And yet, at the same time, I resist categorically sweeping these voices into a simple reductionist box, for the concept of false consciousness has utility only up to a certain point. I found instead that among white Zimbabweans, "false" consciousness exists alongside other kinds of equally important consciousness, creating multiple levels of awareness. In both public and private arenas, on the one hand, was the staunch insistence on denying past injustices, oppression, and exploitation under the colonial regime.[6] On the other hand, in the exclusively private domain, many people revealed glimpses of a much deeper, self-reflexive awareness that acknowledged the many privileges they gained through their status as white settlers in Africa.

Marie and Jon's son Riann expressed such thoughts to me one night as we sat drinking coffee under the vast thatched roof of his parents' safari lodge. "You know why I'll never leave here? I may not be a smart man, but there are so many fools here [in Africa] that I know I can be the boss." Such statements were not uncommon. They revealed a startling arrogance, but at the same time, a defensive vulnerability: a moment of self-recognition in which shortcomings in relation to the rest of the world are acknowledged, along with the realization that their lives are perhaps undeservedly privileged by virtue of circumstance. It seems as if underneath the surface lies a "truth" that everyone recognizes, but that all are complicit in keeping at bay through constant reification of a particular worldview. As a consequence, these multiple levels of awareness, as well as the slippages between them, defy simple classification under the rubric of false consciousness. It would seem that "truths" and "falsities" can coexist side by side, not necessarily at odds with one another, but surfacing according to context. This plurality translates into an important tension recurrent throughout white Zimbabwean discourse, ideology, and practice.

MORAL IMAGINARIES AND THE NARRATIVE FORM

In the edited volume *The Making and Unmaking of Whiteness*, one author describes a moment of epiphany when he realizes that the white supremacist he is interviewing bears striking parallels to himself—they both have three children, wives who work as nurses, and similar homes (Rasmussen et al. 2001). A similar epiphany occurs for the author of *Mukiwa*, an autobiographical account of a boy's childhood in Rhodesia that almost all white Zimbabweans read as a rite of passage. Peter Godwin describes his cousin Oliver's visit from Britain in the following way: "At the time I thought Oliver was pretty strange, really eccentric, with his loincloth and Afro and everything. But in his eyes I saw that he thought *we* were the odd ones. And for the first time I got a glimpse of how we appeared to the outside, of just how far we had strayed from our mother culture and mutated into this quite separate people. And I realized that was why my parents would never really consider going home to England, because England wasn't home any more, even to them" (1996:197).

White identity in Rhodesia and subsequently in Zimbabwe is mutually constituted through its exoticization by the rest of the white world. The exotic qualities of white settlers in Africa have been fetishized especially within liberal Western perspectives as the antithesis against which Westerners identify themselves. The Dutch, for example, call Afrikaners the "Baby Dutch," a label that originally came from the comparatively unsophisticated grammar that was adopted into the Afrikaans language from Dutch, with the sometimes strange effect of Afrikaans-speaking adults sounding exactly like young Dutch children. The Baby Dutch are an embarrassment to people from the Netherlands, who are anxious to disassociate themselves from common cultural and historical ties.[7]

By examining white Zimbabweans' narratives closely, we can identify a self-conscious project to highlight their close engagement with the rest of the world. Sometimes they reclaimed their kinship and ties with an imagined "Europe," but just as often people simply sought to demonstrate their knowledge of world politics as educated, informed global citizens. At yet other moments, they deliberately set themselves apart in a process of self-exoticization, especially when claiming a certain exceptionalism for white Rhodesian history and national character. Building on the idea of plurality discussed above, through close attention to these narratives we begin to see that they are not, in fact, wholly self-contained, self-replicating entities, but instead offer pockets of contradiction, accommodation, subtle concession, and even self-doubt. Ideas about race and racism, even when deeply embedded within cultural ideology, occur through dialogues in which boundaries are tested, discriminations are qualified, and statements invite multiple interpretations.

At the same time, however, these momentary spaces of ambiguity must be subtle enough not to upset the effectiveness of the narrative as a whole. Mikhail Bakhtin (1981) suggests that in the construction of a narrative, a moral choice must be made from amid a heteroglossia of linguistic possibilities. This choice enables a formative moment in the emergence of consciousness as the narrator takes up a specific moral orientation. The key significance of these narratives lies in their articulation of a distinctive moral imaginary. Such strategies play an important role in what Sherry Ortner has termed "serious games," a phrase that captures not only the dialogic aspects through which different groups enter into the realities and imaginations of the Other but also "the constant play of power in the games of life, and the fact that, for most people most of the time, a great deal is at stake" (1999:23). And indeed, what could present greater stakes than the question of one's very future in a nation?

HILLBILLIES AND COSMOPOLITANS

One of the most important lines of differentiation within white communities is the construction of rural versus urban identity. As Hartigan argues in regard to American society as a whole, "A comfortable conviction holds sway among middle-class whites that racism is concentrated in the *lower* classes . . . while certainly present in working-class whites, it bubbles up most vigorously from the hearts of poor whites, as allegorized in the cultural figure of 'white trash'" (1999:8). In Briggs, the poorest white neighborhood in Detroit, certain whites are labeled "hillbilly," a term that inscribes a "stigmatized intra-racial distinction," which, in turn, accredits a sense of sophistication to those who impose the label.

Strikingly, many white Zimbabweans in Harare derided the commercial farmers in the western part of the country by using the same term. "Watch out for those hillbillies," several people joked when they heard where I was conducting research. "Those guys are stuck in the nineteenth century." Although such comments were framed humorously, they belied a subtle anxiety among urban whites who were eager to distance themselves from their rural counterparts. They were insistent that white farmers, especially from "backwater" regions of the country like Mlilo, did not represent white Zimbabweans as a whole. The "hillbilly" stereotype indexed the lack of electricity and satellite television among farmers, but more importantly, it invoked an opposition of cultural and intellectual distinctions, not least of which was how one approached the question of race.

Urban white Zimbabweans often presented themselves as cosmopolitan, liberal, and comfortably accepting of the racial integration of the social spaces they occupied, whether at supermarkets and the cinema, or at banks and offices.[8] This self-presentation was in contrast to their view of farmers, whose interactions with black workers were seen to take place in the comparatively private sphere of the farm where there was less accountability. Urban Zimbabweans assume that farmers are more racist, or "racialist," the more common term in Zimbabwe. In July 2002, when a farmer named Philip Bezuidenhout in Odzi ran over one of the "war vets" who blocked his truck, the ruling party rejoiced, for ZANU-PF had long hoped for retaliatory action by farmers that would provide real-life validation of its ideological campaign against whites.[9] Soon afterward, however, it came to light that Bezuidenhout was married to a black woman. This dramatically altered the meaning of the incident, and people were suddenly uncertain about how to interpret it. For the nation, the fact that Bezuidenhout was married to a black woman seemed to automatically nullify the assumption that he was racist—or at least to throw significant doubt on it—and therefore the death must have been a tragic accident after all. ZANU-PF had lost its easy target, especially when Bezuidenhout turned up at court with a black defense lawyer.[10]

The categories of "white" and "black" severely constrain the possibilities of interpretation in cases like this, and fail to allow for the rich, nuanced texture of these particular events. In her analysis of race in contemporary Brazil, Donna Goldstein refutes the common belief that the country's "color-blind erotic democracy" is synonymous with the absence of racism. Brazilians assume, for example, that "white men who prefer dark-skinned women are 'logically' not racist because they sexually desire them" (2003:109). However, as she goes on to demonstrate, the historical objectification of mulatto women as sensuously erotic only serves to reentrench negative racial essentialisms in Brazilian society. The hierarchy of race is therefore reproduced beneath the surface of public ideology, attesting to the existence of multiple modes in racial discourse. The following sections turn back to Mlilo to shed light on the interplay of such modes as they create locally specific understandings of race.

NATURAL LEXICONS

The cultural poetics that white farmers in Mlilo drew upon in constructing race predictably emerged from the lexicon that lay closest at hand. In this world, where tourism had eclipsed all other economic pathways by the 1990s, wildlife constituted the central axis around which people's lives revolved. Wildlife demographics, both in terms of numbers and species present on a property, as well as the maintenance of infrastructure that ensured their continued presence, monopolized people's obsessions and anxieties, and followed them into their nocturnal dreams. It was hardly surprising, then, that Marie selected the social behavior of wildebeest and zebras in the opening vignette of this chapter to explain her understanding of racial difference.

In a different metaphor, the representation of Africans as "black baboons" is familiar to all who have lived in southern Africa. Why baboons, when they are grayish-brown in color, rather than black? The answer is obvious: baboons have always categorically assumed the role of vermin in African settler history. The denigration of ethnic groups through comparison with animals is an old trick, but one that is tirelessly utilized, with powerful effect. Robert Mugabe himself has been known to rely on this trope in condemning gay individuals as "worse than dogs."[11] Such animal analogies often undergo evolutions in meaning over time. For example, the association of raccoons, or "coons," in eighteenth-century American society with what were perceived to be irresponsible, dandified free blacks in the North was gradually replaced in the mid-1800s by the Whig Party's appropriation of the animal to identify with rural white common people. In this context, raccoons became thoroughly white in symbolism, epitomized by Davy Crockett's coonskin cap and the use of live raccoons to signify party loyalty (Roediger 1999).

In Mlilo, knowledge of the "black baboon" metaphor was always present, but the only time I heard whites apply the term as a derogatory reference was when Marie and Jon had two older houseguests visiting from South Africa. These men were acquaintances who used the house as a convenient stopping point en route to Zambia, and their crude, vulgar personalities and unabashedly racist jokes and comments clearly set the rest of the family on edge. In contrast, the context in which I heard the term used most often during my research was when people in Mfula explained to me how they believed whites saw blacks. Black politicians who visited the communal area were particularly adept at its usage and skillfully employed the phrase to invoke moral reprehensibility on the part of white farmers, without having to make reference to any specific incriminating action or incident. The metaphor was thus a provocative one, and its use automatically set into motion a chain of associations and emotions for black villagers.

When isiNdebele-speaking Zimbabweans refer to whites, by contrast, they use the term "Mukhiwa." The *mukhiwa* is a type of tree, and its equation with whites has become so strongly entrenched that *khiwa* is now a noun root connoting anything related to whites. For instance, *isiKhiwa*, rather than *isiNgisi*, is the word popularly used for "English." When asked about the etymology of this term, black people referred to the wild figs that come from the tree, which are pale pinkish in color (Godwin 1996), resembling a white person's skin. White farmers, however, believed the association was derived from the color of the wood itself, which is pure white once the bark is removed. They also referred to the quality of the wood, which is soft and crumbles under the slightest pressure, rendering it useless for furniture or sculpture. As one white farmer explained to me, "It's a rubbish tree . . . good for nothing, and that's why they like to call us Mukhiwa." Interestingly, during the entire course of my fieldwork, I never once heard this particular explanation given by black farmers.

What, then, might we make of these two examples, in which negative representations of each group are accentuated and given life through opinions projected onto the other? Whites assigning certain racial logics to blacks, and blacks attributing specific racial worldviews to whites, brings to mind the figure of a ventriloquist using puppets to give voice to thoughts that would be considered impermissible under normal circumstances. This is not to say that all white farmers had moved beyond racially denigrating insults, for such was certainly not the case. Similarly, it is possible that black Zimbabweans found the coincidence between their choice of tree for designating whites and the poor quality of the wood a convenient and playful one, even though they chose not to highlight that particular characteristic by way of explanation. In this context, the meaning of race seems to depend just as much on the invention and reproduction of race as it is understood to occupy the imaginations of the Other, as well as on racial judgments and values emerging from one's own cultural worldview. Ironically, then, the production of difference is furthered by reminding oneself of representations that are imagined and reflected onto the other. This should hardly surprise us when we consider the individual discourses of self-deprecation that emerge in the wake of colonialism. What *is* surprising, however, is that this process flows in both directions. White settlers' discomfiture with what they perceived to be negative critique by black farmers—although they never admitted outright that such opinions mattered to them—rendered their own assertions of history, belonging, and moral correctness all the more essential to their self-preservation.

"LIKE AN EMPTY PIECE OF SHIT"

White farmers in Mlilo elevated storytelling to an art form. The narration of each story was a performance in and of itself, a meditated sequence of events and explanation with no element left to chance. The most elaborate versions of these stories were reserved for the unconverted: the new expatriates, foreign visitors, and black bureaucrats and local leaders who displayed any sign of disenchantment with the current regime. Stories were designed to persuade, convince, and win the sympathies of the audience over to the narrator's side. The objective lay in drawing listeners in to witness the country through their eyes, to recognize postcolonial Zimbabwe for the tragedy it had become. One of the most common narrative tropes, as noted, was the juxtaposition of the before and after, images paired in stark contrast to engender a sense of simultaneous loss and crisis. The combination of absolute moral conviction and poetic catastrophe was often commanding enough to sow the seeds of doubt in even the most unsympathetic listeners. The following narratives of postcolonial decline were relayed by individual farmers in conversations with me:

ROB LAWRENCE

It's all a "political thing" now, what they call "indigenization." Indigenization means taking everything from the whites and giving it to the blacks—that's all it means. It's because [Mugabe's] realized that as long as he keeps harping on the white man this, and the colonialists that, he will continue to have national support. But it's not the support of the people on the ground, you know, not the support of the masses. It's the gangsters and the thieves and the politicians who steal all the money. Ask anyone here [in Mfula], and he will tell you that the whites are fair, they pay their salaries and don't steal their money, whereas if they work for a black person, he will never pay and will steal all their money.

So it's all these greasy politicians. They've been wanting to target the white man since independence, but they were under colonial regulations for ten years to not take white people's property away. The day, hour, and minute those ten years were up, he set right in. . . . The day, hour, and minute! Mugabe and these gangsters care nothing about the people in the country, or getting money for them; all they care about is driving the white man out—forcing the whites to leave. If you look at the constitution now, you'll see: there's a statement in there that the government has the right to take any property away from its owner—whether it's land, clothing, motor cars, equipment—as long as they compensate you. This is a law! You know they have the constitution already written up?[12] Mugabe hired a British law firm to write the whole thing—all of these workers asking people what they think—it's all an eye blind; it's just for show. This professor from the university in Britain [on the BBC News] said that nothing the people say will change what's already been written in the constitution. You've heard the rumor that there are people who are keeping groups away from these constitution discussion meetings? The new constitution is nothing—it's another political thing so people in other countries will think Mugabe is doing something good.

But the present state of Zimbabwe is all the work of other countries, you know. If they hadn't always given money when Mugabe was in trouble, he would have been out years ago. The people would have thrown him out. Instead countries like the US and Britain always supported him, and keep giving him more and more money, which is why he's managed to stay. You know what the World Bank said about Zimbabwe after independence? That it wasn't eligible for donor aid because the average income of people in the country wasn't less than $100 US [per month]. The Zimbabwe dollar was equal to the US dollar, and people were earning good salaries. So you know what Mugabe did? Overnight, he devalued the Zim dollar 10:1 against the US dollar, which was just enough to bring Zimbabwe under the average $100 income. Just because he wanted donor money! And now all anybody talks about is donors.

I replied, "That's true. . . . Yesterday, when I was in Mfula, I met an adult literacy teacher who told me that she wanted to become friends with me so that I could contact my friends on that side and find a donor for her."

Rob said, "Ha! You see? Four or five years ago no one knew what a donor was. Now all they can talk about is donors. The first thing they ask you is, 'What have you brought us?' You can write a book about that."

HENDRIK VAN DER VOSSEN

Those British and Scottish guys who worked on the railways before independence, they knew a lot. I had real respect for them. After independence, Mugabe kicked them right out and put black people with no training in their place. He was so stupid, Mugabe could have used these people. . . . They could have given him so much. If he was really smart, he would have used them. The same thing happened in South Africa—it's all because of the racists. When racists drive an economy down, you know it's an awful thing. Okay, he could make them leave, but get them to train people first. And it's not like they can't do it—they can, you just have to find the right one, get rid of the ones who aren't motivated. You know this guy who was doing the culling of the elephants here in the park? He said send me a guy, and I'll train him. They sent him two guys from Harare, and after a week, they were gone, they ran away. They were scared—culling was too dangerous, and they didn't want to do it. But you know, everything in this country has gone down. Everything! There isn't one thing that's operating properly now. Everything has been destroyed— you can't believe it. I can sit here and think about how it used to be, and how it is now, and I can't believe everything can be destroyed so completely like this. And it's just gonna get worse. The only way things will get better is once they hit rock bottom. Look at Mozambique. They're doing much better now because they're inviting the [white] farmers in, giving them land, and the IMF [International Monetary Fund] told them that they'll finance them all, and you won't have to import food—this will be how you get your economy going again. And they have South Africans working with them, giving them help. That's the only way that this country is gonna get better. Even the Wankie [Hwange] Colliery, it's bankrupt now. Because the government owes them millions, ZISCO [Zimbabwe Iron and Steel Company] owes them millions, and the power plants owe them millions. You know there are only ten white guys working there now. You know Don Richards? The open car blasting manager? Now they're investigating him for stealing. Tell me, what can he steal? Nothing! It's only because he's white! And now they're all over the other white guys working there . . . You know there used to be a special train that ran four times a day to pick up coal from the colliery, and then deliver it to ZISCO. It was a clockwork operation, ran smoothly all the time. I haven't seen those trains in ten years. And the warehouse in Bulawayo where tons and tons of machinery sits, doing nothing. Like an empty piece of shit! Spare parts and engines and generators and cranes—I never knew this stuff existed in Zimbabwe. And the workers just sit around and make *sadza* with the acetylene metal-cutting machines while there's hundreds of electric sockets around. They're doing nothing—I tell you, you can't believe it!

ALEXANDER DU BOIS

I asked, "Did you ever consider leaving the country after independence?"

Du Bois responded, "Of course I had to consider it, because I had trained people to kill their fighters—I thought I would be at the top of their list. But then a top general from ZIPRA [Zimbabwe People's Revolutionary Army—the military wing of ZAPU] came to my living room and asked me why I wanted to leave. This country will hit rock bottom, he said, and you and I have to rebuild it. So I stayed. Of course that was when Mugabe broadcast on television that he wanted bygones to be bygones. And it's true, they haven't hurt me yet. At least not physically."

His wife, Jane, nodded in agreement. "Yes, not physically . . ." She trailed off, implying that the damage had taken other, more devastating forms. She picked up where her husband had left off. "There were three hundred thousand whites in this country at its peak, and two hundred thousand left the country. And they were the best people in Rhodesia. The first ones who left because they were scared were the ones you didn't want anyway, the ones you would be better off without. But then the young people—the cream of the crop—left because they had no choice. And they were the skilled people as well. What do they say? First the chickens run, and the old run. And then the wise run."

Her husband continued, "Here's a fact: in 1980, the average person was earning $30 a month. And a 50 kg bag of mealie meal cost $3, so he could buy ten bags of mealie meal a month. Now, the minimum salary is $1,700, and each bag of mealie meal is $900—so he can only buy two bags a month. What more do I need to say?"

.   .   .

Anger, betrayal, and grief lie at the core of these narratives, animating distinct themes and representations. Alexander and Jane explain their decision to remain in the country after independence as rooted in national loyalty and gracious acquiescence on their part to a plea extended by a former enemy. And yet, despite their demonstrated good faith, the promise of reconciliation was broken. Jane's words resound with loneliness and a sense of isolation at being left behind. The narratives by Rob and Hendrik, on the other hand, provide more explicit critiques of the state, personified through the figure of Robert Mugabe, as a regime that is irrational, self-interested, and guilty of conspiring against its own citizens. Both of these narratives display a close engagement with the world through references to global politics and international donor organizations. Rob's sharp critique, moreover, includes other countries, which he sees as playing an equally culpable role in Zimbabwe's demise. As a rhetorical strategy to legitimize his charges of state corruption, he invokes the higher authority of "a professor from the university in Britain" appearing on the BBC News as his source.

If we listen closely to these narratives, we can also identify moments of admission, or sites of compromise, in which people acknowledge that certain things *had* to change after independence. Hence, Hendrik's interjection, presented almost as a retraction: "Okay, he [Mugabe] could make them [whites] leave, but get them to train people first. And it's not like they [blacks] can't do it—they can, you just have to find the right one." The sequence of thought, where this observation follows on the footsteps of the statement "When racists drive an economy down, you know it's an awful thing," seems paradoxical on the surface, but in fact points to the interplay between multiple levels of discourse and awareness. While all of these strategies lend persuasive power, perhaps the most significant lies in the fetishization of catastrophe that seems to be at work here. Hendrik's narrative, in particular, with its evocative imagery, borders on aestheticizing postcolonial disaster and dissolution. Functioning simultaneously to narrow the distance between their own perspectives and those outside the community, the catastrophic sublime exists in farmers' imaginations as the perfect antithesis against which Beautiful Rhodesia is reified time and again.

THE VIRTUES OF HARD WORK

In order to assert moral claims to their lands, many farmers presented artfully crafted "origin stories" describing hardship, and in some cases, destitution, in their childhoods. They rose above such circumstances, these stories argued, by virtue of hard work and tireless effort. "My sons don't know what hard work *is*," Klaas Van Esch grumbled to me one day. "I got my first pair of shoes when I was sixteen years old, and three of my brothers wore those same shoes before me." He sat back in his chair and began telling me the story of his parents, who had a farm in the Orange Free State, where they grew crops and raised livestock.

There were Jew boys back then who owned everything in the community. They owned stores and lent people money, and when a farmer brought back some crops or livestock in payment, the Jewish lender had the power to decide how much the goods were worth. No matter what they gave, or how hard they worked, these farmers would never be able to repay the full amount. In the end, they get your house and farm and you had to work for them. So this is what happened to my father. He lost everything in the Great Depression of 1931 and 1932. He was working for this Jew boy, but he had to leave, and the only thing that was still his was the livestock. So he took his wife, my older brother who was still young, and all the sheep, and trekked up to the railway station, which took seven days. By the time they got there, only one out of the two thousand sheep was still alive. He slit the sheep's throat and shared it with the railway workers. He got a job there, working on the railways for £12 a month. He and my mother got a small cottage, and then a farm, and my father was promoted to loading master. But he could never quit his job, because the family needed those £12—without that, they wouldn't be able to survive. But they always had plenty of food. Cabbages and chickens, meat—we were always giving food away. We always made butter and cheese because we could never sell all the milk. Me and my brothers had to get up at 4 a.m. every morning and milk the cows. When the sun rose, all the milk [had to] be delivered and all the animals had to be fed. It was a rule that nobody in the house could eat until all the animals were taken care of. We were still poor, but I never needed money. I didn't know what to do with my salary once I was in the air force.

As a teenager, Klaas emigrated to Rhodesia and worked as a mechanic for a farmer in Rusape for ten years before he could afford to buy land in Mlilo. "But I paid for it. No one gave it to me—I saved my money and I paid for it myself. And now they want to take it away from me. I'm asking you, is that fair?" The intensity with which Klaas asked me this question left me at a momentary loss for words. But the question was a largely rhetorical one anyway. The narrative that he chose to give here provides testament to individual hardship, distancing him from an anonymous collectivity of white privilege and wealth. To Klaas, the logic of his argument is self-evident, based on cultural values that render hard work and individual achievement sacred and thus unassailable.[13]

LINGUISTIC FAILURES

In order to bolster their own symbolic capital as whites, a favorite pastime among farmers involved recounting moments of linguistic and semantic misunderstanding in postcolonial Zimbabwe. One day over lunch, Jon and Marie and two of their sons exchanged a dozen anecdotes, several of which are included here:

- When Queen Elizabeth visited the country a few years ago, an announcer on TV reported that Queen Elizabeth the Eleventh was arriving the next day (he was reading from his notes, which said Queen Elizabeth II).
- A reporter was announcing the results of the FA Cup [soccer tournament] and read it as "Fa-cup," which sounded as if he were saying "fuck-up."
- On a TV dating game show, a man asked a woman who was a prospective partner, "Where's the best place you've ever had sex?" To which the woman replied. "Agh, the best place I've had sex is the bum." After that, the program was taken off the air.
- During the 1992 drought crisis, maize was being flown in from all over the world to feed the people, and the national railways were completely congested because they were trying to transport the maize. At the same time, because of the lack of water, there was no electricity for half of the country because the Kariba Dam was nonfunctional. A journalist asked a representative from the Ministry of Energy why they didn't import electricity from other countries in southern Africa. The ministry representative replied that the trains were too full from transporting all the maize.
- A reporter asked one of President Mugabe's aides why he needed to take a whole entourage of people every time he attended conferences overseas. "Why not send only Mugabe, and cut down on the spending of foreign currency?" the reporter asked. The aide answered, "But we don't take foreign currency. We always take traveler's checks."
- A broadcaster on the radio reported that a group of beautiful Merina rams had been exported from Australia to breed with the ewes here, but he pronounced "ewes" as "e-ways," which is a Shona greeting [meaning "hey you"]. The white broadcaster who was reporting with him started laughing and couldn't recover her composure, and was fired the next day. She had been broadcasting on the news for years.

blackness as impostor to correct white authority

By the time Martin finished relaying his last anecdote, Marie was in tears from mirth. "Yeah," she said. "At least they keep us laughing."

By highlighting instances of linguistic failure among black Zimbabweans, members of the family reclaimed their imagined authority over the arena of language, which historically served as an important source of symbolic power that was jealously guarded by white settlers. By reminding themselves that blacks were only imperfect imitators at best, lines of black and white distinction between the two groups were reinforced. In *The Grass Is Singing*, Doris Lessing's novel about the gradual psychological breakdown of a farmer's wife in the 1930s, one of the most provocative moments in the story occurs when one of her husband's workers dares to speak to her in English. "Most white people think it is 'cheek' if a native speaks English," and seeing "in his eyes that sullen resentment, and what put the finishing touch to it, amused contempt," Mary explodes into an inarticulate rage (2000:133–134). The concept of "cheek" is a fascinating one, pointing to moments of rupture when existing social hierarchies are subverted, although seldom taking the form of overt resistance. Language and its different applications thus became a significant site of struggle through which colonial authority was continually contested (Bhabha 2004). Perhaps this exercise of periodically cataloguing black "failed performances" in postcolonial Zimbabwe continued a tradition of colonial surveillance, carefully drawing the boundary between imperfect imitation and "true" linguistic competence.

language as contested side of colonialism

THE DANGERS OF INTIMACY

In the postcolonial context, farmers' anxiety centered around the policing of social boundaries between black and white, especially for children. Julie, a frequent guest at the Lawrence house, had been sent to live in Mlilo when she was seventeen because her parents felt that she was spending too much time with her black friends in Bulawayo. The Lawrences were good friends of her parents, and, understanding their concern, agreed to take her on as a secretary for their safari company while they gave her room and board. People generally saw Mlilo as a "safer" space, where spatial segregation was easier to maintain. Ironically, Julie soon became romantically involved with one of the Lawrences' (white) professional hunters and became pregnant. When I met her, she was living in Bulawayo as a single mother, struggling to support her eight-year-old daughter on a secretary's income. The Lawrences, who remained close to her and felt partially responsible, assisted her financially whenever they could.

On the other side of the valley, Liesl Cronje worried constantly about her grandchildren, who attended boarding school in Bulawayo and came home to Mlilo only on the weekends. She seemed more tense than usual as I was having tea with her one Friday afternoon, and explained that her grandson, Brian, was staying at his boarding school on Saturday and Sunday because his parents were too busy to make the four-hour round-trip to town. "It's not good because he'll be alone with ten or twelve black boys from Botswana," she fretted. "I say it's a sin against your child to keep him with black people twenty-four hours a day. They shouldn't have to sleep with them on top of spending the daytime with them. He needs to be with his own kind, his own family." Although Liesl never criticized her son and daughter-in-law outright, she clearly thought they were remiss in not ensuring that Brian had a way to come home that weekend.

Echoing a similar sentiment, Alice Marling told me that her daughter-in-law was considering moving to Bulawayo full-time when her granddaughter started school the following year. Although it would mean that her son and daughter-in-law would have to live apart, and she herself would see her only grandchild much less frequently, she was convinced that it was a better alternative than placing Emily in a boarding school.

> It's better for them, because of the integration. I don't believe it's right for them to have to integrate with black children like that. They can go to school with them, and sit next to them in lessons, but they shouldn't have to sleep with them. And especially in schools now, they're always doing things the African way because they're too afraid to speak up. If they say anything, the government will be on them accusing them of being racialistic. There was a case in a school where the black boys complained that the white children were eating bread faster than they could. So the black parents demanded more bread for their children. Then in Plumtree, the black teachers wanted the white teachers to be fired because of some conflict or whatever. And at Milton Senior, some black students signed themselves out on a Sunday, and went and drank alcohol and brought drugs back into the school. One of them grabbed a white student's towel, and a fight started as the white boy tried to get the towel back. They broke furniture, and both sets of parents were called in. The school wanted to expel the black student, because of course you can't bring drugs into school, but they were too afraid to. So they'll never expel black children.

Life had many paradoxes for children in Mlilo. One of them was having a black "nanny" who often spent more time with the children in her care than they spent with their real mothers.[14] Very close, intimate bonds developed as a result, and the children learned to understand and speak Ndebele alongside English. Jenna, one of Marie and Jon's granddaughters, brought a brand-new stuffed animal to her mother, Carolyn, one day and asked if she could give it to her nanny, Grace, to give to her baby, who lived in the compound. I knew that Jenna sometimes went down to visit the compound even though her mother disapproved. I watched as Carolyn gently pried the doll away from Jenna's hands, and picked up an older, faded-looking teddy bear from the living room floor. "That one's too new, my girl. Why don't you give her this one?" Jenna looked pleased that her mother had been so responsive, and went off to find Grace.

At a certain point in time, however, an important reversal in power occurs, when the child realizes that there is a social order to things, in which her nanny occupies a subordinate position. She has the right to talk back to her caregiver; she can be disrespectful and get away with it. On many occasions, I witnessed children yelling at their nannies and calling them names in ways they would have never dared with their mothers. In her study of whiteness in transition in South Africa, Melissa Steyn provides an account of an Afrikaans man attending an anti-racism workshop, and confessing his grief and regret at having mistreated his nanny during childhood:

> As a little boy on the farm in the Northern Transvaal where he grew up, he had loved his African nanny. He had loved to snuggle his head between her full breasts; he had loved the songs she sang to him in her language; he had loved the food she fed him. But as he grew up, his friends had taunted him for his affection for her, as she was "net'n kaffirmeid" [just a nigger servant girl]. He had learned to deny his love for his first friend in life, and to call her names to prove his indifference. Now he was articulating a deep sense of loss and waste, anger at a social system that had raised him on lies and damaged his humanity. He had feelings of personal shame for not having somehow managed to transcend his social conditioning. (2001:x)

Thus, social rules defining appropriate versus inappropriate intimacies involved complicated negotiations that children navigated through trial and error, correction, and learned intuition. The result, however, created a strange tension between suppressed desire and feigned insensitivity, which resulted in experiences of fragmentation for many individuals.

FRIENDSHIP AND AFFINITY

In discussing whiteness in the context of Africa, what is often mistakenly over-looked is the extent to which whites feel most comfortable when surrounded by blacks. Despite the professed fear of cross-racial intimacy, many white Zim-babweans I knew felt most at home when the majority of people surrounding them were black. People did articulate, of course, the need to have at least some white presence within reach in order to preserve a sense of identity. The con-cerns voiced by Liesl, Alice, and Julie's parents reflect this idea of proper iden-tity formation as contingent upon unambiguously white social spaces. At the same time, however, the relationships of genuine affection that many whites seemed to have with blacks contradicted assertions of incommensurable dif-ference.

At any given moment, Jon had at least four or five workers who helped him in his workshop and assisted in maintaining the boreholes and water pans on his property. His favorite employee, Peter, had worked beside him six days a week for over ten years. Jon had no qualms about claiming that Peter was his best friend, and in fact, Marie often seemed envious, if not jealous, of their closeness. When Marie and Jon took an extended trip to visit relatives in South Africa in 1999, Jon decided that he would take Peter also, because Peter had never seen the ocean, and Jon wanted to show it to him. He helped Peter apply for a passport, paid all of the application fees, and bought Peter a plane ticket and a new traveling outfit. It was of course understood that Peter would have to help out on the trip, carrying bags and perhaps doing some work in their relatives' household once they arrived. During their stay, he would sleep in the compound along with the family's regular workers. Nonetheless, it did seem like an extraordinary gesture on Jon's part.

Over the course of that year, Peter's health steadily deteriorated. Marie and Jon took him to the clinic regularly and covered all of his medical expenses, but he died of AIDS early in 2001. Although I was not in the country at the time, Jon's daughter emailed me to tell me how devastated he was by Peter's death. When I returned later on that year, I discovered that there was a new person installed in the position of favorite worker, who turned out to be Peter's younger brother. After Peter's death, his father had arrived at the Van den Akker house with his younger son in tow, and proposed to Jon, "Now that my older son is gone, you must take my younger son." Jon had agreed without hesitation, as white farmers often developed close ties of moral obligation with specific fami-lies in neighboring communal areas. Fortunately, Peter's brother seemed to be possessed of the same talents for hard work and meticulous attention to detail with which Peter had been blessed. What I found surprising, however, was that Jon had decided to call him by the *same name* as his brother Peter. Whether this was because he wanted to honor Peter's memory or because it was too much trouble for him to distinguish between the two men was difficult to discern. Perhaps Jon thought of Peter's brother as part of a corporate lineage in the anthropological sense, where individual identities were less relevant than that of the collective group.

We can infer, however, that to some extent, at least, Jon considered the original Peter substitutable. Would Jon have been so quick to ascribe interchangeable identities to Peter and his brother had they been white? Does this alter the significance of their friendship? Or more importantly, disqualify it altogether from the very category itself? Perhaps what had appeared to be a social transgression in the closeness shared by these two men was in fact never in danger of transgressing boundaries at all. Firmly situated within a hierarchy understood by all participants (except for the anthropologist/outsider), Jon may have glossed what was always fundamentally an employer-employee relationship with the fiction of friendship.[15] This was, moreover, a friendship occurring in a nondomestic space, with fewer opportunities for spontaneity and intimacy, where the patterns of daily life were structured by the demands of work. Thus, the stakes may have lower, with an underlying formal relationship remaining in place at all times. And yet, I prefer to think of friendship differently, to expand, if necessary, our definition of the term. Even where hierarchy exists (and when does it not?), close sociality also exists in different configurations. I choose to privilege Jon's own interpretation, and find within this particular example a moment where once again, understandings and experiences of race were far more pluralistic and complex than ingrained ideologies—cultural, political, and intellectual—would have people believe.

PATRIARCHALISM AND LOCAL RULE

One day, Charlie Oakeshott, a farmer who lived at the eastern tip of the valley, told me about a local Peace Corps volunteer named Gabe who was working in a communal area neighboring his property. Gabe asked if he could borrow Charlie's tractor for the day, and, Charlie, feeling magnanimous, also "lent" him three of his workers to help run the machinery and offer assistance wherever it was needed. Gabe came back later that morning, sweaty and grimy because he had just run 6 km from the dam where the tractor had broken down. He had gotten lost in the bush while trying to take a shortcut to the communal area. Charlie was convinced that his workers had deliberately directed Gabe down the wrong road so that they could sit back on the tractor and relax for the subsequent two hours. "They know that Gabe is different, and they take advantage of him. You think they're stupid, but they're clever, these guys." He went on to describe each of his workers in detail.

CO: There's Johan, who's the instigator of trouble. He's too clever—he even outsmarts me sometimes. . . . He'll stand up quietly when I'm working hard and walk silently behind the workshop to the onion beds, where he'll sit and pick plants out one by one, resting and taking his time. He'll tell me he's "deweeding." . . . He's been deweeding for two months now.

YS: And Philip?

CO: Philip you also have to watch, but not so much—only 10 percent of the time.

YS: And Jealous?

CO: Jealous will also do these things, but he's clever—when he wants to get something done, he'll do it quickly. His hands know what to do even without anyone telling him. He's a better mechanic than Philip—he doesn't know more than Philip, because he's only been here for a year and a half, but he's clever. You know, he has no mother and no father. His mother died, and his grandmother went all the way to Zambia to fetch him and take care of him. I had three youngsters here, working on a contract basis. And this little guy [Jealous] was the cleverest. But then Cathy comes and says this one is a gangster—that he beats up his grandmother.[16] So I took the first two paychecks that Jealous made here and gave them to his grandmother directly. I told him it's a fine for beating up his grandmother.

YS: What did Jealous say when you told him that?

CO: He didn't say nothing. He knows that if he complains, he'll lose his job, and he'll be just like those other unemployed guys, wandering around in the communal areas there.

The actions that Charlie undertook in "fining" Jealous for wrongdoings committed in his own home reveal extraordinary presumption on Charlie's part. His approach reproduces colonial patriarchalism in assuming the right to dispense justice not only within the boundaries of his own property but also in a sphere extending well beyond it. In this instance, Charlie most likely believed he was acting to protect the interests of the innocent by compensating

Jealous's grandmother for abuse she had suffered at the hands of her grandson. In this way, farmers became key participants in complex webs of local moral economies, wielding power by virtue of their monetary wealth. What was striking, moreover, was that certain factions within the communal areas actually expected and relied on these kinds of interventions by white farmers. Farmers who were deemed unjust in their practices toward communal farmers became subject to various forms of resistance, but individuals such as Charlie Oakeshott were recognized publicly as figures of moral authority.[17]

To decipher the workings of such residual sites of power, Eric Worby provides a useful conceptual framework in his analysis of parallel structures of self-governance that emerged in northwestern Zimbabwe during the 1980s: "What happens if . . . we dispense with our organic vision of the state, if, instead of picturing an amoeba or octopus, we see instead a dispersed residue of specific and very different sites of power—tidal pools in which micro-environments of power are iteratively nurtured, but never irrevocably submerged, by the sea?" (1997:75). Within rural areas, many white farmers acted as ghostly shadows of colonial authority, dispensing alternate forms of justice in their own residual pools of power. While echoing certain forms of cooperation that existed during the liberation war (Lan 1985), the alliances between whites and blacks in upholding local moral economies once again complicate typical assumptions of deep-seated antagonism between the two groups.

"BAMBA ZONKE"

Mlilo's location in Matabeleland North, which historically has been peripheral within the nation-state, is an important factor influencing alliances between black and white farmers. Primarily Ndebele in ethnicity, black Zimbabweans in this area are marginalized in both material and symbolic spheres.[18] This added an interesting element for white farmers, who drew upon an intense dislike for the ruling party that was shared by local blacks, creating images of themselves in opposition to the immorality of ZANU-PF. During the Gukurahundi campaign, the period of sustained ethnic genocide in the mid-1980s outlined in the previous chapter, Fifth Brigade leaders ordered white farmers to stay in their houses when their workers were being beaten. Many farmers, however, refused to leave these scenes and faced down brigade soldiers, which resulted in fewer atrocities overall.

During the late 1980s, moreover, three incidents occurred in which white farmers from Mlilo were arrested on charges of conspiracy against the government. In prison, they occupied the same cells as leaders from the local communal areas who had been incarcerated on similar charges.[19] They described their shared experiences of interrogation and torture by ZANU henchmen as a basis for solidarity, and the belief that regardless of differences in race, both groups had been persecuted by the current political regime. In this context, white identity took backstage to a larger, regional identity in which parallel marginalizations established a foundation for co-identification and alliance.

People living in Matabeleland North refer to Mashonaland as the region of the politically corrupt, the greedy, and the dishonorable, where the reigning logic is *bamba zonke*, or "take all." Many farmers, while recognizing the disadvantages of the dry climate and poor soils in Matabeleland, expressed a clear preference for this region because it enabled them to stay out of the government's grasp. Interestingly, a parallel valuation is also mapped onto imagined ethnic hierarchies, as the Shona are described as the "snake-eyed" and "shifty Shona," while the Ndebele retain a reputation for honesty, hard work, and courage. These typologies circulate among both blacks and whites in the area, and fierce regional loyalties emerge as overlapping spheres of allied sentiment. When in 1999 a group of angry Ndebele passengers forcibly removed a man from a bus on the road between Bulawayo and Victoria Falls upon discovering that he was Shona, white farmers rejoiced in the story and celebrated the courage of the individuals who had momentarily reversed the oppressive structures of postcolonial power. These black "allies" constituted a vitally important element in white-authored critiques of the state because people understood that they lent a legitimacy of voice that the contemporary nation routinely denied white farmers based on their racial identities.[20]

TO BE WHITE EUROPEAN, OR WHITE AFRICAN?

While in the public domain these racial identities remained more or less fixed, among white Zimbabweans, identities are in the process of transition. Emerging out of deeply embedded colonial worldviews, the idea of racial hierarchy itself exists as an absolute certainty within the minds of most whites in Zimbabwe. Social categories according to this perspective are typically divided into white Europeans, colored Europeans, colored Africans, and black Africans, in this order. However, white "ethnosociologies" of race extend further in categorizing and distinguishing between groups. In one conversation that took place between Jon and one of his childhood friends who was visiting from South Africa, the two men recounted how they had experienced race growing up in

Heidelberg, a rural community outside of Cape Town. The following passage is drawn from my fieldnotes relating to this conversation:

> Chinese people were classified as colored, and Japanese people were classified as whites. I asked Jon and Gert why that was, but they didn't know. Indians, or "coolies," were colored, along with the Portuguese and Chinese, and Italian (eye-ties) women were referred to as "mates" (Afrikaans for "maids") because they were so dirty. Jon said that the Chinese women were ugly enough to make you run in the middle of the night. He and Gert also talked about how Jewish people owned everything—how they acted as banks and ended up owning all the farms. According to Jon, they left right before South Africa gained independence in 1994, and all went to the US. Now the "coolies" own half the Parliament, although there used to be a law that no coolies could even get off the bus in the Orange Free State—they had to drive straight through. Gert remarked wistfully that the world had changed.

Given the importance placed on race as a marker of social difference, the resistance that many white Zimbabweans expressed to changing articulations of identity came as no surprise. At the same time, however, a small minority of people in Mlilo had begun to claim the label of "white African," rather than "white European" at the turn of the millennium.[21] Although most likely motivated by strategies of self-representation, a key shift in the conceptualization of identity seemed to be at work. The expression of loyalties to Africa for the first time superseded people's imagined ties to Europe, once staunchly insisted upon as the very essence of their beings and the most important source of their symbolic capital. Such changes, while perhaps enacted as simple linguistic shifts at first, opened up spaces for new forms of identity, liberated from the constraints of old categories. While the question of race will always be a contentious one, the emergence of new identifications offers the promise that even seemingly inflexible ideologies can undergo revision in response to changing contexts.

THE GOVERNOR'S FAUX PAS

In a departure from the rhetorical language and themes outlined above, the final section of this chapter recounts a sequence of events that demonstrates how certain narratives are created and circulated to validate white perspectives. The most visible public index of a white farmer's morality was determined by the role he took in caring for his workers, as well as the relationships he built with neighboring communal areas. In Mlilo, where wildlife ranching required very few workers in comparison to commercial agricultural farms, white farmers' reputations were built through a spectrum of interactions with communal areas that were carefully observed and catalogued in black farmers' memories. Mlilo shared boundaries with four different communal areas; typically, families concentrated most of their energies on the communal areas directly bordering their properties. Some maintained hostile relationships, as in the case of one farmer who became infamous for brandishing guns and unleashing graphic threats on each occasion he discovered communal farmers grazing cattle on his property, a pattern that earned him the nickname the "devil." In most cases, however, farmers were at least occasionally obliging when it came to responding to requests for the provision of transport, loans, technical assistance in building and fixing boreholes, providing bricks for the construction of schools, and contributing game meat for community celebrations. I found it striking, for example, that on more than a handful of occasions when I had been invited over to a farmer's house for dinner, we were interrupted by a phone call from the local schoolmaster, who was requesting a ride from his school to the main road.[22] Although they expressed exasperation, farmers were surprisingly accommodating when it came to these kinds of requests.

From 1996 to 1998, the Van den Akkers had contributed technical assistance to the construction of a health clinic in the communal area that neighbored their property. The sparkling white clinic was a source of immense excitement for the community, for which the closest health care facility up until that point had been an unpaved 26 km to the east. Although the Mfula clinic had already been operational for two years, in September 1999 the village hosted an official clinic opening to celebrate the completion of its construction. The celebration was of unprecedented magnitude in Mfula, with the attendance of the deputy minister of health, the governor of Matabeleland North, both provincial members of Parliament, nineteen district councilors, the Hwange district administrator, traditional chiefs from the entire province, and five representatives from a church congregation in Britain that had raised funding for the clinic. In recognition of their substantial technical assistance, Jon Van den Akker and his three sons were ushered to seats in the center of the second row, immediately behind the major politicians. Members of the Mfula community had prepared for months for this event, and the schoolchildren's songs were painstakingly rehearsed, the women's dances seamlessly coordinated, and the politi-

3.1 The new health clinic in Mfula that was commemorated in the official opening celebration. Photograph by author.

cians' speeches flowery and verbose. The audience, numbering well over three thousand, settled in comfortably for the long program, which was already two hours behind schedule before it even started.

When it became Governor Mabhena's turn to speak, he stood—short, round, and bald—and commenced in Ndebele to congratulate Mfula on the community's cooperative efforts in building the new clinic. Halfway through his speech, which had subtly shifted from the topic of health care to the subject of the nation-state, he switched abruptly into English and declared, "There are people here who think we're all baboons on this side of the fence. They call us baboons, and they want to chase the baboons to the other side of the hill to the driest land in the area, and keep us there so that they do not have to be bothered by the baboons." The interpreter was clearly distressed, and haltingly translated the words into Ndebele. There was a collective intake of breath, and the sleepy lull that had descended upon the audience instantly evaporated. "We must tell these people that they *cannot* chase us off the land!" Mabhena shouted triumphantly in an atmosphere now electrified with tension. Then, just as abruptly, he switched back into Ndebele and espoused the glory of the country—a rote regurgitation of ZANU-PF propaganda—for the remainder of his speech.

The Van den Akkers sat rigidly tense, the audience shifted nervously, and the British fund-raisers were puzzled but uncomprehending as to what had happened. By code-switching, Mabhena had targeted the white Zimbabweans present as clearly as if they had been marked with bull's-eye targets, effectively slapping them in the face during an occasion that was meant to honor them for the part they had played in setting up the clinic. The Van den Akker men barely waited until the end of the speeches to leave the premises. They unceremoniously dumped the thirty crates of bottled soft drinks they had brought for the festivities from the backs of their trucks, and drove off in a swirl of dust.

Later that night, a telephone call interrupted us during dinner. It was the retired district councilor, uncle to the young traditional chief, and the unofficial head of the Mfula community. He was calling from a telephone—the only other one in the village besides the one in the clinic—that a Norwegian NGO had installed in his house over a year ago. He apologized profusely for the morning's incidents and expressed his outrage at Mabhena's bad behavior in destroying the spirit of celebration and collaboration at the clinic opening. "These politicians!" he spat disgustedly, saying that the village was writing a formal letter of apology to Jon and his family, which would be signed by all. According to Jon, who relayed the substance of the conversation to the rest of the family afterward, the councilor narrated the course of events that happened later that evening: "Mabhena came back, but all of us, we chased him away. 'This man gives us meat all the time for all our events,' we said to him, 'and now it's finished because of your speech at the opening. You, Mabhena, have six farms and you haven't tried to resettle anyone on them, and you go and *shupha* this old man who helps us.'"[23]

Addressing Jon again, the councilor continued, "We saved the cool drinks you brought, and we want to have another party tomorrow night. This time just with you, this time no politicians."

Jon gruffly declined, making it known that his deep irritation would not be so quickly dispelled. He appeared disgruntled as he got off the phone, but it was clear as he walked back to the table that he was somewhat mollified. When I asked him if it made him happy to know that the people felt this way, he responded: "Ja, but I've always known this. It just goes to show again that the politicians are just doing their own thing. They have nothing to do with the people—they don't care. They just use them during elections to vote for them and do their dirty work, and then they go and do whatever they want. No one uses people like they do in Africa."

During the next two days, for a community of such isolated households, it was astonishing how quickly the story spread in Mlilo, flying across scratchy telephone lines and relayed during visits to the post office. It seemed inevitable that this too would be incorporated into the artillery of narratives that oppose institutionally racialized national mythology.

In this development of events, it was entirely likely that the retired councilor was simply being politically strategic: later, Mfula villagers confirmed that Mabhena had in fact faced considerable hostility when he returned to the celebration in the evening, but realistically, the councilor was not above a little embellishment in his own narration of events if it meant repairing relations with his white neighbors. Nonetheless, I could not help but feel excitement at the possibilities of subversive alliance between black and white Zimbabweans that challenged dominant racial politics in the country at that point. Upon telling the same story with gusto to a young black political science professor at the University of Zimbabwe, however, I was crestfallen at his response. With a laugh, he dismissed the villagers' reaction to Mabhena as not surprising in the least, declaring, "Oh, that's just because Mabhena's unpopular to begin with. It's a well-known fact that he's one of the two most despised governors in the whole country." Thus, what the white farmers had imagined to be the villagers' courageous defiance of a powerful politician because he had insulted their white "friends" was after all an action within the scope of political acceptability, backed by a notorious lack of support for Mabhena on a regional scale. The symbolism of the act therefore turned out to be not quite as significant, and the possibilities not nearly as daring. These subtleties, if fleetingly felt, would undoubtedly be sublimated as the narrative of this story was repeated and entrenched in white farmers' memories.

PLACING RACE IN PERSPECTIVE

In postcolonial Zimbabwe, where the question of race transects every social and political landscape, assumptions about racial difference constitute an interpretive grid through which people make sense of everyday experience. Race is seized upon in an absolute manner, positing overarching distinctions between black and white. But in practice, understandings of race continually change, as they are negotiated and renegotiated in microcosms of performance and power. For whites in Zimbabwe who finally began to realize that a quarter-century of "waiting and seeing" was drawing to a close, the urgency to reassert their identities in the face of dissolution grew ever more pressing.

This chapter has focused on central themes that emerge in the way white Zimbabweans situated themselves in relation to race and the nation-state. The use of metaphors from nature to naturalize cultural assumptions concerning race reflected the local specificity of how race was experienced and understood. The wildebeest and the zebra never transgress social boundaries, even as they share the same physical spaces; in contrast, among people, the potential for intimacy as a site of transgression demanded constant policing. As a consequence, an essential component in the formation of "proper" white identity lay in the assurance of physical segregation whenever possible. Women in Mlilo worried for their grandchildren especially in the context of sharing dormitory spaces with black classmates. Symbolic distinctions played an equally important role in the production of ideas about race, as whites claimed exclusive authority in spheres of practice such as language.

Through their elaborately constructed narratives, moreover, white farmers in Mlilo presented contrastive geographies between an idealized pre-independence past and a post-independence catastrophic present. By highlighting instances of unscrupulousness and corruption, they crafted eloquent critiques of the state, positioning themselves in opposition to a self-serving and destructive government. Narratives of belonging, on the other hand, invoked individual hardship and perseverance to persuade their audiences that economic privilege was based solely on hard work and merit. In crafting these narratives, farmers chose a definitive moral orientation, and yet multiple voices also existed within that framework. Switching back and forth between different voices never threatened to decenter the overall moral position, but instead offered moments of possibility through a range of interpretations.

Reinforced by these types of rhetorical devices, whiteness always acts as a marker of higher authority. At the same time, though, social constructions of difference operate within webs of everyday practice that are in fact deeply inconsistent and contradictory. Where cross-racial affections and intimacies arose, some relationships were categorized as transgressions, while others were implicitly condoned. Farmers who routinely articulated the basis of white superiority would claim black individuals as their friends in the same conversation. In their relationships with neighboring communal lands, they extended acts of generosity and kindness even as they exercised forms of intervention with a "beneficent" patriarchal gaze. Finally, in direct contrast to institutionally racialized national narratives, blacks and whites in this region were allied in sentiment and collusive in their opposition to the state.

These surprising affinities reveal the fundamental unevenness of racial topographies. This points not to an *imperfect* system, but rather, to a plurality of existing discourses and practices that circulate in continual recombination. These different perspectives do not necessarily contradict or compete with one another: they exist in multiplicity, allowing people to adopt flexible positions and articulate understandings of race through different frameworks. On one occasion, an American missionary working in Zambia who had known Jon and Marie for many years came to stay with us for two nights, bringing a guest with him. David was African American, a member of the Southern Baptist Church, and visiting Africa for the first time. I remember a distinct sinking feeling in my stomach when I first saw him, for I dreaded the inevitable mutual embarrassment when Jon and Marie would let slip their essentialisms about racial difference, no doubt to David's horror. I was torn between wanting to protect David and wanting to protect Jon and Marie. But as it turned out, I had not given either side enough credit. During David's visit, Jon and Marie consciously invoked a different set of understandings about race that was based on their cosmopolitan knowledge of racial politics in other places. They were social chameleons, changing their colors and earnestly debating issues such as affirmative action and its relative merits. They were not in the least bit paralyzed by David's out-of-place-ness in their world, as I imagined they would be. For his part, David situated Jon and Marie within a specific social framework, and if they said anything that bordered on contentious, he took no visible offense.

Why was it, I wondered, that I was the one who was most tense during these conversations, waiting for the fallout that never actually materialized? I realized through this extended encounter that racial understandings were not singular—that invoking one set of discourses does not necessarily displace or disable all others. Upon David's departure, Marie reached up to give him a hug and kissed him on the cheek. I was startled by this sight. And I recognized, in that moment, that I was guilty of continuing to exoticize the very same people who had become such a familiar presence around me. Operating under assumptions of what I believed was a single, unyielding worldview on their part, I had overlooked the basic fluidity of processes through which ideas about race and difference are produced. Thus, while there is no doubt white Zimbabweans retain a distinctive, clearly articulated, and hierarchical understanding of the world when it comes to racial difference, it is, as with most other things, impossible to reduce into black and white.

4

REINSTATING NATURE,
REINVENTING MORALITY

O N a crisp August morning, Jon Van den Akker taught me how to shoot a rifle. The first shot made me feel like I had wads of cotton stuck in my ears, and then the ringing started inside my eardrums, becoming louder with each successive shot. Jon walked across the yard to the target and looked surprised. I had hit the target eight out of ten times. "Not bad for a beginner," he yelled over his shoulder. I grinned back at him.

Like every other farmer in the valley, Jon had taught Marie and their children how to shoot during the liberation war. Marie slept with a gun under her pillow whenever her husband was away. She never went anywhere, not even the front yard, during those years without a loaded pistol strapped to her waist. To this day, her left hip bears a mark where the holster used to rest, the embodied memory of a war three decades past. Her children were all accomplished in the use of firearms also. Jon claimed that their daughter was a better marksman than their three sons combined.

Afterward, Jon and I sat companionably together on the verandah and sorted through a large box of loose bullets. We carefully separated the tracers from the regular bullets and set them aside. Jon regaled me with stories of shooting competitions he had won in his youth, when he was an undisputed champion marksman. Hunting had been a part of his life since he was seven years old.

"Did you always like hunting?" I asked.

"It's not bad, when you're shooting an elephant or eland or buffalo," he replied. "But when you hunt zebra, it can be terrible. If you hit them without killing them straight away, the injured zebra will start biting itself, and the others in the herd will gather around it and make a big commotion. It's sad. You don't want to hunt after seeing that." He studied the pewter-colored bullet between his fingers, and continued.

"In the old days you didn't need nothing to hunt. No permits, no papers, no writing exams. People who were professional hunters learned from experience, years and years of experience in the bush. Hunters who weren't good got killed, so if you survived you were a professional hunter. Now these guys who write exams, they don't know nothing. And everyone wants to be a professional hunter. They don't want to be lawyers or doctors anymore, they want to be professional hunters. They want to make big money."

At that moment, Mapinky, one of Jon's workers, announced that the vervet monkeys were back to steal fruit from the paw-paw tree.[1] Jon told me to grab the rifle and go and shoot them. I shrugged and replied that I would just have a look first.

Jon brought the gun, and Mapinky brought the bullets. Jon started shooting the vervet monkeys high up in one of the trees above the house. It looked like he was shooting around them, rather than directly at them, but the muted cracks of the rifle and the frantic scurrying of the monkeys created a dull knot in the pit of my stomach. I slipped away and went back to my room, knowing that Jon would probably give me a hard time later.

THE TURN TO WILDLIFE

This chapter focuses on the entangled histories between settlers and landscape, the initial fall of wildlife, and its subsequent reinstatement. Two parallel trajectories occurred in this context, when the transformation of nature as cattle ranching gave way to wildlife production, accompanied by a transformation in farmers' identities. Few visiting Mlilo in the late 1990s would have guessed that this valley, with its rich wildlife reserves and tree-dotted vleis, the perfect picture of "what Africa should look like" (Neumann 1998), was a comparatively new landscape. In contrast, the presence of wildlife just a few years beforehand would have caused consternation and anger. Tracing these developments is critical to understanding how environments are naturalized and conceal histories of intervention and change. In terms of larger economic shifts, game ranching has come to constitute a critical element in the agrarian politics of southern Africa over the past few decades, giving rise to sites of immense wealth and capital investment, and bringing into alignment new forms of political conflict and social differentiation. This reflects broader shifts as ecotourism gains popularity throughout the world, and species that were once decimated are reintroduced. Mlilo claims the distinction of being the very first community in Zimbabwe to make the transition to wildlife production.

On the ground, wildlife production presents an interesting puzzle for us to think through. Because of its potential for generating greater income, it was considered until recently to be one of the most desirable land use paradigms in Zimbabwe. Its unique configuration, however, also gave rise to conflict within the community, fueling existing tensions and creating new ones. This is because the success of wildlife ranching relies on the conceptualization of animals as fluid, communal property, which runs counter to Western notions of private ownership. Moreover, the creation of a conservancy requires the dismantling of fences between individual estates to allow the uninterrupted movement of wildlife, thus blurring the boundaries of land as discrete private properties and giving rise to new conflicts between neighbors. Ironically, farmers find themselves in a dilemma where modern, cutting-edge wildlife production techniques are predicated on the configuration of property as *communal*, a system historically associated with black Zimbabweans and denigrated as illogical and doomed.[2]

Despite this dynamic, which often generated antagonism within the community, wildlife ranching became the predominant form of production in the 1990s in Mlilo because it was far more lucrative than cattle ranching. As this new paradigm took root, it also enabled farmers to reinvent themselves and legitimize their continued presence in the context of an increasingly hostile nation-state. Through interactions with biologists, international donors, politicians, and tourists, wildlife production won farmers a public, global identity vis-à-vis the emotionally and morally charged domain of conservation. From this depoliticized angle, people were able to enter into dialogues at both the national and international levels, invoking their self-articulated roles as conservationists working in the interests of the nation as a whole. Through such representations, as this chapter demonstrates, farmers staked their hopes on the belief that their role in preserving nature as something of scientific and objective value would somehow transcend, if not erase, the political and social stigma of being white in postcolonial Zimbabwe. In short, wildlife ranching enabled its practitioners to reinvent themselves as good citizens despite the liability of their skin color. The historical transformation of this farming community unfolded over the course of a century, with a gradual turn from cattle ranching to wildlife ranching.

4.1 Two white farmers in Mlilo. Photograph by author.

CATTLE CONUNDRUMS

At the beginning of the twentieth century, when small-scale cattle ranching first began as a state-designed initiative in the area that would become Mlilo, families coming from South Africa settled far in from the main road with a minimum of infrastructure and access to cosmopolitan conveniences. They found circumstances much harsher than they anticipated, with dry, nutrient-deficient soil, which made grazing difficult, and a stubborn weed that was poisonous to their cattle (Palmer 1977). The area's population remained minimal; today, long after the disappearance of these families, small graves with Afrikaans inscriptions left forgotten in the bush are the only remnants of that period.

The community of Mlilo that I encountered in the late 1990s was founded in the 1930s, when the approach to cattle ranching shifted dramatically from small-scale to large-scale production. The nation's cattle industry experienced its first crisis in the early 1920s, when a decrease in European markets in the aftermath of World War I resulted in a parallel reduction in South Africa, the principal country to which Southern Rhodesia exported its beef (Phimister 1988). Although veteran ranchers and scientists from across the world agreed that Rhodesia's climate and terrain created an exceptionally favorable environment for cattle ranching, the adverse economy at the time stirred a profound sense of alarm. The drop in export outlets coincided with a period when cattle stocks in the nascent industry were maturing for the first time, and ranchers entered the markets only to discover that their supplies far exceeded demand. A report commissioned by the government in 1923 to explore the future of the industry captures this sense of crisis: "A most serious state of financial embarrassment of cattle owners has gradually arisen and is to-day acute, with every prospect of becoming steadily worse, and unless a prompt remedy is found there must follow the ruin of a large number of our farmers and farming companies" (Government of Southern Rhodesia 1923:1). This "remedy" consisted of new refrigeration techniques through the Cold Storage Company to enable exports to more distant markets, substantial subsidies for the acquisition of land, tax exemptions for the purchase of equipment, loans for the construction of fences, new educational programs in cattle husbandry, and special railway rates for the transportation of beef.

In Mlilo, the government consolidated the existing ranching properties, which averaged twenty-five hundred acres each, and created a much smaller number of new properties ranging from thirty to one hundred thousand acres. This new policy was based on the proposition that small-scale ranching would always be inadequate in Natural Regions IV and V, with the most arid soils in the country. An optimal ratio of thirty acres for each individual head of livestock was established for these dry areas, which entirely changed the landscape of cattle ranching in the region. By this time, most of the original settlers from the turn of the century had abandoned their ill-fated ventures, so the demographics of the region had shifted dramatically as well. The government awarded portions of land to long-serving civil servants, while others bought thousands of acres at substantially subsidized prices.

Eventually, two dozen extended families settled permanently in Mlilo and formed the core of this remote community. The 250 km distance to the nearest city, Bulawayo, made frequent visits prohibitive. Moreover, in a setting where one's nearest neighbor typically lived half an hour's drive away, social gatherings clearly carried more significance because of the effort they required. Strong relationships developed among families even though they were all engaged in cattle ranching, making them competitors in a tough market. Given the 30:1 acre to animal ratio, along with the average dimensions of these properties, families could easily own at least one thousand head of cattle, and sometimes up to two or three times that amount without endangering optimal levels of sustainability. While tensions arising from broken fences and animals grazing on neighboring properties always existed, farmers overall worked under a code of cooperation, helping one another by sharing prize steers for breeding and returning neighbors' calves accidentally born on their properties to their rightful owners in good faith.

Despite community solidarity, however, just like their predecessors, most families in Mlilo found cattle ranching frustratingly difficult when it came to realizing profits. Over time, they repeatedly confronted the harsh reality of living in close proximity to Hwange National Park, with its high density of predators that preyed upon livestock. The settlers embarked on systematic projects of wildlife eradication, citing irreconcilable conflict between cattle and wildlife, and received the blessings of the state. This practice continued throughout the 1950s and 1960s, focusing on species—particularly buffalo—that were potential carriers of contagious diseases when domestic and wild animals shared grazing lands.[3] Natural predators such as lions, cheetahs, leopards, and wild dogs were vilified, and became the targets of systematic extermination campaigns (Beinart and Coates 1995; Carruthers 1989; Mutwira 1989). Officially classifying these animals as "vermin," the government paid bounties for the skins of hyenas, jackals, lynx, mongoose, baboons, gray monkeys, cheetahs, leopards, and lions. Clearly, in the eyes of the state as well as its citizenry, "the interests of game" had to give place to the "claims of crops and cattle" (Mutwira 1989:254–255) for the civilizing project.

The ease with which game was sacrificed for the sake of agriculture is counterintuitive for a country that has since highlighted its environmental policies as a cornerstone of its national identity. However, this anti-game stance perhaps makes more sense when we consider the roots of certain traditions within Christianity, which condemned the "wildness" of wild animals as a "satanically incited rebellion against man's divinely constituted authority over nature" (Cartmill 1993:54). Because of this doctrine, disobedient wild beasts have often been viewed as symbolic demons and sinners; they signified the fallen condition of humans in Christian thought and thus represented the "very abstract of degenerated nature" (Cartmill 1993:54).

By some accounts, the concentrated energies directed at wildlife eradication proved enormously effective. By the late 1970s, when the idea of wildlife production first emerged, those who ventured into it discovered to their disappointment that they had a virtually nonexistent faunal base to build on. People who still invested their faith in cattle ranching, however, continued to face persistent predation. One family reported that they lost 165 head of cattle, the majority of which were calves, to predators in a single year. Despite efforts to outwit returning lions and leopards by changing kraal locations, reinforcing fences, and increasing nocturnal security, the losses due to marauding animals continued to be too great.

Other factors increased the odds against cattle ranching considerably, such as the liberation war in the 1970s, when freedom fighters traveled in the bush and launched attacks on white farms in the area, making regular patrols to monitor the movement and safety of cattle virtually impossible. In many cases, moreover, men left their homes for months at a time to fight in the Rhodesian Armed Forces, leaving their families to live a subdued and fearful existence behind barricaded walls. In such instances, people had no choice but to leave cattle to fend for themselves. Incidents of stock theft by freedom fighters proliferated; they specifically targeted white-owned cattle of imported pedigree; other cows and bulls were shot or mutilated in symbolic defiance and left to die in their pastures (Grundy and Miller 1979).[4] In the Tribal Trust Lands,[5] where the policy of compulsory cattle-dipping had long been regarded with suspicion and resentment, the issue became deeply politicized.[6] The physical structures of the dip tanks, which also served as assessment points for government taxes and fees, soon came to be seen as tangible embodiments of colonial oppression. Liberation war fighters encouraged villagers to destroy tanks by filling them with stones and lumps of concrete, while dip attendants risked death if they continued to carry out their jobs. Two years after the compulsory dipping ceased, tick-borne diseases began spreading like wildfire in the communal villages, and panicked villagers sold their cattle as quickly as they could get rid of them. As a result, prices in the overall cattle market plummeted, creating an even bleaker scenario for white ranchers (Grundy and Miller 1979). The stage was set for the decline of cattle, and the subsequent return of wildlife.

REINTRODUCING WILDLIFE

Given these political and economic obstacles, the turn to wildlife production occurred at first as a tiny ripple in the water in the mid-1970s and gradually expanded to become the only viable form of production in Mlilo twenty-five years later. Numerous people recounted to me the advent of wildlife ranching, and the distinctive forms of conflict and heartache it precipitated within the community. Although the actual process of transformation was variably interpreted and often bitterly contested at each turn, with the rising importance of the wildlife industry in the country as a whole, many people tended to forget their initial reluctance and instead asserted—and sometimes even embellished—their roles in bringing about this shift in land use paradigms. In their conversations with me, farmers often competed with each other in laying claim to certain key roles; for example, in bringing the largest number of animals into the area or cofounding the Wildlife Producers Association (WPA), an organization that represented the interests of over a thousand wildlife producers nationwide by the late 1990s.[7] On one occasion, while attempting to reconcile two very different accounts given by individuals who both claimed sole authorship for the idea of establishing the WPA, I remarked offhandedly, "I guess everyone has a different story." The farmer I was interviewing replied sharply, "Other people tell stories; I tell the truth." Clearly the issue was a sensitive one. While acknowledging these divergent perspectives, I begin with Jon Van den Akker's narrative because he in fact was the very first person to actively cultivate the presence of wildlife on his property.

Even back in his cattle-ranching days, Jon had always been regarded by his neighbors as somewhat suspect, with too many outlandish, unsettling ideas. Surprisingly, of all the farmers in Mlilo, he was the only one who articulated a preexisting interest in animals as part of his rationale for experimenting with wildlife production. The idea took root in 1975, when the newly enacted Parks and Wildlife Act gave landowners the right to manage and benefit from wildlife found on private property (WPA 1998). This act emerged from a fifteen-year period of tentative institutional reform in attitudes toward wildlife, precipitated by the Wild Life Conservation Act in 1961. Up until that point, as was the case in Mlilo, wildlife numbers had suffered tremendous decline across the country due to their presumed incompatibility with development in Southern Rhodesia. It was only in the 1960s that the government came to the realization that even the animals within game reserves set aside exclusively for their protection were falling under the threat of agricultural expansion (Child 1995). At that point, the administration recognized that the policy of centralized protectionism, in which animals held value only for the state, had become largely unenforceable. With the change in governance brought by the Unilateral Declaration of Independence in 1965, the state adopted a deregulatory stance toward wildlife based on its inability to manage game on a national scale (WPA 1997). The idea of extending the value of wildlife to individual landowners was thus proposed with the goal of turning animals into resources, the intended effect of which was to dissuade farmers from eradicating game on their properties.

What Jon anticipated early on, and what other farmers were much slower to recognize, was a gradual shift in the country toward a philosophy of sustainable wildlife utilization. During the early 1980s, Zimbabwe became a radical advocate for the paradigm of utilization as a conservation strategy—as opposed to the strict fortress-style preservation model far more prevalent throughout the continent—unleashing censure from the international arena. However, just as wildlife production came to eclipse cattle ranching in Mlilo, so sustainable utilization gradually gained traction over the course of the next decade to become the dominant form in today's global conservation practice.

Seeing the exponential growth in the number of foreign tourists who visited Hwange National Park each year following independence, Jon decided to turn Mlilo's proximity to the park—the very factor that had been its greatest liability in terms of cattle ranching—to his advantage, and he began to draw the benefits of the tourist industry into the private sector. In the 1980s, he embarked on the previously unimaginable by opening up his property *to* wildlife, the very opposite of what he had been conditioned to do as a cattle rancher for the past twenty years. He also began establishing contacts with hunters overseas, who quickly became devoted clients, and built the first luxury lodge in Mlilo. His business rapidly expanded to include a hunting camp, a backpackers' rest, and an upmarket bush camp in addition to the original lodge. Jon's family ultimately became one of the wealthiest and most influential in Mlilo largely because of his vision, as well as the entrepreneurial mind-set of his children, who later comanaged the business. During the time I spent in the household, he never tired of telling the story of an American ecologist he befriended during the 1980s who pronounced that Jon was "a hundred years ahead of his time."

It was in the early years, however, before the benefits of his schemes became clear, that Jon encountered the most resistance from the community, which harbored a deep-seated distrust of and animosity toward wildlife. He began his efforts to entice wildlife onto his land by dismantling all of the fences that lay along boundaries shared with Hwange, and creating new water pans by pumping water from underground aquifers.[8] One of the more noteworthy landmarks on Jon's property was a beautiful vlei that soon became a favorite roaming spot for a small herd of zebra. Although this addition represented a triumph for Jon, his neighbors were alarmed by the new presence. From that point on, if any of the surrounding ranchers happened to find wildlife on their properties, they assigned blame to Jon, regardless of the unestablished origin of the trespassers. The zebra, impala, or wildebeest that appeared on their properties could

4.2 A typical luxury accommodation in Mlilo, where guests stayed in "rondavels" with thatched roofs that reflected an "indigenous" aesthetic. These camps usually charged US$300–$400 per night for guests. Photograph by author.

easily have come from the national park, as such animals had been known to do in the past, but now people automatically assumed that they came from Jon's farm. For a period of several months, he received weekly invoices from an especially bad-tempered neighbor who insisted on charging him for "zebra [or other wildlife species] found grazing on my land on x date for y amount of time." In a heated encounter during a meeting of the local Commercial Farmers Union chapter, the neighbor threatened to kill Jon if he discovered that his cattle had contracted foot-and-mouth from any kind of wildlife. Most of the farmers rallied around the neighbor, and Jon found himself blacklisted within the community for a period of time.

Nevertheless, determined to persevere, Jon set out to purchase and transport some of the rarer, high-profile species that were less likely to make a spontaneous appearance on his property. He reached an agreement with the Department of National Parks and Wild Life Management (DNPWLM), and bought two white rhinoceroses from Hwange National Park at a cost of over US$4,000.[9] Soon after the rhinos were released onto his vlei, however, they found their way over to a neighbor's property, where they quickly sparked controversy. Declaring that this was the last straw, members of the community finally voted to force Jon to repatriate his rhinos back to the park. Regrettably, he had little choice but to comply, and bid farewell both to his rhinos and his $4,000 investment. Twenty years later, he derived some degree of satisfaction from watching the rest of the community struggle to acquire rhinos for their wildlife populations, but without success because the value of the species had risen too high.[10] "One hundred years before my time," he often muttered over tea during our afternoon conversations on his shaded veranda, stirring the contents of his cup vigorously. "They should have listened."

WILDLIFE FORTUNES

Despite the initial opposition to Jon's project, it was only a few years before others began to see the potential of his vision. Ranchers with more financial resources at their disposal began investing heavily in the acquisition of wildlife, as well as the construction of lodges and hunting camps to serve the growing number of visitors to the country. Often, if a family had sons, one or more of them trained to become a professionally licensed hunter, which enabled the family to run a self-sufficient business without contracting high-priced outside professionals. Households lacking the capital to set up enterprises for themselves leased hunting concessions on their lands to safari operators who needed a place to bring their clientele. Alternatively, some people chose simply to lease portions of their property to companies looking for picturesque sites on which to build the newest trendy accommodation.

By the end of the twentieth century, everyone in Mlilo had turned to wildlife production and found themselves involved in the industry in one form or another as their primary source of income. Those who were not actively involved in the acquisition of animals hoped to reap benefits simply by opening up their properties, converting their cattle troughs into water pans that blended more aesthetically with the landscape, and sitting back to wait for wildlife to appear from their neighbors' properties and the national park.[11] In large part, this 180-degree shift emerged because of the visible connection between length of investment in wildlife production, on the one hand, and increase in profits on the other. A survey conducted in the early 1990s by the World Wide Fund for Nature compared ranches across the country engaged in the production of cattle, wildlife, or both wildlife and cattle on the same property, and concluded that wildlife-*only* ranches were the most financially viable, with an average return on investment of 10.5 percent, compared to 3.6 percent for "mixed enterprise ranches," and a mere 1.8 percent for properties exclusively ranching cattle (Jansen et al. 1992). The same study found that domestic cattle were far less resilient than wildlife in droughts, which are frequent in Zimbabwe. The researchers reported, moreover, that the viability of the cattle industry demonstrated more sensitivity to government pricing, marketing, and exchange rate policies than did wildlife. Wildlife production enabled ranchers to retain more autonomy and stability in their enterprises, a factor that became increasingly significant as the state's policies during the 1990s caused drastic economic decline.

Almost without exception, the people in Mlilo who ventured into wildlife ranching the earliest, as in Jon's case, became the wealthiest in the valley. By the 1990s, they were driving sleek new Toyota Land Cruisers rather than battered old Land Rovers, living in houses equipped with home entertainment systems, and traveling abroad more frequently.[12] Not surprisingly, the remaining skeptics were eventually won over. At the same time, the uniform dependence on wildlife belied a great deal of ambivalence as people attempted to come to terms with the changing place of animals in their lives. The transition to wildlife ranching was by no means synonymous with people shifting their worldviews to one that magically transported animals into the realm of the good. For the majority of the community, the turn to wildlife was not articulated as an ethical decision or "natural" progression; the choice was principally an economic one. As a consequence, the acceptance of wildlife in Mlilo was still very much an incomplete project when I arrived in 1998. Many of the conflicts in the community arose from the widely divergent attitudes that farmers held toward nondomestic animals and conservation in general.

During one of my visits to his house, Jack Hallowell, a seventy-four-year-old farmer born and bred in Mlilo, sat back in his worn armchair, clasped his hands over his spectacular paunch, and fixed me with the hawk-eyed glare to which I had grown accustomed. In a tone that would brook no challenge, he declared, "Whenever I see an animal in the bush, I feel like shooting it. That's what I've always done in the past." For Jack, this fiercely defiant position presented no problematic contradictions with his self-proclaimed love for the bush, and the certainty that he would perish if he were ever forced to live in the city. Jack's conceptualization of nature did not depend on the presence of "charismatic megafauna," as Western sensibilities are inclined to do, but in fact decisively excluded it. His own family's transition to wildlife ranching occurred in the late 1990s—his property was one of the last in the valley to do so—as the power of Jack's influence in determining the family's economic decisions waned. Conflicts with his sons over the fundamental wisdom and soundness of wildlife production erupted frequently, and his only sense of security came from the small herd of one hundred cattle they continued to hang on to as a safety net.

Members of the old guard like Jack were left behind as the values attributed to wildlife changed, giving rise to a new order within the community. In dialogue with global conservation discourses, white farmers like Jon, who pioneered the wildlife industry, rose to prominence in the 1990s, and were recognized as being "cutting edge," "modern," and "enlightened."[13] Their houses were among the first in the valley to acquire electricity, private telephones, computers, internet connections, and email to coordinate with clients overseas. Because they were wildlife "stakeholders," moreover, their presence was actively solicited at meetings and conferences called by Hwange National Park management, giving them greater presence and influence in the region.

On the national level, the rising prestige of successful wildlife producers also served to overturn key relationships between core and periphery. Black and white Zimbabwean youth growing up in cities such as Harare and Bulawayo internalized the same rural-urban stereotypes that existed elsewhere in the world. By the end of the 1990s, however, identifying the wildlife industry as *the* place where money flowed, thousands of cosmopolitan Zimbabweans in their twenties and thirties competed aggressively to work as wildlife guides and lodge managers in remote and isolated places.[14] Moreover, they came to work for people they had previously disdained as the most provincial in the country, often jokingly referring to them as "hillbillies" who lived by generators rather than proper electricity.[15] This collision between worlds often coincided with generational conflicts as well, leading to considerable tension in employer-employee relationships. A wildlife guide who lasted for longer than two or three years in a single locale was considered a true anomaly. In contrast to the United States and Europe, where professionals in animal-related industries are expected to articulate devotion to the natural world, many wildlife guides in Mlilo framed their occupational choice as originating not from a long-engaged interest in wildlife, but from economic strategy.[16] Thus, the groundswell of transformation in attitudes toward conservation at both local and global levels, the changing nature of consumer markets, and the desire to keep pace with modern developments rendered the shift to wildlife impossible to resist.

OWNERSHIP UNDONE

With almost everyone in Mlilo involved to some degree in wildlife production, members of the community voted to form a conservancy in May 1993.[17] Following the pioneering model developed by the Save Valley Conservancy,[18] the farmers decided on this change in a conscious bid to re-create Mlilo as a more enticing potential investment for NGOs and donor agencies.[19] This marked the turning point at which wildlife producers no longer just welcomed serendipitous coincidences between their economic endeavors and global opinion, but began to publicly rearticulate their businesses in increasingly apolitical and moral terms. The new strategy emerged as a result of the realization that for the first time since independence—as the initial ten-year period of protected ownership came to an end—the security of tenure for white farmers on their own properties had come under serious threat. It was in their interest to represent their livelihoods as contributing to the nation-state and to reinvent themselves as long-standing and dedicated conservationists, stewarding the country's faunal resources with beneficent knowledge and expertise.

As previously noted, one of the defining characteristics of wildlife conservancies in southern Africa lies in the transition to a paradigm of communal property. This practice emerges from the objective of attracting and maintaining extensive wildlife populations, which flourish through unrestricted movement between different properties. A thirty-thousand-acre private estate could successfully support a self-contained cattle-ranching operation, but an ideal regime of wildlife production calls for land managed on a much larger scale, given considerations such as genetic health, grazing patterns, and predator-prey equilibrium.[20] In order to ensure their individual success, therefore, farmers in Mlilo found themselves in a situation where they first had to buy into the goal of the conservancy's *collective* success. As a result, hundreds of kilometers of wire fences that ranchers had painstakingly constructed had to be torn down at great cost. It was common to see a farmer's workshop surrounded by piles of thickly coiled, rusty fence wire. Characteristic of the frugality for which white Zimbabweans are famous, this wire was saved and set aside for the future, when farmers might feel compelled to return to cattle ranching as their primary livelihood.

Because the transition to wildlife production occurred gradually over two decades, differential levels of investment created deep fracture lines among members of the community. The first few individuals who embarked on this new enterprise had to spend tremendous amounts of capital in the process of

purchasing and transporting wildlife to their lands. As people began opening up their ranches, some animals did venture into Mlilo from the national
park, as in the case of the zebra on Jon's vlei, but these usually consisted of the
less "glamorous" species, such as impala, kudu, and warthogs, which would fail
to attract enough ecotourism consumers and big game hunters to make the
enterprise worthwhile. In the 1980s, this group of pioneering farmers began
importing wildlife in earnest, sinking their financial resources into animals
from all over the country. As a result, a decade and a half later, many of the
giraffes in Mlilo originated from Gonarezhou in the southeastern lowveld, the
elephants and leopards from Hwange, and the zebra from a population originally translocated from Mana Pools in the north.[21]

Due to the efforts of this handful of producers, by the time the rest of the
community jumped on the bandwagon in the early 1990s, Mlilo could celebrate
both abundant numbers and impressive species diversity in its resident wildlife
populations. Even more significantly, Mlilo carried the distinction of being the
only private wildlife reserve in the country that could boast the presence of the
"big five," a commonly used index of prestige that included elephants, buffaloes, lions, leopards, and white rhinos. The valley was also home to three of the
continent's most endangered species: black rhinos, wild dogs, and cheetahs, an
achievement that was routinely cited with great pride. When the community
eventually came to a consensus on the formation of a conservancy, however,
the initial investors had to face the troubling reality of losing control over their
wildlife property in favor of an ethic of communal stewardship.[22] On the frequent occasions when animals moved off to explore potentially sweeter grazing lands, the original purchaser-owner could do nothing but stand and look
on. Ultimately, despite the knowledge that a larger spatial range would benefit
the overall welfare of wildlife in Mlilo, certain individuals continued to have
difficulty relinquishing their attachments to what they perceived as their rightful property. One prominent farmer who had bought a total of 150 buffalo over
several years in the 1980s recounted bitterly how his neighbor, "a good enough
fellow," had all of his buffalo now, even though he had never paid a cent for
any of these animals in his life. With ties of ownership coming undone, social
relationships in the community began unraveling as well.

RENEGADE FENCES

Time would soon prove that not everyone was content with simply submerg-
ing their dissatisfactions and accepting their losses. When the conservancy's

constitution was first drafted in 1993, the document was designed around four main principles:

- Internal game fencing must be kept to a minimum, and no new game fences may be constructed in order to avoid interfering with the natural movement and breeding of animals.
- If a conservancy property passes into the hands of an owner whose land use and wildlife management practices are not consistent with those of the conservancy, that property may be excised from the conservancy, and conservancy assets retrieved.
- Members are jointly responsible for meeting the recurrent costs of conservancy management, such as administrative expenses and anti-poaching patrol salaries.
- Management of wildlife and other natural resources in the conservancy must be based on scientific knowledge and the principles of sustainable use.[23]

Although the constitution was straightforward in concept, combative personalities, lingering grievances, and a steady influx of newcomers to the valley all presented obstacles to implementing these rules in practice. Many of the original farmers who signed the constitution insisted on retaining their own individual visions even when they were at direct odds with the interests of the collective. Among the conflicts that arose, some became so polarized that the entire community was swept in, forcing people to take sides and causing deep schisms in the valley.

One of the most controversial cases in Mlilo unfolded between 1994 and 1995, ending only when the offending party was permanently ousted. David Heron was a wealthy businessman who had made his fortune elsewhere and acquired property in Mlilo from a family who had emigrated to South Africa. The fact that he was an outsider automatically pitted the rest of the farmers against him, but the unconventional ways in which he began pouring money into his ranching operation sealed his reputation as a troublemaker. From wildlife reserves and producers in South Africa as well as Zimbabwe, Heron imported rare and extremely costly species such as Liechtenstein's hartebeest and steenbok, in addition to large numbers of more common animals.[24] Then, in outright defiance of conservancy policy, he proceeded to construct a fenced enclosure around his entire thirty-thousand-acre property to protect his investment.

Although there most certainly would have been voices of dissent, Heron might have succeeded in his operation had it not been for the misfortune of having one of the most ill-tempered men in Mlilo as his neighbor. Incensed by Heron's actions, Henry Gordon accused him of fencing in large numbers of his own wildebeest when Heron constructed the enclosure, in effect committing wildlife embezzlement. The local Wildlife Producers Association and Mlilo Conservancy committees recognized the larger implications of Henry's accusations; Heron had in all likelihood fenced in not only Gordon's wildebeest but also wildlife belonging to the whole community. At the same time, because the conservancy only had a constitution voluntarily mandated by its members rather than a legally binding contract, the appropriate path of action remained unclear. In the meantime, Gordon had taken matters into his own hands, setting upon a nocturnal campaign in which he and his workers hacked through the fence and left a gaping hole as large as a living room wall to allow the passage of animals onto his own estate. Upon discovering the damage, Heron furiously repaired the fence, only to have Gordon return to the same spot a few nights later. This cycle continued for months, and the conflict grew more explosive. In the end, Heron swallowed his losses, sold his ranch, and left Mlilo.[25] The subsequent owners removed the fence, but with associated histories remaining vivid in people's memories, they found Mlilo's established social circles less than welcoming.

The blurred boundaries between private and communal property under the wildlife regime created similar feelings of isolation and alienation for almost everyone in the community, although few people openly admitted it. Heron's refusal to fall in line with the conservancy's vision was only one example of the new conflicts that emerged; along the same spectrum, smaller battles occurred on a daily basis concerning ownership and rights to specific animals. When a buffalo was shot on one farmer's property, for example, but managed to escape with a nonfatal wound across a boundary into another farm, who would have the right to claim the trophy fee? The farmer on whose land the animal was originally tracked and sighted, or the individual on whose property it was eventually killed?[26] Heated disputes like this occurred regularly, and at any given moment one could find feuding neighbors. In the most difficult cases, mediation by district courts served as a last resort. Because of the lack of faith people had in the judicial system, however, in the majority of instances, conflicts were kept within the community itself and often continued to brew unresolved. The once tranquil days that people recounted, with tennis games and Sunday picnics hosted alternately by different families, had long since disappeared; what remained instead was rivalry, mistrust, and jealousy that unsettled a once firmly anchored sense of community.

FLUID PROPERTY

Fences function as more than physical markers in the land; they constitute archetypes of division (Peters 1994). In her account of land use in Botswana, Pauline Peters describes the contested process of dividing communal property for the creation of privatized areas, with fences gradually cropping up across the landscape. This transition presents a narrative that is more common these days. The transformations in Mlilo portrayed in this chapter, in contrast, move in the reverse direction through the transition from private to communal property as an essential step in the remaking of wildlife as fluid resource.

The uniqueness of this equation presents an interesting paradox for those conditioned more conventionally in the practice of private ownership. Ben Cousins (1992) argues that property regimes often constitute a terrain of struggle because they are intrinsically linked to income distribution and thus to power. Since the articulation of Hardin's "tragedy of the commons" model in 1968, the question of common property has been passionately debated, with the general conclusion that the system itself is not a flawed one. Rather, problems arise when strategic individuals fail to act in the interests of the group, which undermines the purported logic of collective action (Olson 1971). Consequently, in the absence of force, people lack the ability to coordinate and enforce actions in situations of collective interdependence (Runge 1986).

The tensions in Mlilo that emerged from contests over communal wildlife appear to substantiate this assessment. At one conservancy meeting where the questioned ownership of animals yet again surfaced as the topic of debate, ideals of honor and gentlemanly behavior were swiftly invoked to mask the unspoken accusations and angry looks that flew across the table. It was then that Charles Murphy, a farmer of quiet disposition, removed his pipe from his mouth and declared philosophically, "We are all gentlemen, except when it comes to money." An uncomfortable silence settled upon the group following this frank admission, which cut to the very heart of the problem underlying the fragile fiction of communality. With illusions of civility and integrity cast aside, as long as wildlife was fluid, it remained a source of deep conflict in Mlilo.

4.3 A Commercial Farmers Union (CFU) meeting in Mlilo. Photograph by author.

ELEPHANTS AND THE STATE

As the private wildlife industry began to thrive in Mlilo during the 1990s, the state's perceptions of wildlife also shifted, recognizing its value as a resource with far greater potential than simply generating national park entrance fees. With this growing interest on the part of the state, Mlilo lost a measure of its autonomy. From this point on, debates over wildlife property surpassed arguments between individual farmers to create new tensions between community and state. One of most public controversies surrounded a proposal to introduce elephants from Hwange National Park into the Mlilo Conservancy. The heart of this conflict lay in the question of who exactly held sovereign rights over wildlife.

The public scale of this struggle also owed much to the species itself. Elephants are animals that have been familiar to many parts of the world since the seventeenth century through their recruitment in circuses, menageries, and zoos, but they hold a particularly significant place in Zimbabwe's social and political imaginaries.[27] For their distinction as the largest living terrestrial animals, and for stories of strength, wisdom, and compassion, elephants are perhaps unrivaled among their animal peers in inviting sympathy and admiration from people. In many African countries, they have joined the cast of elite charismatic megafauna that have become synonymous with conservation movements worldwide, symbolizing the high moral standing of animals. These representations in turn allow animals to be stripped of their contexts—political, historical, and social—transforming them into subjects of a global sovereignty rather than a local one.

While other areas of the continent continued to fight against declining numbers, countries in southern Africa witnessed an efflorescence in elephant populations during the second half of the twentieth century. During the 1980s Zimbabwe was the most successful country in southern Africa in promoting its elephant population, with elephant demographics burgeoning to the point where they actually surpassed sustainability thresholds in many national parks. The formidable impact elephants have on their environments led to growing concern over landscape degradation, eventually leading to an initiative to cull what were termed "surplus" animals.[28] As noted earlier, this practice brought harsh criticism from Western critics to Zimbabwe's doorstep, culminating in the global categorization of elephants as a Level I Endangered Species, which effected a moratorium on all traffic in elephant products.

This ban dealt Zimbabwe a double blow: not only did it bring an end to a working model of sustainable utilization that had already proven successful, but it also prevented the government from selling its existing ivory stocks, which spelled a significant loss in the country's revenue. Zimbabwe, however, refused to concede defeat, and continued to argue its case over the next several years. In 1997, the Convention on International Trade in Endangered Species (CITES) voted to relax the ban on ivory[29] and empowered Zimbabwe to engage in limited sales with Japan.[30] In what was heralded as a historic moment, the elephant was transformed into a symbol not only of Zimbabwe's success in conservation but also of the very nation itself, as a country that the global North could no longer afford to ignore.

Elephants thus held special status in the national landscape. Among national parks, Hwange boasted more elephants than any other place in the country, earning it the nickname of "Elephant Park." During dry seasons, visitors were guaranteed the spectacle of at least a dozen elephants even before they reached the main entry gate to the park. While obviously adding to the enchantment and appeal of the park, from an ecological perspective, the explosive reproduction of elephants became a problem of critical proportions for park management. As culling programs continued to remain under strict prohibition by global conservation regimes, the only other option was translocation, a costly and ambitious project because of the sheer size of elephants, as

4.4 Two elephants walking next to a water pan in Mlilo. Elephants were a common presence in the conservancy before the land occupations. Photograph by author.

well as the complex structures of their social groups.[31] Although translocation schemes have been successful on a limited scale in the past, it was clear by the turn of the millennium that the Zimbabwean government lacked the technical skills and financial resources to carry out such projects, faced as it was with much larger political and economic difficulties.

Under these circumstances, the Mlilo conservancy hatched a plan that its members believed would create a win-win situation for everyone involved. The conservancy itself remained below the level of saturation in elephant numbers, and would happily accept new immigrants from Hwange into the area. The only problem lay in the fact that the wildlife ranchers themselves could not produce the capital to finance the translocation costs. They decided to take out an advertisement in a British magazine inviting the public to "adopt an elephant" and donate money for the translocation of elephants from Hwange to Mlilo, at £400 per elephant. To their surprise, donations began flowing in, accompanied by letters of support and encouragement from readers in Britain.

Several weeks later, however, the Department of National Parks and Wild Life Management (DNPWLM) headquarters in Harare sent a formal inquiry to the conservancy board about exactly who had authorized the advertisement. The elephants in Hwange belonged to the state, they objected, and it was unlawful for a private conservancy to raise overseas funds for property that the state had not yet even agreed to sell. After two years of complicated negotiations by Mlilo residents during which the government remained unbending in its decision, the conservancy finally returned the funds to each individual donor in Britain with a letter of apology and explanation.

Needless to say, members of the conservancy were deeply embarrassed by this turn of events, and bitterly resented the actions of the DNPWLM, which they assumed were driven by the desire to assert power rather than to act in the genuine interest of elephants. Given the rising valuation of wildlife property, combined with an increasingly tenuous political landscape, farmers interpreted the state's actions as a deliberate and unjust punitive measure against the community. In their eyes, the state was threatened by the conservancy's success, and used this opportunity to stage yet another performance of authoritarian power.

Although obviously a politically convenient interpretation on the part of the farmers, this rendition of events was perhaps not far off the mark. For the state, an issue much larger than alleviating environmental pressures on Hwange lay at stake: instead of seeing this project as an opportunity to provide surplus elephants with a better habitat, the conservancy's actions were understood as an attempt not only to usurp national resources for private gain but also to undermine the very authority of the state itself. Such concerns were highlighted in a letter addressed to the Mlilo Conservancy on November 18, 1993, in which the Ministry of Environment and Tourism suggested that farmers had created the conservancy in order to subvert national land designation schemes. This type of accusation was not atypical: because conservancies have no statutory definition by law, many in the government view their motives with a great deal of suspicion. William Wolmer et al. suggest that "at best, conservancies are regarded as 'white self-indulgence,' and at worst, as attempts by large-scale farmers to hide and privatise wildlife, exploiting a national heritage and challenging the state's control over wildlife" (2003:4). This was illustrated during a seminar in Masvingo, when the secretary of environment and tourism made his distrust of conservancies clear by issuing the following declaration: "Government will not allow the privatisation of wildlife resources through the back door, that is, through unplanned and uncontrolled private conservancies. We are fully aware of such Machiavellian plots to privatise wildlife resources from Kenya to South Africa" (quoted in Wolmer et al. 2003).

This episode of failed elephant translocation, moreover, was by no means the only one of its kind; such entanglements with the state occurred time and again, particularly revolving around the sale and purchase of wildlife. In 1999, for example, the conservancy board was involved in a lawsuit against the government, which had failed to deliver two dozen giraffes from Gonarezhou National Park that had been paid for in full four years before. These acts of "bad faith" fueled people's critiques of the state, further entrenching the conviction that the government cared nothing for the welfare of wildlife. It is possible that inefficiency and lack of coordination on the part of the DNPWLM had something to do with its failure to deliver the animals.[32] However, it was the imagined reality of corruption and conspiracy that was socially meaningful in this context, and thus it was in opposition to this "failed state" that white farmers began articulating their own reinvented moralities.

REINVENTING MORALITY

The state, as it lives in the imagination of white farmers, straddles a boundary between administrative incompetence on the one hand and consummate skill in effecting its desires on the other. In analyzing the workings of statecraft, farmers accredited the postcolonial government with an intimate knowledge of how to deploy the politics of crisis as a strategic tool. Long before the land invasions began, people recited countless examples of how the state engineered situations that did not just invite interventions from foreign countries but made them absolutely imperative. Jon Van den Akker was in the habit of declaring that it was in the interests of the state to keep the country in a perpetual state of disaster so that the government could receive more donor money and line its deep pockets even further. On one occasion, as the family sat in the living room watching television after dinner, he was spurred on by a segment on the Zimbabwe Broadcasting Corporation news announcing that Japan had agreed to donate Z$300 million to build a hospital in Gweru.[33] Jon related this news back to the 1980s, when the Lions Club International had built the St. Luke's eye hospital in Ken Maur, which now stood derelict and crumbling.[34] Raising his voice, he articulated the following critique:

> There has to be thousands of people wandering around in the bush blind
> with cataracts. Then the doctors from America will come, and they'll donate
> millions of dollars. These bloody guys [government officials] don't care. They
> make *us* care. It's the same as in the parks—the water holes must be dry,

the pumps all buggered, and the animals sick and dying and having to eat mud—and then the donors will come in with money, like the $192 million for the Hwange Park Management Plan. You should tell those Americans to just keep their money and feed their poor people back home, because it won't help anyone here.[35]

As skilled strategists themselves, farmers highlighted their own steadfast commitment to conservation in contrast to the state's failures. The great majority of farmers adhered faithfully to hunting quotas set each year by the DNPWLM. In 1996, a number of Mlilo Conservancy members submitted a proposal to institute a separate quota system for the conservancy that would serve as a safeguard in addition to quotas mandated by the state, in order to ensure "true" sustainability. Although ultimately the motion was not passed, some of these members felt so strongly about the quota that they threatened to resign from the conservancy if the new system was not put into effect. Mlilo farmers also recounted how in 1992, when the Hwange National Park administration ran out of funding in the middle of one of the worst droughts of the century, they worked tirelessly to maintain their water pans even when every single water source in Hwange had dried up. During those months, thousands of animals made their way into Mlilo to find water, and people often claimed that all of them would have died had it not been for the hard work of local whites. By playing up their own role in conservation, wildlife ranchers strategically portrayed themselves as working wholeheartedly in the interest of nature and the moral good, or in this case, for the animals that routinely fell victim to a callous and ineffectual state.

Finally, and perhaps most significantly, underlying much of the relative ease with which farmers reinvented their morality was the confluence between the past and the present. While the form of ranching may have changed, in local worldviews, the successful management of wildlife was just as dependent on the ability to discipline and control nature. In ideological constructions of difference, the power to domesticate the environment is used as a common trope in establishing the dividing line between the civilized and the primitive, and the scientific versus the irrational. Rooted within Judeo-Christian theology, ideas about maintaining and controlling nature circulate within a valence of abstract associations, including knowledge, wisdom, industriousness, determination, and God-like authority (Thomas 1983). Hence, the moralizing position farmers assumed was a comfortably familiar one. Combined with the global status of conservation, these values inscribed a particular moral order upon wildlife production, which, in turn, reinforced the argument for rights of tenure in one's settled environment. The original economic logic favoring wildlife production was thus cast aside in favor of a cultural understanding that provided testament to the superior morality and pure intentions of whites.

In contemporary identity politics, claims of distinctive and indispensable ties to the environment have become a critical site of self-articulation (Comaroff and Comaroff 2009; Li 2000; Tsing 1999). Most often framed together with constructions of indigeneity, such claims rely upon the symbolic capital of cultural identity. As a consequence, as many scholars have shown, indigenous struggles have undergone gradual "greening" in recent decades as groups tap into the language of Western environmentalism and incorporate themes such as "respecting Mother Earth" and "being close to nature" within activist discourses (Conklin 1997:712). Reessentialized, the "ecological noble savage" speaks with authentic authority on behalf of the environment, flora and fauna, and indigenous rights, conveniently packaged into one. The fact that the argument for indigenous rights must attach itself to the shining star of the environment in order to gain visibility is deeply unsettling. Nonetheless, this constitutes a form of what Peet and Watts (1996) call "liberation ecologies," or the collective sense of identity and empowerment that emerges from imagined social connections to the environment.

Here, once again, Mlilo defies the typical narrative. The ecological noble savage is absent; instead, the ignoble colonizer is the one fighting for rights and recognition. White farmers represent the Other in postcolonial Zimbabwe, but without a marked ethnicity, and with their *un*marked—yet extremely visible—whiteness, they lack access to certain types of symbolic capital in hierarchies of cultural legitimacy. The language of articulation therefore shifts from the particular to the universal: farmers speak on behalf of global nature, in the language of scientific authority. This carries powerful weight in the modern world, where science is seen as standardizing and perfecting knowledge, unencumbered by bias. Accordingly, by framing wildlife production in terms of its scientific value to conservation, farmers invoked a context larger than the nation-state. Within the global framework, their whiteness not only ceases to matter, but in fact suddenly makes absolute sense in conjunction with their claims to environmental consciousness. In the context of the global, whiteness is rendered invisible once again, along with all of its associated privileges. Conservation operates as a safe haven in which representations can circulate stripped of unfavorable social, historical, and political contexts.

Thus, despite the inherent contradictions built into wildlife production as a form of land use, farmers for the most part embraced this paradigm because it enabled them to re-create their public identities. The concept of articulation in Tania Li's (2000) work captures the delicate balance between historical contingency and self-conscious strategy that is achieved in such formations. For the Lindu in Indonesia, Li suggests, articulating indigenous identity is a creative act, opening up new political possibilities unavailable to "ordinary villagers." The "tribal slot" opens up room for the Lindu to maneuver within existing fields of power. Li's understanding of these dynamics is particularly useful here because it highlights the "uniqueness and contingency of articulation, and its necessary occlusion of the larger flows of meaning and power, the practices of everyday life and work . . . and the structures of feeling which form the larger canvas within which positioning occurs" (2000:166). Despite radically different fields of power, white farmers are also engaged in a high-stakes strategy of articulation, drawing upon "historically sedimented practices, landscapes, and repertoires of meaning" (Li 2000:151). The "white slot" is as legible as the tribal one; although often implicit rather than explicit, it conjures equally powerful meanings.

Interestingly, black Zimbabweans working for the national park, the Forestry Commission, and the Natural Resources Board routinely sought out Mlilo residents for advice on environmental management issues as well as technical support in maintaining vehicles and engines. In a handful of instances during my visits to different households, individuals dropped by to explain that they were applying for higher degrees in environmental training and were requesting assistance with tuition. More often than not, to my surprise, farmers such as Jon Van den Akker and Charles Murphy obliged. In these cases, it was the type of degree that was important, for I witnessed the same benefactors turning down requests for help with other kinds of professional degrees without a second thought. They clearly felt a stronger obligation toward promoting environmental education, and rewarded those who acknowledged their authority in relation to nature.

There is something very telling about these interactions. Within such negotiations, we see that wildlife ranchers were to varying degrees successful by the end of the twentieth century in reinventing themselves as public brokers of conservation. In a number of situations, they were acknowledged as experts. In a world where perceptions of environmental practice often have the currency to legitimize or delegitimize whole groups and even entire nations, the "enlightened white conservationist" card holds obvious social and political utility. Even as they used this card to position themselves in the global landscape, people in Mlilo simultaneously appealed, with increasing desperation, to the nation-state to take notice of their efforts. While perhaps buying extra time, however, this articulation was ultimately trumped by other interests aligned with the state's evolving agendas. The next chapter takes a closer look at the animals implicated within these articulations, and how particular species were employed to symbolize and reinforce economic inequalities and imagined social hierarchies.

5

THE USES
OF ANIMALS

IN July 2001, on a cloudless wintry afternoon, I sat on a hard sofa in the sparse, well-scrubbed home of Charles and Ella Murphy, an elderly white couple who lived near the tiny post office in the center of Mlilo. The Murphys ran a small, two-chalet lodge during the tourist season and derived the rest of their modest income from leasing out the hunting rights on their property to safari operators in the area.[1] Charles and I had first become acquainted at a Commercial Farmers Union meeting in February 1999, when he took his pipe out of his mouth, gave a shy smile, and held out his tobacco-stained hand for me to shake. He invited me home to meet his wife, Ella, who was a fragile-looking, anxious woman, polite to a fault and disarmingly sincere. Since then, I had made it a regular habit to drop by the Murphys's house whenever I had an errand at the post office. My afternoons there were usually spent chatting over cups of milky tea and store-bought biscuits; cooking was not one of Ella's strengths, and unlike the rest of the families in the valley, she and her husband employed no domestic servants. Charles and Ella's only daughter lived in the United States, so they seemed to enjoy the company, and professed that my spontaneous visits reminded them of days gone past, when people in the valley had been much more social.

This particular visit turned out to be different: the atmosphere was palpably tense, and the teapot lay untouched on its tray. The land invasions of white commercial farms that had begun in February 2000 had finally reached this region the month before, despite what had gradually grown into a comfortable complacency that here in the arid bush, far removed from the politics of the capital, they would be for the most part forgotten. For the past sixteen months, in fact, farmers in this area had been relatively unhindered in going about business as usual on their lands. With the arrival of the war vets in June 2001, however, Mlilo's residents were rudely awakened from such naive expectations as the new land occupants quickly laid the foundations for thatch houses, created their own bus stops, and claimed formerly private roads for their own exclusive use. In each of these stages of land invasion, the local government officials not only turned a blind eye but actually offered infrastructural support, substantiating the popular belief that these land occupations were state sanctioned despite their constitutional illegality.

My earlier conversation with Charles and Ella had been interrupted by an official from the DNPWLM who had come to investigate urgent complaints by the war vets that they had been harassed by lions at their campfire the night before. The officer had stopped in at the Murphys's house to report that they were now looking for an officially designated "Problem Animal."[2] In the brief, heated argument that ensued, Charles declared vehemently that under no circumstances would he allow the DNPWLM to shoot one of his lions, which by rights belonged to him as his private property.

Ritual subtleties in the performance of power between black and white Zimbabweans had changed dramatically since the land invasions had begun, and the officer's only reaction was to shrug dismissively as he led his team off onto the Murphys's farm. I sat waiting with Charles and Ella, who looked grim and had given up any pretext of normal conversation. The DNPWLM team returned two hours later, and the officer, somewhat less confident this time, stated ruefully that they had failed to find any signs of lions around the war vets' campsite. Instead, what they had discovered were bushpig tracks, revealing the recent presence of a solitary wild pig. The officer quickly explained that although bushpigs are not large, their grunts can sound similar to those of a lion, and the mistake was therefore perfectly understandable. The terrified war vets' fears had been calmed, and the potentially explosive action of tracking down and killing one of the Murphys's lions was temporarily deferred.

Upon the departure of the DNPWLM team, the tension of the encounter slowly evaporated, and Charles's taut expression transformed into a grin stretching from ear to ear. "Can you believe it?" He shook his head incredulously. "The war vets couldn't even tell a bushpig from a lion!" He laughed uproariously, and Ella joined in his revelry. Very soon a celebratory atmosphere filled the room, and the Murphys, whom I had always known to be very restrained and formal, were slapping their hands on the coffee table and wiping tears from the corners of their eyes.

The story quickly circulated around Mlilo, and farmers breathed a collective sigh of relief to find themselves once again on comfortable terrain. They chose to interpret the incident as evidence that the land occupiers were fundamentally out of place on their newly claimed lands—not just from the white farmers' perspective, but also from the occupiers' own point of view—if they had failed to identify even the most elementary differences between a bush-pig and a lion. The story winsomely illustrated not only the war vets' obvious unfamiliarity and lack of ease with the local landscape, but also their basic fear of it as an imagined space of "wild" animals and "untamed" bush. Thus, the ill-fated encounter between war vets and bushpig served to delegitimize the moral authority of the land issue that had been so carefully propagandized by the government. Here, adding fuel to already deeply ingrained practices of critiquing state corruption, was a local example that perfectly illuminated the fundamental contradictions and flaws of the land redistribution project.

It was in this context that the tale of the phantom lion grew in dimension as it was relayed with increasing hilarity among the farmers of the valley. Jokes revolving around landscape and (in)competency appear as a common theme in many societies, usually with a clear subtext aimed at undermining a group's right of residence.[3] The strategic appropriation of this case of mistaken identity served as a way for people to contest their marginality within the national arena and engage in the creative reconfiguration and discrediting of state agendas. After weeks of growing uncertainty augured by the arrival of the land invaders, the white farmers seized on this particular story as a safe yet powerful means through which they could dismiss the government's blundering efforts as doomed to failure. Through this process, the state, ordinarily perceived as a menacing threat, was transformed, at least momentarily, into an object of laughter.[4] The next section turns to the centrality of animals in our social worlds more broadly, and explores their significance as markers of status, identity, and hierarchy.

ANIMALS, POWER, PRIVILEGE

John Berger begins his influential essay "Why Look at Animals?" by disavowing a certain perspective: "To suppose that animals first entered the human imagination as meat or leather or horn is to project a 19th century attitude backward across millennia. Animals first entered the imagination as messengers and promises" (1991:4). Animals figure prominently in our social and moral landscapes because they make themselves readily available as mirrors and metaphors. These days, as boundaries between local and global disappear and people mobilize increasingly creative ways of debating difference, animals have become deeply intertwined in human identity politics. Whether in the

construction of gender, race, class, indigeneity, or citizenship, animals constitute sites of political struggle, serving as cornerstones for "progressive" social
movements and the focal points around which "traditional" cultures are reified.
As a consequence, animals are *fundamentally constitutive* of human societies,
or, as Claude Lévi-Strauss (1963b) would say, animals are "good to think" with.

While many of anthropology's classical texts engaged the role and function
of human-animal relationships in culture, the animals themselves were seldom objects of interest. The past two decades, in contrast, have seen a renewed
focus on animals, in an "animal moment" that attempts to include animal
perspectives (Emel and Wolch 1998). The impetus for the animal moment is
articulated in close dialogue with movements in popular culture, where conservation discourses proliferate, marketing empires are built on dinosaurs, and
cloned sheep are presented as scientific triumph. With their increasing visibility, moreover, animals have become subjects of intense contestation. With
the changes brought by transnational migration, for example, contemporary
conflicts within nation-states often erupt around "animal-based practices," or
cultural practices that involve the use of animals in some form (Elder et al.
1998). Through the decontextualization and racialization of subaltern animal
practices, immigrants and minorities are stigmatized as savage, primitive, and
uncivilized, while dominant groups remain comfortably within the zone of
the ethical and humane. Masquerading under the guise of concern for animal welfare, xenophobia and racism thus find a convenient entrée into public
discourses where they might otherwise not be tolerated. As a consequence,
certain animal practices are used as "tools of cultural imperialism designed
to delegitimize the subjectivity and citizenship" (Elder et al. 1998:73) of those
labeled Other in the nation-state.[5]

The use of animals in justifying contemporary inequalities extends to other
dimensions as well; animals are often utilized in symbolic representations of
power and privilege. The custom of designating certain creatures—the more
majestic, the fiercer, the better—as the distinctive province of monarchies and
aristocracies recurs across space and time (Hay 1975). The hunting of such animals was usually conducted with a great deal of fanfare, emphasizing exclu-
sivity of access and reinscribing power differentials between classes. Imperial
policies were often patterned on the same model by transforming wildlife into
a highly charged domain restricted to government officials and settlers (Mutwira 1989; MacKenzie 1988); at the same time, colonial hunts functioned as
spectacles in the enactment and performance of imperial sovereignty, winning
colonial subjects through a form of "predatory care" (Pandian 2001). Such ico-

nicization of white colonial power continues to operate in veiled ways today, perpetuating images of wildlife as a resource for which access has been flagrantly undemocratic.

These symbolic conquests of empire were in turn imported back to the metropole through the display of dazzling "exotica" from the colonies. Zoos and museums paraded animals in ornate enclosures with racialized depictions of their native environments (Rothfels 2008; Davies 2000), accompanied by "exotic" human attendants who became part of the exhibits themselves (Ritvo 1987). These spectacles functioned as a stage for "domesticating, mythologizing, and aestheticizing the animal universe" (K. Anderson 1998:28). In these "centers of calculation" (Latour 1987), hierarchies were aligned according to an evolutionary master narrative that ultimately culminated in the triumph of the Great White Hunter over nature (Haraway 1989). The critical agenda lay in educating the public with a doctrine that placed European expansionism at the pinnacle of moral, political, and commercial imperatives. From this point on, it is easy to imagine how such displays would translate into larger discussions on global hierarchy, exoticism, and perceptions of difference.

Thus, animals are routinely used as mechanisms to cement power and privilege. Beyond spectacular displays of hunting and animal captivity, power is consolidated by redefining the human-animal boundary, rendering certain groups of humans more beastly and other types of animals more human. One example of this boundary-shifting comes from Nazi socialist ideologies during the 1930s and '40s, which pronounced animal protection as a top concern and created an enormous bureaucratic organization known as the Reichs-Tierschutzverein (Association for the Protection of Animals of the Reich), the membership of which was confined to individuals of Germanic blood (Arluke and Sax 1995). Experiments involving the use of vivisection were illegalized because of their perceived cruelty, and the scientists who employed this technique, most of whom were Jewish, were persecuted. Hunting and meat consumption were condemned as signs of decay in national culture. German shepherds, on the other hand, were celebrated as embodying the spirit of nationalism, and the loyalty and bravery of Hitler's canine companions achieved mythological status.[6] This culture of elevated moral status for animals in turn enabled the dehumanization of Jewish populations, making it possible for National Socialists to commit horrific atrocities within a framework of rationalization (Arluke and Sax 1995).

Focusing on this same volatility of the human-animal boundary, Jacques Derrida (2008) more recently revived the discussion of how philosophers have drawn ontological distinctions between human and animal across time. In response to his famous question as to why he feels naked, rather than nude, under his cat's scrutiny, Donna Haraway (2008) issues a challenge: Derrida never considers what his *cat* might be thinking, but focuses only on how the cat's gaze affects *him*. She exhorts us instead to look back reciprocally at our companion species, to hold their gaze in mutual respect, to be curious about what *they* are thinking. Pushing Lévi-Strauss's classic insight further, animals, Haraway insists, are not here to think with; they are here to live with. Inspired by Haraway's call, scholars such as Eduardo Kohn (2013, 2007) have proposed an anthropology "beyond the human," seeking to restore to the center creatures that ordinarily appear only on the margins of the discipline. Hugh Raffles (2010), for example, unravels in beautiful detail how insects—arguably the most marginal of animal Others—have become thoroughly entangled in our day-to-day practices, sentiments, and imaginations. More recently, these theoretical concerns have come together in a field known as "multispecies ethnography," which explores how "a multitude of organisms' livelihoods shape and are shaped by political, economic, and cultural forces" (Kirksey and Helmreich 2010). Multispecies ethnographers strive to rethink and undo natural and cultural categories, locating biosocialities in our engagements with meerkats, cup corals, honeybees, microbes, and orangutans, among other living things.[7]

In Mlilo, a multispecies lens illuminates the complex ways in which animals were embedded in both physical and symbolic landscapes. Animals were an indispensable part of farmers' social worlds; they were fluid in their meanings and symbolisms, but were unwaveringly constant as a point of reference. Animals in Mlilo were routinely utilized, moreover, as vehicles for reinforcing authority and reproducing racialized hierarchies. People used charismatic animals as a narrative focal point, mapped social logics onto their pets, and employed particular species as metaphors for political critique. This chapter explores both changing and enduring uses of animals by focusing on four different typologies: charismatic animals (lions), reinvented animals (African wild dogs), criminal animals (elephants), and domesticated animals (cats and dogs). The consolidation of power, privilege, hierarchy, and understandings of difference in white farmers' worldviews was entirely dependent on the multiple uses, and utility, of animals.[8]

Now, picking up where we left off with the story from the beginning of this chapter, the delight that the farmers took in the war vets' misreading of the landscape was derived from another important dimension: the fact that the bushpig had been mistaken for a lion. The next section turns to lions to explore their significance in the social and historical landscapes of Mlilo.

TRACKING LIONS IN THE LANDSCAPE

In Mlilo, lion imagery recurred regularly throughout farmers' stories, alternating between representations of magnificent, awe-inspiring creatures and despicable predators that preyed upon livestock. Not surprisingly, more than any other animal in Mlilo, the lion was powerfully evocative in both symbolic meaning and sentiment, always present as a critical point of reference for the formation of rural white Zimbabwean identity.

Within the larger context, lions occupy an uncontested space as the most magnificent animals in the contemporary Western imaginary. From the Lion King to the lions of Tsavo, popular culture has anthropomorphized the lion by gifting it with cunning, wisdom, nobility, blood thirst, and sovereignty over the entire Animal Kingdom.[9] Similar symbolisms can be found in different historical contexts, as in the use of lions in the Roman gladiatorial arena and of captive felines in the private menageries of eighteenth-century French aristocrats, which demonstrated wealth, power, and prestige on the part of their owners (Ritvo 1987). In China, dogs were once bred to resemble miniature lions, and roamed around imperial courts as living symbols of the greatness of the Chinese empire (Tuan 1984). These representations are typical of the role that many "supreme predators" take on in cultural worldviews, as in the example of the jaguar in Aztec society, which stood as a metaphor for spiritual power and elite status (Saunders 1994), or the polar bear for the Inuit, which carries powerful associations with male authority and prestige (D'Anglure 1994). The investment in a particular conceptualization of the lion's predatory nature was in fact so strong that for many years, studies revealing that lions were often opportunistic scavengers that exploited the kills of hyenas were met with indignation and resistance by popular audiences (Glickman 1995).

In Mlilo, lions have always been complex in symbolism, moving through a mosaic of meanings across time. By tracking lions in the social and historical landscape of Mlilo, this chapter replicates the chronological history presented in chapter 4, but privileges lions as the narrative axis. The point of departure in telling tales about lions began with a particular origin myth, when white Rhodesians first arrived in the region at the beginning of the twentieth century and set out to transform it into the site of a successful cattle-ranching industry. As noted previously, because of its close proximity to Hwange National Park, the landscape in Mlilo was plagued with wildlife, which was officially labeled "vermin" and subject to systematic extermination (Mutwira 1989). The colonial government instituted a cash reward policy for the predators of the area, such as leopards, cheetahs, wild dogs, and hyenas, all of which posed serious threats for newly acquired cattle and ran counter to the "civilizing project" as a whole.[10] Among these animals, lions were especially notorious for their unflagging persistence in tracking down the *bomas* where cattle were sheltered, despite the painstaking lengths farmers went to each night to move the location of these enclosures. Moreover, lions would hunt in groups, targeting structural weaknesses in fences to gain access to the precious cattle. Up until the 1970s, the losses brought by lions remained discouragingly constant, resulting in the harsh reality that most farmers in the area struggled each year simply to break even.[11]

Narratives of this time were interlaced with the language of hardship, but also with an undercurrent of romantic longing, as men recounted how they spent countless nights guarding their livestock from the flatbeds of their pickup trucks, rifle in one hand, lantern in the other. The solitude of those deep nights, lying alert and watchful under the luminescent starlight, drew emotive power from the timeless mythology of human desire pitted against nature as an adversary. Skilled marksmanship was glorified, and the number of feline bodies a man could claim was transformed into an index of masculinity. Fusing history, political necessity, and ideology, white Rhodesian nationalism in the mid-twentieth century emphasized qualities of ruggedness and resourcefulness, epitomized by the spirit of the *voortrekker*, or frontier experience. The celebrated history of pioneers migrating northward from South Africa to conquer the unknown wilderness was the pride and essence of Rhodesian-ness. In this context, lions were key, for their strategic identification as the most dangerous and cunning adversaries enabled the convenient metonymic leap from conquering *them* to symbolically conquering nature as a whole. The narrative of continual struggle between humans and lions—both usually coded male—was incorporated into the ongoing reproduction of a "mythico-history" (Malkki 1995) that asserted entitlement to the land through an unassailable logic of conquest.

Memories of this period were always perched at readiness on the edge of consciousness, creeping into the language of the everyday and shaping the discursive limits of self-representation. In material form, memories were assembled in the taxidermic specimens that littered people's houses: buffalo head stumps, whole civet cat skins, and the beautiful spiraling symmetry of kudu antlers adorned living room walls, memorializing an age whose glory had long since faded. In other shadowy corners, perfectly preserved lions stood in eternal alertness, radiating intelligence and power. These dusty specimens, while often becoming one with the overstuffed chairs around them, nonetheless served an important purpose. They represented a specific ordering of the world—one in which the encounter between Man and Nature takes center stage, where identity is articulated *through* human mastery over the landscape. In this world, intimacy with nature, along with the courage and skill that enable its subjugation, are privileged. As with the history of race, sex, and class that Donna Haraway (1989) extracts from the African Hall in New York's Museum of Natural History, these animals served as a microcosmic representation glorifying Christianity, pioneering adventure, white masculinity, and authority over the landscape. Capturing nature glorified the magnificence of white achievement in a primitive and savage environment. Disobedient no longer, the vanquished stood quietly in civilized space, offering up evidence of their own taming. Thus, even once they had been killed and stuffed, animals served as an important part of the groundwork for contemporary senses of belonging.

Farmers in Mlilo routinely contrasted an idealized past with a negative present. Jon Van den Akker's critique of professional hunters, presented at the beginning of chapter 4, typifies the sentiments expressed by many other farmers in the valley, who invoked an era when true hunters were created from the harsh realities of the physical landscape rather than through a bureaucracy of papers. The authenticity of one's position as a hunter was determined not on the basis of state-administered exams, but instead from hard-won survival in the face of repeated tests imposed by an unrelenting nature. In this worldview, animals rationalized as vermin aroused feelings of hatred, anger, disgust, or detachment, immediately disqualifying them in terms of moral worthiness of protection. Jon had thus issued a challenge in assigning me the task of chasing the vervet monkeys away from the papaya tree. Reluctance when it came to the killing of animals—especially vermin—was coded as soft, frivolous, and feminine. Jon's criticisms of me when I emerged later on that evening were framed in jest, but also seemed to belie genuine disappointment.

PUTTING THE LION OUT AT NIGHT

In the 1970s, a key shift occurred as people began turning their attention to the untapped potential of wildlife tourism. A gradual conceptual reconfiguration emerged during this period in which wildlife was transformed from an abominable presence into one that could actually be desirable in the landscape. This was when Jon Van den Akker embarked on the previously unimaginable: the domestication of lions. Jon's inspiration came in the early 1970s when he came across two lion cubs who had been orphaned when their mother was killed by a Problem Animal Control team. Stirred by a combination of pity, curiosity, and whimsy, he brought the two cubs back home to his family. Despite initial protestations by Marie, and to the delight of the children in the family, the lions became family pets. N'anga ("traditional healer" in Shona) and Lwane (short for *isilwane*, meaning "wild animal" in Ndebele) enjoyed special privileges. Unlike the family's dogs, who were not allowed to cross the threshold into the house and had to sleep on the verandah, they moved freely in and out as they pleased. With a wry laugh, Marie recounted how they used to put the lions out at night, but inevitably, by the morning, they had found their way back in and were sprawled across the living room carpet.

In exploring this instance of lion domestication, it is worth noting that the Van den Akker family chose to give their pet lions African, rather than Afrikaans or English, names. Furthermore, these names were based on terms for general categories of animals and people in Ndebele and Shona, rather than individual identities. These choices are interesting given that the more conventional pets in the household all had English names. Although drawing conclusions on the basis of two lions is difficult, we might speculate that these names equated the wildness and intractability of these animals with racialized wild landscapes. This in turn may have served to symbolically reinforce hierarchies between whites and blacks in a setting where claims to ownership and domination were never complete or certain. Thus, even within micropractices such as pet-naming, we can identify the use of animals as a vehicle to communicate ideas about human social hierarchy.[12]

During the height of the liberation war, N'anga sometimes accompanied Jon and his unit during their foot patrols in the bush. The image of a dozen armed white Rhodesian men dressed in drab military gear walking through the bush with a fully grown adult lioness by their side is a startling one, as it was intended to be. "Having a lion with us gave us protection," Jon explained as we sat over lunch one day, eating brown bread, pickled beets, and potato salad together. Marie was away in Bulawayo, and it was one of the very rare occasions when there were no visitors stopping by, no grandchildren to mind, and Jon and I were alone. "Whenever people saw her, they ran. No terrorists would ever *shupha* us when she was around."[13] N'anga obviously contributed her services as a guard animal, but her value must have gone beyond simply decreasing their chances of being taken by surprise. One can easily imagine how her presence, and what must have appeared to be her own volition in accompanying these men, might have lent the unit a kind of power that bordered on the magical.

"We used her to interrogate them," Jon lowered his voice, looking at me closely for any sign of a reaction. "A black man can get beaten up, but threaten to put him in a cage with a lion, and he'll tell you anything. So we would take them to her pen, and threaten to lock them up with her. We knew she wouldn't touch them, but they didn't know that. After that, they told you everything. Exact locations of camps in Zambia, where their weapons were, whatever you wanted to know. You never saw anything like it. These guys, they've lived in the bush here all their lives, but they're shit scared of lions. I don't know why." Jon shrugged and began spreading another thick coat of butter on his bread. Deeply troubling as it may be, here we see yet another example of how humans achieve power and authority through the strategic manipulation of animals. And with his statement, Jon conveyed his clear conviction that even though they had lived in this area all their lives, blacks could never master the environment in the same way that whites could.

In the 1980s, Jon expanded his vision and built a pen enclosure for twenty-eight semi-domesticated lions on his land. The lions were prodded into action whenever a large tourist group descended upon the famous safari lodge in the national park and needed to be guaranteed a spectacular lion sighting. Jon trained the cats to follow his pickup truck, and after depositing a hunk of animal carcass in the middle of a scenic grassland, drove quietly away. The tourists would then "happen" upon this huge group of lions feasting upon a "fresh" kill, and their safari would culminate in the fulfillment of what they imagined to be a quintessential encounter with "wild Africa." Later, after the tourists had returned to the lodge for cocktails at sunset, Jon would retrieve the lions and restore them to their pen. With the ferocious roar of these great cats echoing regularly on the property, the household achieved a legendary regional reputation among both white and black Zimbabweans as people who magically held lions at their beck and call.[14]

In the late 1980s, according to Jon, the family's lions became regional stars who were the highlight of the agricultural show in Hwange Town each year. One year, just as the family was about to leave for the event, a woman from the Bulawayo chapter of the Society for the Prevention of Cruelty to Animals (SPCA) pulled into the driveway. She had heard about the lion, she announced, and demanded that it not be subjected to the long trip to Hwange. Mrs. Harrison then proceeded to inspect the pen in the backyard and declared that it needed to be expanded by one meter. She turned next to the lion, who was pacing in the trailer attached to the Land Cruiser, and diagnosed the animal as being overstressed. "The only one on this property who's stressed is you," Jon retorted, to Mrs. Harrison's indignation.

Jon had had enough, however, and decided not to go to the show at all. Mrs. Harrison drove to Hwange Town and announced to the Agricultural Show Committee that Mr. Van den Akker had kindly agreed not to bring the lion. The committee members, however, knew that without the lion, there would be no show. They continued calling Jon's house throughout the day, begging him to bring the lion after all, and he finally agreed, but only if he received a signed letter from the governor saying that he would take full responsibility if Mrs. Harrison and the SPCA decided to press the issue. A signed fax arrived within half an hour, so they took the lion and spent the next four days in Hwange, "making speeches to the black people and putting up an exhibit of photographs and the animals."[15] As with N'anga accompanying the Rhodesian soldiers on foot patrol during the liberation war, this captive animal spectacle served to reinforce assertions of white dominance and authority over the most dangerous of animals, thus naturalizing constructions of hierarchy, power, and difference.

LION KILLERS

By the early 1990s, the project of converting wildlife into valuable capital was still incomplete in its ideological dimensions, but on the level of practice, almost everyone in the valley had entered the new industry in some form or another. As recounted in chapter 4, those who identified themselves as "enlightened," "modern," and "progressive" were the farmers who converted their properties entirely to wildlife ranching very early on; and they in turn discounted as conservative and nonprogressive any neighbors who insisted on retaining part of their land for cattle in case the wildlife industry failed. Amid such tensions, a series of stories began to circulate about one family whose members were rumored to be "lion killers." Unlike many of the farmers in the valley, the Hallowells had no electricity and lived very modestly, and were labeled "primitive" and "backward" for their staunch advocacy of cattle ranching as well as their refusal to allow wildlife onto certain areas of their property.

When several dead lions were mysteriously discovered around the valley, the community demonized the family and accused them of tracking down and exterminating these lions under cover of darkness. The Hallowells were thought to represent a dangerous threat to the integrity of the community as a whole; as nonconformists and "deviants," they were particularly vulnerable in a situation that resonated with accusations of witchcraft. They were taken to court by their neighbors and eventually acquitted for lack of evidence, but the rumors were so pervasive that people in the capital 800 km away knew of the infamous Hallowell "reputation." Consequently, in dramatic contrast to the cultural meaning of lions under cattle-ranching regimes, the protection of lions had become an index of morality, modernity, and productive *Zimbabwean*, as opposed to *Rhodesian*, citizenship.

In distinguishing between the colonial and postcolonial, we see that animals often act as benchmarks in the construction of modernity. The performance of certain attitudes toward lions becomes essential in demonstrating one's participation and self-conscious engagement with the modern world. For families like the Hallowells, contrasting attitudes were worn as a defiant mark of anti-modernity and the refusal to acquiesce to global trends. Given that colonialism itself was understood to be a vehicle for the practice and dissemination of modernity, there is a certain irony to the fact that a "colonial mentality" toward wildlife was subsequently refigured as anti-modern. Modernity thus extends into yet another realm of social practice, reinforcing old oppositions between "enlightened" and "backward" based on attitude and conduct in human-animal encounters. Closely paralleling farmers who chose to reinvent themselves and become more modern, certain species of wildlife have also undergone refigurations in meaning. The next section turns to the African wild dog and its transformations, as it was "modernized" and given a new persona.

REINVENTING THE AFRICAN WILD DOG

Just as landscape has gone through aesthetic shifts and changing uses throughout the world over time, so the creatures occupying these spaces have experienced transformations in meaning. In upstate New York, as soon as deer entered a gilded age in which they were equated with the "tame yet wild" ideal embodied by the Adirondacks, their predators—wolves—suddenly became animals that were considered "out of place" (Brownlow 2000). Like the "vermin" policies in Southern Rhodesia, wolf extermination projects took the form of aggressive bounty systems, resulting in their complete eradication by the end of the nineteenth century. Many decades later, restoration campaigns seeking to reintroduce these animals to the region reflected the triumph of an urban-based ideology that transformed the Adirondacks into a "playground" of leisure and recreation for affluent urbanites. The idea of restoring wolves into the physical landscape, however, could be conceived only after these animals had been thoroughly redefined and resituated within the *cultural* landscape. With their public images reinvented, wolves these days have come to represent intense sociality, untamable independence, and most interesting of all, Native American spirituality.[16]

The African hunting dog—also known as the wild dog or painted dog— shares a strikingly similar story. Drawing on Sandra Swart's assertion that "a dog is social history that can bark," I consider hunting dogs a key example because their refiguration over the past century closely parallels farmers' own reinventions. As Jody Emel has argued in relation to the American frontier, Western European imaginations aligned the figure of the wolf with the wild, the savage, the diabolical, and the lustful, calling for complete annihilation: "The wolf failed to live up to European and North American expectations of the proper hunter. A true hunter was supposed to be humane, to make the kill quick and clean; the true hunter was also supposed to hunt alone. Ganging up on the prey was [considered] inappropriate sporting form" (1998:104). In much the same way, hunting dogs in Rhodesia were the most reviled of wild creatures for settlers because of their techniques in hunting. Taking turns in relay formation and running their prey down through sheer exhaustion was reprehensible enough, but once the animal fell, dogs pounced on it as a pack and literally ripped the body apart by pulling its limbs in opposite directions. Falling woefully short in terms of moral standing, the hunting dog became the most verminous of vermin, condemned to the most killable category of life (Derrida 2008; Haraway 2008). Indeed, for a number of the farmers who recounted their hatred of hunting dogs to me, I detected a glint of satisfaction in their eyes as they revisited memories of a time when exterminating them was common practice.

Half a century later, as hunting dogs take on new status through their global circulation at the top of endangered species lists, they have moved into an entirely different echelon of value. With newly legible "biographical and political lives" (Kirksey and Helmreich 2010), hunting dogs have become one of the most celebrated and coveted wild species in this region, often surpassing the traditional animals of the Big Five—the lion, leopard, rhino, elephant, and buffalo—as an index of desirability for tourism destinations. Much as advocates of killer whales attempted to restore the reputation of orcas by calling them "sea pandas," hunting dogs have been reincarnated as African wild dogs or painted dogs. Emphasizing geography, autochthony, and visual appearance,

5.1 The African wild dog, *Lycaon pictus*, also known as the African painted dog or African hunting dog. Image from Wikimedia.

these new names attempt to erase past histories of complicity with violence. Just as the wolf has become a symbol of the wild, the free, and the uncommodifiable in North America, so the African wild dog has been culturally redefined and resituated as a subject with intense social affects that are mapped onto our own and newly enveloped within a larger universe of human-canine recognizable affinity (Haraway 2008).

In conservation discourses, painted dogs join a select number of species falling under the category of "charismatic megafauna." Those creatures lucky enough to be gifted with "aesthetic charisma" (Lorimer 2015)—giant pandas, cheetahs, spotted owls, and polar bears, to name a few—are mobilized as the spokesanimals of conservation movements, which sensationalize their endangeredness, uniqueness, and lovableness. Practitioners of conservation thus display remarkable skill in inventing new personae for animals with already long-established reputations. Through such representations, some animals become global mascots, and previous repertoires of meaning are left behind.

NATIONAL SYMBOLS

Given the tendency for animals to be reinvented and ascribed new cultural meanings, they are often appropriated as national symbols in "iconographies of power" (Baker 2001). In Zimbabwe, the national symbol is a bird that adorns the national flag and all forms of coin and paper currency. Many currencies in sub-Saharan Africa feature animal imagery, closely intertwining geographic imaginaries with representations of nature.[17] States, however, by no means hold a monopoly on the use of animals for signifying nationhood; people in Mlilo often creatively imagined their own symbols to represent the nation-state. Andrew Graham, a newcomer who arrived in Mlilo in 1998, erected a signpost emblazoned with a zebra at one end of the valley, strategically placed so that it would be the first thing a visitor would see when entering the area from the direction of Bulawayo. The sign advertised his lodge, announcing "Kingdom Cottages, 3 KM Ahead" in large, bold letters. Upon meeting him for the first time, I complimented him on the sign, which was a novelty in a place where farms, boundaries, and lodges were often poorly marked.

"I chose the zebra, you know, because it stands for what Zimbabwe *should* be, black and white, getting along and working together," Andrew explained, unprompted by any inquiry on my part about his choice of animal. The zebra in this context was called upon for its sharply defined, vivid stripes, and the idea of black and white occurring side by side, in equal representation. The metaphor of the zebra as a symbol of the ideal nation was one that I heard often in Zimbabwe, particularly among whites, but also among blacks. Thus, representations of animals, whether imbued with charisma or employed in the making of national identity, can precipitate strong emotions.

Returning to the proverbial leopard that appeared at the very beginning of this book, we can take note of the metaphorical language in which discourses about race and nation circulate in Zimbabwe. Both animals and nature figure prominently in dialogues about nationhood, coinciding with forms of signification found throughout the world. The snow leopard is the national animal of Afghanistan, and the dugong represents Papua New Guinea. As we know, such symbols are used to consolidate state power, but in Zimbabwe, nature has played an equally important role in *contesting* power as well: its putative separation from society makes it a perfect site for political intervention. The leopard represents one example of this use of nature as political critique. As in Andrew Graham's explanation, the zebra was another animal that made regular appearances

Even when there is no cockerel, the sun rises.

Ndebele proverb

5.2 This image was circulated by the Movement for Democratic Change. The cockerel proverb is intended as a critique of the ruling party. Image by Chaz Maviyane-Davies.

in both politics and popular culture to symbolize the ideal nation. In envisioning nationhood, nature can serve as a powerful indexical tool.

The state is well versed in such processes of signification, and the ruling party in Zimbabwe claims the cockerel as a symbol in constructing its political authority. Such identifications are not objects to be taken lightly. In 1997, one farmer in Mlilo was arrested on treason charges for killing five of his own roosters. He had two hunting clients staying with him who had complained that the roosters woke them up too early each morning. The farmer decided that it was easier to get rid of the roosters than to risk incurring the continued displeasure of his clients. Local authorities, tipped off by someone who had witnessed the event, interpreted this as an act of insurrection against the state. While this response might seem excessive, their intuition about the vulnerability of such political representations was absolutely correct. Symbols designed to strengthen party solidarity can be manipulated in equally effective ways to undermine the state. Thus, the Ndebele proverb "Even when there is no cockerel, the sun rises"—translating into the idea that "no one is indispensable"—

gained popularity during this time.[18] Not surprisingly, this saying was featured prominently among the opposition party's campaign posters. The reference to Robert Mugabe, of course, was patently clear.

There is something particularly arresting about the use of animals in these contexts. For the leopard and the zebra, nature is displayed as an ideal because black and white appear organically, in the absence of human design, and so represent the way things should be. The rooster, on the other hand, is called upon in the making of power, but also enables its undoing. Constructing social meaning through nature is an inherent component of culture itself; in Zimbabwe, these links run especially deep. In founding mythologies, in proverbs, in politics, and in daily life, animals recur as a constant point of reference. Much of this stems from the centrality and importance of wildlife within the country's historical, political, and economic contexts. The second half of this chapter looks more closely at wildlife as a broader category, beginning with the crowning of Miss Wildlife at a national beauty pageant in 1999.

MISS WILDLIFE CROWNED

On January 17, 1999, Harare's *Sunday Mail Magazine* featured a front-page color photograph of a young black woman with a radiant smile, bearing the triumphant caption of "Miss Wildlife Crowned." Her image, with delicately fluted eyebrows and bleached, straightened hair, speaks eloquently of a trendy, cosmopolitan woman; the article on the next page confirmed this by describing her active modeling career. The woman is not attired, however, in a swimsuit or evening gown, as one might expect of a beauty pageant contestant; instead, she wears a green and orange cloth wrapped around her head in a more traditional style, and a cloth of the same material swathed around her torso, with shoulders left bare. Elaborating on the qualities that distinguished this particular pageant from others, the promotional representative explained, "Our aim is to see people being enlightened with ideas on the preservation of natural resources, and the preservation of our African culture which is being eroded."[19]

The very idea of a beauty pageant centered around the title of "Miss Wildlife" illustrates the changing landscape of national concerns in contemporary Zimbabwe. A number of scholars have focused on the ties between beauty pageants, nation-building, and dominant ideologies (see Cohen et al. 1996). For postcolonial nations, pageants have come to function as a badge of modern status (Borland 1996). The crowning of a winner becomes a profoundly political act when it transforms a single individual into a symbol representing an entire nation. The *title* of the crown, moreover, is useful in identifying what people imagine to be most emblematic of a country at any given time. In this case, the initially curious pairing of wildlife with a beauty pageant reflects a historical moment in which tourism, and wildlife in particular, ascended to unprecedented heights of importance in the national arena. Perhaps most striking of all in this context, however, is the promotional propaganda—the message that the successful preservation of *African cultural heritage* hinges upon the preservation of the *natural environment*. Somewhere along the line, the symbolic spheres of race and nature have become one.

WILDLIFE AS POLITICAL ECONOMIC CAPITAL

Images of wildlife are inescapable in Zimbabwe. Postage stamps depict regal leopards and groups of tourists seated in safari vehicles; posters advertise lush lodges by water pans where animals congregate at sunset; buses emblazoned with sprinting cheetahs roar across the country's highways; and clusters of stone and wood animal carvings grace urban street corners, lying in wait for the uninitiated tourist. Yet in reality, wildlife in its most celebrated form—beautiful, exotic, alive, and "wild"—remains outside the reach of most Zimbabweans. The prohibitive costs of game-viewing limit local tourists to the exceptionally wealthy elite, while those living in rural areas near national parks confront wildlife primarily as threats to their crops. Clearly, then, the idealization of wildlife in popular representations emerges not from local experiences, but rather through engagement with global audiences.

The significance given to wildlife in Zimbabwe has been articulated in close dialogue with global ideas and assumptions surrounding conservation. The rapid ascent of the conservation paradigm is a startling one given its comparatively short history. In the early 1900s, the popularization of wildlife films unified international approaches to conservation, consolidating different national visions of nature, including those that privileged dramatic landscapes and others that celebrated wildlife above scenery (Beinart and Coates 1995). The introduction of automobiles further altered the dynamics of tourism in regions such as the United States, when national parks suddenly became accessible to the motoring middle classes. This entrenched an American conceptualization of "pristine wilderness," a landscape freeze-framed at the point after the eviction of Native Americans but before the arrival of settlers. By fusing together nature and nation, national parks took on premier importance as symbols representing nationhood. Thus, the designation of nature is fundamentally political; as

Beinart and Coates argue, "God may have created the world, but only Congress can create wilderness" (1995:72). Given the powerful significance of national parks as a national symbol, the very act of visiting such a park came to function as a badge of assimilation for immigrants in the performance of national belonging.

The symbolic potential of national parks quickly caught on in other countries of the world, which suddenly felt the need to establish parks of their own.[20] In South Africa, the political climate of Afrikaner nationalism in the 1920s led to the fictive linking of cultural heroes with a love of nature. Kruger National Park was established to commemorate Paul Kruger, who was dubbed a devoted conservationist despite biographical sources to the contrary (Carruthers 1989). The creation of a national park also emerged out of an explicit desire to find common ground that would unite both the poor and the wealthy among the white population; in this case, the most salient common ground lay in the racial exclusion of Africans from vast territories of land. This displacement coincided with the development of a distinctive landscape ideal that facilitated nascent formations of South African nationhood (Foster 2008; Dubow 2009). Accordingly, national parks and nature appreciation came to serve as symbols of white supremacy, and in that capacity engendered a strong sense of solidarity despite significant class differences within the white population.

In its approaches to wildlife, as noted in chapter 4, Zimbabwe began to diverge from a conventional model of preservation within designated protected areas in 1975, when the Rhodesian government passed the Parks and Wildlife Act, giving landowners the right to claim any wild animals found on their farms as private property. This legislation reinscribed the social role and meaning of wildlife—it became, all at once, something that was potentially profitable, rather than a constant thorn in farmers' sides threatening agrarian production. To convert wildlife into property was the equivalent of assigning animals with individual, quantifiable value. Up until this point, the eradication of wildlife by private landowners was legal if animals were understood as coming into conflict with agricultural interests. By legislating this act, the Rhodesian government hoped to make farmers think twice before shooting animals on their properties. The next step was to create outlets that would allow the application of the value assigned to wildlife. As a result, in the late 1970s, Rhodesia challenged Western environmentalists by espousing sustainable utilization as a new alternative to conservation.[21] This was a daring, audacious act, provocative to a degree that is difficult to imagine these days, when utilization has become the prevailing paradigm. Despite the censure the country received from around the world, the government refused to be deterred and stuck to its new model.

Initial experimentation with the utilization paradigm resulted in the development of a program called Wildlife Industries New Development for All (WINDFALL), which was designed to distribute the benefits of wildlife resource use to residents of communal lands most affected by the presence of wild animals. Within a decade, WINDFALL gave way to the famed Communal Areas Management Programme for Indigenous Resources (Campfire), which reinstated management rights over wildlife to communal areas bordering national parks. Weathering much controversy, Campfire since then has been celebrated for its principles, as well as strongly critiqued for its failures in practice.[22]

What this program excelled at most was establishing a high profile for sustainable utilization. Within this framework, the commodification of wildlife occurred in three different ways. The first was through the culling of "surplus animals"—a term that represents a shift to the vocabulary of markets—harvesting their skins, tusks, and meat, and selling these products for revenue; the second involved contracting with "safari operators" whose clients paid handsome fees for the trophy animals they hunted; and the third was based on bringing visitors into communal areas for photographic safari tours. Of these, the third option proved to be the most logistically difficult because communal areas never had a consistent critical mass of wildlife, and the animals that were present were perceived by tourists to be "out of place" when situated against a backdrop of village houses and crops.

After independence, the Zimbabwean state continued in its pioneering role, gradually winning recognition and respect from its former critics. The country continued to arouse conflict on specific issues, however, as in the example of the sale of surplus elephant ivory. The topic became the center of global debate in November 2002, when 160 countries gathered in Santiago for the United Nations Convention on International Trade in Endangered Species [of Wild Flora and Fauna] (CITES).[23] In a world where the geopolitics of power between northern and southern hemispheres is consistently difficult to upend, Zimbabwe won its first triumph in 1997 when CITES voted for a partial relaxation of its 1989 ivory ban. This resulted in an amendment that allowed Zimbabwe to sell limited quantities of its raw ivory stock to Japan.[24] With this ruling, the world's governments officially acknowledged the effectiveness of Zimbabwe's wildlife management strategies and reinstated a right of resource stewardship as yet unexercised by most developing countries. The significance of this historic moment was not lost on many Zimbabweans, who understood that the country had regained a level of sovereignty over its national resources that was unprecedented in Africa.

From that point until the end of the 1990s, Zimbabwe achieved recognition as one of the foremost authorities on wildlife and tourism, and one to which other African countries turned. This distinction carried added significance given the context of what we might call an "environmental modernity," which engages questions of environmentally conscious policy, responsibility, and accountability at the level of the nation-state. Negotiations between sub-Saharan countries have thus increasingly taken the form of wildlife or environmental expertise, as illustrated by an agreement between Zimbabwe and Nigeria in 2001 to export non-indigenous species such as giraffes, rhinos, leopards, and cheetahs to West Africa.[25] The focus on wildlife has even generated new geographic entities, such as the Gaza-Kruger-Gonarezhou Transfrontier Park, which was engineered by Zimbabwe in partnership with Mozambique and South Africa. Inside the continent's first transfrontier park, tourists would be able to travel freely across national borders (Duffy 1997), participating in new experiments in regional governance.[26] Thus, over the course of the 1990s, during which tourism soared to become the second highest income-generating industry in the country, the successful wildlife story in Zimbabwe became, in essence, an all-important currency through which global recognition and symbolic capital were won.[27]

Wildlife is Zimbabwe's bargaining chip—iconic in national imagery and foundational in the construction of the country's identity—and this is how we arrive at the Miss Wildlife pageant of 1999. The importance of wildlife in the global arena, moreover, transforms it into a wellspring of tension and contradiction at the national level. In Zimbabwe, wild animals circulate across a shifting and often contradictory spectrum of meanings. They are constructed, at various moments, as elemental to national heritage, objects of colonial fantasies, detestable vermin, resources translating into foreign currency, and crop and livestock raiders spelling ruin for rural farmers each year. These images coexist at any given moment, reflecting tensions between the capital and the periphery, white and black Zimbabweans, and tourist and nontourist enterprises across the nation. Given these divergent interests, policies toward wildlife are fluid and inconsistent, and constantly come under revision as they are subject to the state's evolving agendas.[28] In 2000, these shifting policies toward wildlife took perhaps the most dramatic turn of all, as we will see in the next chapter.

Finally, it should be noted that the contradictory images projected by the state are symptomatic of an array of perceptions surrounding wildlife at the local level. These vary so widely that it begs the question of whether the very category of "wildlife" itself, in its semantic, legal, and social meanings, carries any validity across differing cultural contexts. Societies draw different boundaries between different kinds of animals, classifying them according to criteria that might not be immediately obvious. For example, while *wildlife* and *game* signify different things within Western frameworks, Zimbabweans often use the terms interchangeably: they refer to wildlife safaris as "game drives," while the 4x4s with elevated, open-air seats for viewing wildlife are known as "game vehicles." Moreover, while urban schoolchildren from Harare encounter "ellies"—an affectionate nickname for elephants—on field trips to game parks with undistilled awe, black farmers stay awake at night guarding their crops against these very same animals, the sight of which fills them with fear. The only commonality between these two examples lies in the exceptionally powerful reactions that these animals evoke.

The diverse meanings that animals embody are complicated even further when they transgress socially inscribed categories and are seen as being "out of place" (Douglas 1966). Nonhuman animals exercise agency, too, continually disrupting anthropocentric boundaries and desires. In Mlilo, animals were constantly in motion and were thus frustratingly unpredictable when it came to availability. In marked contrast, within the communal areas, animals were synonymous with crop-raiding and thus constituted a feared and hated presence. Drawing upon a recent controversy surrounding bears in the United States as a point of departure, the next section explores processes set into motion by the criminalization of animals who transgress human boundaries.

CRIMINAL ANIMALS

While the idea of a vanishing nature shapes many narratives of the modern world, more recently we find ourselves confronted by the *re*appearance of the wild, often in inconvenient places. Cougars find their way into suburban playgrounds in California, feral cats patrol the borderlands of urban spaces, and coyotes ride subways in New York City. The reemergence of animals that were once assumed to have been permanently displaced—deer, wolves, and peregrine falcons, among others—might initially be seen as representing a partial restoration of balance between humans and nature. But the situation quickly becomes more complicated. These animals do more than enhance the quaintness of local landscapes: they are animals out of place, and as such, routinely upset the boundary between nature and culture, the wild and the domestic.

In recent years, incidents of bears breaking and entering into homes, attacking people, terrorizing pets, and demolishing bird feeders have dramatically increased in the northeastern United States. In response to this new "criminal" bear, the New Jersey Fish and Game Council instituted a black bear hunting quota two summers ago for several counties in the northern part of the state. Although well aware of the controversy that it would create, state officials ultimately supported this action, adopting the argument that designating bears as "game" would protect them from being labeled a public nuisance, which in turn would protect them from extermination. As in the case of Zimbabwe's utilization paradigms, there is a certain irony in the idea of conserving something by putting it in the line of fire. In this case, the qualities attributed to bears in our society made the notion of reducing them to common vermin somehow unpalatable. Instead, the path chosen was to elevate bears to the status of game, to remove the ambiguity of their presence in suburban backyards, and to restore them to the role of worthy adversary.

This legal transformation of bears enabled the state to deal with criminal individuals more swiftly and decisively, and yet the problem of the crime itself still remained. Animals that upset anthropocentric boundaries cause distress and fear on the part of communities and people. In the context of the communal area of Mfula, which shares two of its four boundaries with Hwange National Park, having to contend with criminal animals constitutes a part of everyday life. Enticed by fruit trees and garden crops, bushpigs, baboons, warthogs, kudu, and vervet monkeys, among other animals, regularly venture into Mfula. One nocturnal visit by an elephant, for example, can ruin the efforts of a household for an entire season. The placement of people's gardens reflects subtle hierarchies within the community; those who are the worst off must cultivate on land adjacent to the national park, where crops are most vulnerable. If they can marshal the human resources, family members take turns guarding their crops at night, banging pots to scare elephants away. A determined elephant is a formidable thing, however, and very little can stand in its path once it sets itself on a course of action. A single elephant can easily destroy a quarter acre with one visit, an area larger than most people's plots.

As transgressors, elephants are despised and condemned for "overrunning" their habitat, as if they intentionally ignore designated boundaries and fences. This type of representation generates contradictions in the level of agency and intentionality assigned to elephants. Their behavior is explained through infer-

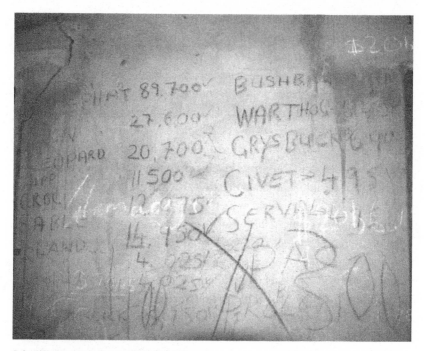

5.3 Wildlife values listed on the wall of the village community gathering space in Mfula. These numbers represent wildlife revenue generated through the Communal Areas Management Programme for Indigenous Resources (Campfire). Photograph by author.

ences about their character, and as crop-raiding increases, their moral worthiness for the state's continued protection is questioned. While Problem Animal Control (PAC) teams within the DNPWLM serve to eliminate criminal animals guilty of repeat offenses, in reality, PAC teams often arrive long after the animals in question have absconded. In the face of such conflicts, Campfire presented itself as an ideal solution that would counterbalance negative sentiment toward wildlife in the communal lands. Under the aforementioned program's principles, a community could lay claim to individual wild animals found within its boundaries and contract with a safari operator who would bring clients into the area to hunt the animals. The revenue brought by the trophy fees would then be divided among households in the community or applied to collective village development projects.

Although the program worked well on paper, the difficulties of revenue distribution, cumbersome administrative structures, and existing local tensions hindered the program's actual operations. Moreover, the situation was complicated once again by the fluidity of wildlife. Animals refused to stay in place long enough for villagers to derive more than token benefits from Campfire. Disregarding such inconsistencies in practice, wildlife producers in Mlilo mobilized the language of transboundary cooperation and mutual benefit in describing the conservancy's relationship with its neighboring communal areas. The logic that growing populations of wildlife in the conservancy, which are free to roam into communal areas, would only augment Campfire profits seems clear-cut. But in reality, many communal farmers complained that the turn to wildlife production in the area had created a safe haven from which animals could crop-raid more frequently, with relative ease. As a consequence, they experienced just as much crop damage as before, but with the close proximity of the conservancy, the offending animals were quicker to vanish back into the commercial lands, thus freezing Campfire operations before they could even be set into motion. Despite the democratic access once promised by Campfire, therefore, in reality existing inequalities are not only reproduced but also intensified, this time through the criminal misdemeanors of animals.

PUTTING PETS IN PLACE

The discussion thus far has focused primarily on wildlife, but other animal actors also played a role in the construction of meaning in Mlilo. Pets figured significantly in farmers' lives, with most households having at least four or five pets at any given time. These ranged from the conventional to the unusual: there were civet cats, donkeys, and, in one case, an impala named May who came running at the sound of candy shaken in a biscuit tin. The Hallowells, who appeared earlier in this chapter, had a beautiful African gray parrot who was over fifty years old. Polly had a fascination for brooms and would spend hours each morning daintily stepping around the circular motions made by the stiff straw ends as one of the domestic workers swept the cement floor.

Numerous scholars have explored the ties between pets and social identity as markers of gender, status, and national belonging. Historically, pets served as instruments of subversion because they symbolized differences in social class. Artisanal apprentices in eighteenth-century France, for example, subjected their mistress's pet cats to violent deaths in order to protest the poor treatment that the apprentices regularly received (Darnton 1985). In Victorian London, kidnapping aristocratic women's dogs and holding them for ransom was a common crime (P. Howell 2000). Today, the idea of pets as a site of social differentiation remains just as strong; different dog breeds, for instance, are understood as signifying particular social categories, ways of life, and even personalities on the part of their owners.[29] In her history of canine breeds in southern Africa, Sandra Swart observes in relation to the Rhodesian Ridgeback, "Although the rough, tough colonial is now a civilised member of the canine community, the Rhodesian Ridgeback still retains the virtues of its hardy ancestors, and wherever a handsome hound of character is required, be sure it will be there—a living reminder of *veld* and *vlei*" (2008:286).

Gender constitutes an equally important sphere in which pets convey powerful meanings. Perceived as aberrant and fickle creatures, for instance, cats were historically associated with women and symbolized "all that was suspect in European life" (Kete 1994:119), including sensuality, mystery, marginality, darkness, evil, and danger. Negative associations of nonconformity and marginality remain surprisingly intact in modern contexts, where the quintessential image of an elderly spinster always includes a cat companion, and cartoon villains caress devious-looking felines. Subject to playful whimsy, pets are critical to the construction of social difference and central to human vanities.

One evening I sat with the Hallowells' daughter-in-law, Trisha, in the small house that she and her husband David had built on the plot of land given to them by David's parents. Trisha was lamenting once again the fact that David's parents took him for granted, how they abused his kindness and ordered him around, while their daughter Rebecca, who contributed nothing to the farm, got the better house and always managed to coax more money from her parents. At that moment, one of Trisha's friends who ran a lodge on a neighboring property drove up to the house, sending the dogs into a barking frenzy. As she appeared at the door, two dogs, one large and one small, jostled her as they angled to get inside. "Oh, look at you two. Are you inside dogs or outside dogs?" she addressed the animals at her feet.

"Zoe's an inside dog; Prince is an outside dog," Trisha replied, and called to the little Jack Russell Terrier, "Come, Zoe!" while patting her knees with both hands. Zoe came dashing inside and catapulted herself into Trisha's lap. Prince, who was a Dalmatian, watched this scene and gave a plaintive whine before the door slammed shut on his face. Neither woman seemed troubled by this display of blatant favoritism.

The distinction drawn between "inside dogs" and "outside dogs" led me to wonder about the ordering of pets in Mlilo, and the implicit division of labor and hierarchy among them. For outside dogs, Mlilo was not an easy place to live. Many died prematurely, killed by baboons or bitten by poisonous snakes, or from swallowing sharp thorns that slowly choked them to death.[30] Pecky, a stalwart terrier who had once stood his ground against a lion while other larger dogs cowered, met his death when he was snatched by a crocodile off a shallow embankment by the river. The dogs that survived often had large zigzag scars on their stomachs where they had been ripped open by sharp baboon teeth and then stitched back up.

These dogs, for whom the smooth slate stones of the verandah were the closest they would ever get to a house, led a very different life from the inside dogs, who had the freedom to go outside but always returned at night to sleep in cushioned baskets or at the foot of their owners' beds. While outside dogs ate from a large shared bowl of dry dog food or leftover maize meal porridge (called *sadza*), house dogs dined on canned dog food and bits of toast handed down to them from the table.[31] Inside dogs often wore sweaters that were custom-knitted for them because "the poor things suffer from the cold in winter," even though their beds already had warm blankets, while the other dogs, with no sweaters, were left to fend off the elements outside. When I began to look more closely, I was surprised at the many ways in which the distinction between the two types of dogs was continually reinforced. Outside dogs sat on the flatbeds of Land Cruisers; inside dogs sat in the passenger cabs. The "working" dogs accompanied farmers on their daily rounds of the property, while the "nonworking" dogs went to Bulawayo on shopping trips with their owners. These boundaries proved to be surprisingly impermeable, with the only exception occurring for puppies, who were considered liminal because of their youth. Even if destined to become outside dogs, puppies were allowed to come and go as they pleased until they grew into adolescents.

The designation of a dog as "inside" or "outside," moreover, depended not so much on the breed or size, but rather, on the human individual with whom the animal was primarily identified. In most cases, farmers in Mlilo conceptualized pet ownership as an individualized domain rather than an experience shared by the household as a whole. In the Van den Akker family, for example, each of the three sons had his own dog who was a constant companion, so that one could gauge exactly which men were present by first looking for their dogs.

Quite predictably, gendered differences came into play in determining the *type* of animal one might choose as a pet. Cats remained firmly within the feminine realm, even though they too are divided into inside and outside animals. Interestingly, outside cats were considered "more wild" than outside dogs, illustrating once again how intractability and deviance are characteristics culturally ascribed to cats. Inside cats, on the other hand, were characterized as much more indolent and self-indulgent creatures than their indoor canine counterparts.

Another important sphere in which pet-based practices form the basis of constructed difference revolved around ethnic background. Unlike whites of British descent, Afrikaners never allowed any kind of dog inside the house, because dogs were animals that belong outdoors according to Afrikaans culture. The English claimed this practice as yet another example of essential difference between the two groups, implying with a subtle shake of the head that their way—to allow animals indoors—was the kinder, more civilized way to treat animals.

Given the absolute convictions people have about what constitutes proper care for pets, it should hardly surprise us that white farmers also extended this moralizing terrain to construct arguments about socially important *racial* differences. They frequently expressed concern for dogs in the communal lands, which they claimed were neglected and starving most of the time.[32] Many of these dogs are, in fact, very thin in appearance, with their rib cages clearly defined, even from a distance. At the same time, as they walk to and fro between people's houses, trot along main roads, and sleep under trees, they seem remarkably self-directed and independent. Most of them have never known the restraint of a leash and are entirely their own agents. Thus, we might argue that these dogs are actually better off than their counterparts in the commercial lands. By representing them as victims of neglect, whites strategically claimed for themselves the practice of responsible, compassionate, and humane care for nonhuman creatures. The flip side of this equation, of course, was that blacks were, by implication, irresponsible and callously indifferent to animal suffering.[33]

Finally, and perhaps most intriguingly, I encountered time and again the theory that dogs have the ability to recognize the difference between blacks and whites.[34] This belief circulated among both groups, who pointed out that dogs belonging to white farmers are uniformly hostile to black strangers, while they greet white strangers with friendly curiosity. Because of the almost universal affinity for canines among landowners in Mlilo, it was virtually impossible to arrive at any house without being surrounded by a profusion of madly barking dogs. Black visitors who arrived in their vehicles at the Van den Akkers' house—Hwange National Park officials, members of Parliament, and the local police inspector—often refused to leave their cars, sitting in the dirt driveway until Jon personally came out and called off all of the dogs. He usually did this with poorly concealed impatience, attributing their behavior to ignorance and cowardice, even when they were highly educated. "Ja, man. They would sit there forever, they're so afraid of these dogs," he grumbled on one occasion after a member of the Rural District Council had repeatedly honked his horn from the driveway, eventually rousing Jon from his afternoon nap. Given the historical precedence of dogs that were trained to be aggressive guard animals serving in the interest of whites, any trepidation expressed on the part of black Zimbabweans today would be entirely justified. This context, however, was rarely acknowledged. From the dogs' perspectives, from what I observed during my fieldwork, I saw no discernible difference between how they interacted with white versus black visitors. And yet, it was the *imagined* difference that was salient in this context. Dogs were represented as animals who instinctively recognized superior beings and were neatly co-opted within white ideology. This logic dictated that the affections and loyalties of dogs belonged to whites because their owners commanded it, but more importantly, because they were entitled to it. Here, we see yet another example of how animals are utilized in the ongoing construction of racial hierarchy and difference.

N'ANGA'S LAST DAYS

In the mid-1990s, Jon transferred the few domesticated lions that remained on his property to a large pen located near the family's lodge. There, when the lions roared, guests staying at the lodge would assume they were listening to wild lions, and experience a visceral thrill. In July 2001, the last lioness of the group—also called N'anga, after her grandmother—miscarried at a very late stage in her pregnancy. Her cubs were stillborn, but her body refused to expel them and she was in obvious pain. As soon as the problem was discovered, Jon called a veterinarian from Hwange, who performed an operation to remove the dead cubs from N'anga's uterus. Afterward, Jon and I maintained a close vigil for several days trying to coax her to eat with fresh zebra meat that had been set aside especially from a hunt. N'anga never recovered her strength, though, and died quietly a week later.

Jon was inconsolable. He refused to leave his room for the rest of the day, and when he finally emerged late in the evening, he looked haggard. He shrugged in response to my questioning glance. "I'm tired," he said, his voice hollow. "My heart's broken, Yuka." It seemed a strange thing to say. After all, N'anga had been caged for the last several years of her life, and Jon rarely saw her. The extent of his grief seemed disproportionate to her actual role in the everyday workings of the farm. Looking back now, though, I realize that Jon was refer-ring at that moment to more than just the lioness. In her death, N'anga had evoked something deeper, signaling the beginning of an end.

In the 1980s and 1990s, Jon's domestication of lions was seen as providing vis-ible testament to his superior mastery of the wild, as well as the achievements of the valley as a whole. But with N'anga's demise, the golden age of wildlife produc-tion, in its most concrete, material form, had vanished. The land invasions that began in 2000 foreshadowed the end of a way of life for Mlilo. The epoch of wild-life tourism, with its new wealth and prestige, was drawing to a close. Thousands of animals in conservancies like Mlilo around the country were killed by war veterans in protest against white commercial farmers. Here, once again, animal bodies were employed as potent metaphors and tools for metonymic critique, this time in order to reverse long-standing racial inequalities.

By drawing upon a range of different categories, including the charismatic, reinvented, criminalized, and domesticated, this chapter has illustrated how animals are routinely annexed, both literally and figuratively, in the making of social hierarchies and racial identities. Animals play a critical role in the pro-duction of moral cosmologies and the idea of the nation itself in Zimbabwe. Put more broadly, the poetics of animals, with the artistry and license employed in metaphor, narrative, and memory, places them at the very heart of culture, where they mediate and transform our worlds. In the final chapter, we turn to the land invasions, where animal deaths—this time wrought by a different form of spectacular violence—would signal the end of an era for wildlife pro-duction in Mlilo.

6

WILDLIFE CONTESTED

THE beginning of the twenty-first century marked Zimbabwe's entrance into a political crisis of unprecedented scale.[1] Following the defeat of a state-drafted constitutional referendum in February 2000, a series of land occupations swept the country, and within a few short months, thousands of white commercial farms had been overtaken by new occupants. These new settlers claimed entitlement to the land as war veterans, pointedly ignoring the reality that many of them were too young to have fought in the liberation war. Despite repeated court rulings pronouncing these invasions illegal, the self-styled war vets were seemingly untouchable, confirming the widely held suspicion that the ruling party was responsible for orchestrating these events. The occupations often entailed violent conflicts, as both white farmers and black farmworkers were beaten and killed. By the end of 2004, forty-three hundred of the country's forty-five hundred commercial farms had been claimed, their owners had been evicted, and hundreds of thousands of farmworkers had been displaced. Commercial agriculture, once the most important source of national revenue, came to a standstill, paralyzing an already crumbling economy.

Tucked away in the western corner of the country, Mlilo remained unnoticed for sixteen months after the land invasions began. Because of its distance from the capital and the poor quality of its soils, few people seemed interested in occupying the valley's farms. The arrival of the war vets was inevitable, however, and by June 2001, Mlilo's landscape had been transformed. The distinctive markers of occupation could be seen everywhere: white triangles were fastened to trees along the main Bulawayo–Victoria Falls road, designating new stops for the commuter buses that formerly bypassed the valley; gates at the entrances of once private roads were adorned with leafy branches, indicating no-go zones set aside for the exclusive use of war vets; tree trunks were marked with the brightly colored initials of the new occupants; and thatched houses sprang up throughout the bush.

Having returned to the United States at the end of 1999, I returned to Mlilo in July 2001, a few months after the war vets' arrival. Properties in the valley were large enough that farmers at this point could continue to live in their homes and drive around as long as they steered clear of the areas settled by the war vets. The occupation mosaic shifted constantly as new individuals arrived in the valley, giving rise to close communication among Mlilo families seeking to keep track of areas that had been taken over. Many people compared this renewed solidarity to the way neighbors had come together and looked after one another during the liberation war years. There was a deeply felt sense of history repeating itself, for the valley was understood to be at siege once again.[2]

To compound such feelings of uncertainty, the exact identities of the "war vets" remained unclear.[3] Farmers informed me that one property had been occupied by the principal of a local primary school; others pointed to the district administrator from Hwange Town and the head manager of Hwange National Park. These individuals fell squarely within the category of "cell phone farmers," or elite black Zimbabweans with the means to hire people to do the day-to-day work of establishing an occupation "presence" while they themselves carried on with their usual lives. White farmers took this as evidence exposing yet again the fallacy of the state's argument that redistribution would primarily benefit the poor and landless. Other rumors circulated that occupants had been brought into Mlilo by the busload all the way from Lupane, 120 km to the east, because the war vets were unable to convince local black farmers to resettle within the conservancy. According to white farmers, their neighbors knew better than to try to cultivate the nutrient-deficient soil; they maintained, moreover, that long-standing relationships of cooperation and respect between the two communities made the involvement of local black communal farmers in the invasions unthinkable.

Sensing my curiosity, Jon Van den Akker offered to take me to the area on his property that was occupied so that I could see the war vets for myself. We drove a few kilometers from the main house and drew up slowly alongside their encampment. Although tensions were high, there had been no open conflict or violence in the valley up to this point. With his sun-blotched skin, bulky frame, and dark sunglasses, Jon was immediately recognizable as a white farmer. When his initial greeting elicited no response, he changed tactics and announced suddenly, "Look, I've brought you a visitor, a donor from Japan!" directing everyone's attention toward me. People immediately began to relax: the protocol for donor-beneficiary encounters was a familiar one, in contrast to rules yet to be established for farmers and occupiers. By highlighting my Asian background, Jon was in effect distancing me from North Americans and Europeans, who might be seen as too similar to white Zimbabweans. I returned their smiles awkwardly, hesitating to correct Jon's misrepresentation for fear that it would stir up more tension. Jon spoke up again, cheerfully oblivious and seeming genuinely interested, "So! What are you guys planning to do with this here land?" We spent the next several minutes tagging along with individuals who were proud to show us their newly acquired land and describe how they planned to develop it. Once the government constructed a borehole to supply water for their new farms, they explained, they would irrigate the land and grow crops, and eventually build a school for their children and shops for the families who lived there. The sense of excitement was unmistakable.

Back in his vehicle, Jon stated the obvious: boreholes were expensive to build and even more expensive to maintain, and the government would never build a single one for the newly settled farmers in the valley. Moreover, even with a hypothetical borehole and the water that it would provide, the soil was too poor for any form of extensive cultivation. Exasperated as I was with Jon for his deliberate misrepresentation earlier, I knew the encounter he had initiated was meant to highlight how little knowledge these new residents had of the local topography, and how haphazard and ultimately doomed the fast-track land reform program was. These new occupants came from distant places, without any intuition for local conditions and oblivious to the intricate web of social and ecological dynamics of the region. Thus, white farmers understood these invasions as engineered by strangers and elites outside the boundaries of the local moral economy, ultimately discrediting their claims to legitimate and meaningful reform.

ANIMAL MASSACRES

Across the country, in the southeastern lowveld, the land occupations took on much more urgent stakes as local and international newspapers headlined reports on the decimation of wildlife by war vets.[4] In the Save Valley Conservancy, over three thousand animals were killed by land invaders in a period of two short months. Game scouts who attempted to subdue these poaching activities suffered abductions and beatings, tourists were forced out of their camps by militant war veterans, and mopani forests were burned to the ground to give way to cultivation. Ironically, less than two decades before, the state had declared this 340,000-hectare region unsuitable for resettlement due to the poor quality of its soils, and readily supported the initiative to transform the area into one of the most successful wildlife conservancies on the continent.[5] As the invasions gave way to an official state policy of fast-track land reform, however, the government designated the white commercial properties in the Save Valley as land eligible for immediate takeover and resettlement by black farmers.

Forced to respond to escalating pressures about the fate of the region's wildlife, the governor of the province accused conservancy owners and workers of conspiring to frame war veterans by slaughtering the animals *themselves* in order to "tarnish the name of Zimbabwe and the president."[6] Wildlife was seen as a key site for defining the state's accountability and governance. Outside observers reacted quickly to this development, as in the case of Germany, which threatened to withdraw Z$1 billion in funding for the clearance of unrecovered land mines—remnants from the liberation war—unless threats to the Save Valley Conservancy ceased.[7] Investing partners in the new Gaza-Kruger-Gonarezhou (GKG) Transfrontier Park, faced with the growing likelihood that the park would fall prey to politics and poachers, voted in 2001 to cancel funding for the entire project.[8] Even the DNPWLM, an organization well known for turning a blind eye to unlawful state practices, condemned the situation in a widely circulated report: "The decision to resettle people in parts of the Save Conservancy not only defies logic—particularly under current economic circumstances—but undermines the country's credibility and conservation image *beyond redemption*."[9] The state was not unaware of the damaging effects of these critiques and made a point of dispatching high-ranking officials to the region to investigate the extent of the animal massacres. This public staging of concern, however, was followed by a noticeable lack of direct action by the government, sparking further protests from observers.

The violence in the Save Valley was mirrored by massacres in other conservancies throughout the country. By the following year, an estimated six hundred thousand animals had been poached by war vets and resettled farmers, obliterating entire populations of wildlife, including protected species such as the endangered black rhinoceros and the African wild dog.[10] This poaching most often took the form of circular wire snares made from stripped fences and set up throughout the bush. Given the vast number of snares, many of the animals caught were simply left to die and rot in the sun. People coming from areas where the only wildlife had been baboons and vervet monkeys were said to have acquired a "taste" for bushmeat, and butcheries and black markets sprang up to supply the new industry. Evidence in some cases pointed to rural authorities who knowingly sanctioned the shooting of animals—often with automatic weapons supplied by the government—to feed a paramilitary youth force organized by ZANU-PF known as the Green Bombers.[11] Others used hunting dogs and smoke to flush animals out of hiding, as described by one farmer in Matabeleland North: "You hear dogs barking and people whistling even at night. . . . We make reports to the police about these people but no action is taken against them. Some of them who call themselves war veterans walk into one's farm with a troop of dogs and start hunting. If you confront them they will tell you that they fought Ian Smith to liberate the land."[12] According to yet other accounts, young boys engaged each other in competitions to shoot wild birds with slingshots, with no regard for their species or their endangered status. By 2002, conservation organizations and former landowners estimated that approximately 60 to 70 percent of the wildlife in the country's private conservancies had been lost as a result of the land reform program.[13]

These wildlife massacres came to be referred to as the "unholy slaughter." It was widely recognized by experts, including a growing number of voices within the government itself, that the decimation had caused irrevocable damage to the nation's natural heritage. As one example, the parliamentary portfolio committee for mines, energy, and the environment produced a report the following year strongly censuring resettlement in the nation's private conservancies. According to the report, the newly resettled farmers lacked the most basic infrastructure; much as Jon Van den Akker had predicted, boreholes were never built and therefore farmers had no water. In Mlilo, this meant that people were forced to share open water holes with wildlife and livestock, which created serious health hazards. Furthermore, no schools were constructed, leaving 258 children in the community without education. Finally, lacking access to dip tanks and other veterinary services, 90 percent of the two hundred head of cattle originally brought in by the new settlers had already perished.[14] The wildlife massacres were understood to have been precipitated by the unsound logic of allowing people to resettle on lands that were too arid, which prompted them to turn to hunting instead. Thus, the fast-track land reform program was interpreted as deeply flawed in its execution, resulting in ultimately disastrous consequences.[15]

ANIMAL VICTIMS

When we explore the implications of this violence within the larger context of the invasions, it is essential to factor in the symbolic dimensions of wildlife, with its connotations of white wealth and privilege. As Roderick Neumann

(1998) has argued in the context of Mt. Meru in Tanzania, such "resource crimes" provide both material gain and meanings of resistance against dominant environmental visions. A well-executed resource crime has the dual benefit of delivering sustenance as well as symbolic retribution. Far beyond everyday poaching, however, the quantity of deaths in the Save Valley clearly signified something greater. Animals were yet again utilized for their powerful symbolism, and their destruction was the physical manifestation of erasing, in one violent act, the wildlife ranching industry painstakingly built by white farmers over the previous three decades. We might think of this as a new national vision, one finally liberated from colonial pasts, where citizenship is rightfully based on race. Long associated with white power, animal bodies served as the vehicle for leveling racial privilege once and for all.

Beyond Zimbabwe, responses were swift and predictable, with global audiences expressing outrage and dismay at these deaths. Throughout the language of critique, we see the appearance of a familiar trope: the animal as "victim." Western attitudes toward animals frequently represent them as voiceless, innocent, and passive, bringing them under our protective gaze. Animals cannot speak for themselves, and thus we must speak for them. The animal as victim carries profoundly emotive qualities, evoking both sadness and pity on the part of audiences (Atwood 1998). Animal victims can stir people's sympathies and indignation in a way that stories about human tragedy often cannot. In a literal application of this idea, an action group called Voiceless Victims emerged as the violence escalated, with the explicit mission of tracking the number of animal deaths and campaigning at international forums to highlight the situation in Zimbabwe. The group's strategies included postering at events such as the Earth Summit and the World Summit for Sustainable Development, and distributing a film called *A Voice for the Voiceless* that depicted images of fallen cheetahs and elephants missing the ends of their trunks where they had been cut off by snares.[16] Through the circulation of such images, the victimization of wildlife became a morally urgent issue worldwide, rendering these animals subjects of a *global* sovereignty rather than a national one. As a consequence, in a setting where issues of democracy and human rights, complicated by colonial legacies, economic inequalities, and racial injustice might be perceived to lie beyond the jurisdiction of external observers, the rapidly deteriorating welfare of wildlife invited immediate condemnation by outside forces.[17]

Strikingly, the idea of animals as victims extended to the domestic realm as well. As the land invasions intensified, the Zimbabwean National Society for the Prevention of Cruelty to Animals (ZNSPCA) began to embark on high-profile rescue missions for the pets and livestock of white farmers who had either been arrested or evicted, and were prevented from returning to their farms. Images of Great Danes and Rhodesian Ridgebacks being beaten by war vets flooded the international media, only to be removed less than twenty-four hours later because they were considered too shocking and distressing for viewers to watch (Buckle 2014). This spurred the ZNSPCA together with the Commercial Farmers Union (CFU) to begin negotiations with Chenjerai Hunzvi, chairman of the War Veterans Association. After several months, Hunzvi granted the ZNSPCA admittance to invaded farms, but only with the repeated reassurance that the organization was entirely nonpolitical. While this may have been a fiction given the nature of its work, a detailed protocol was established: the ZNSPCA inspectors had to arrive in marked vehicles and wear uniforms at all times; they were required to inform the base commander, or war veteran in charge, of their presence; they could only take the animals specified upon arrival; and there would be no media or publicity allowed (Buckle 2014).

Over time, Meryl Harrison, chief inspector of the ZNSPCA, gained world renown for her work in the invasions, and received several international awards, including the BBC Special Award for Outstanding Work in Animal Welfare in London in 2002. As with the wildlife slaughtered in private conservancies, the idea of the animal victim significantly raised the stakes of these daring "rescues." Stories of domestic animals left ownerless, neglected, and often subject to acts of symbolic violence by war vets provoked a public outcry against the war vets' actions. Images of hamstrung cattle, starving pigs feeding on the carcasses of other pigs, and dogs with broken jawbones created an unparalleled sense of urgency in denouncing the violence of the invasions. Here again, we see how animal welfare becomes a site of seemingly apolitical intervention, or a safe zone from which other groups' practices can be criticized.

In important ways, these sympathies for wildlife, livestock, and pets cloak a much darker discourse in which perceptions of difference in animal-based practices are understood as racial distinctions between the morally "upright," responsible West and "savage," "amoral" Zimbabweans.[18] Representations of the breakdown in civil society were intensified by critiques surrounding the care and respect for animals, where Zimbabweans were deemed to fall far short. As a result, the country lost much of its standing as an upwardly mobile nation, predicated in large part on past achievements in environmental conservation.

This begs the question of why the state would allow things to spiral so rapidly out of control, when for two decades following independence, the government went to such great lengths to cultivate wildlife populations and new approaches to conservation as a cornerstone of national policy. One interpretation might be that the lack of direct counteraction by the government even after visits by high-ranking officials to these areas indexed a radical shift in state priorities. Perhaps the state failed to act due to its changing interests, in this case, prioritizing the attenuation of white industry over the safekeeping of national wildlife resources. The state's passivity in failing to curb the destruction of wildlife, moreover, echoed a striking change in the nation's stance toward the international arena. In the months following the advent of the land invasions, President Robert Mugabe shocked the world with his accusations against Western countries for conspiring to reinstate neocolonialism in Zimbabwe. When faced with increasing pressures from the International Monetary Fund and the World Bank to account for donor money expenditures, he dismissed their funding as unwelcome, much to the dismay of the national community.

In a visit to the United States in September 2001, Mugabe spoke to a large African American congregation at the Mount Olivet Baptist Church in New York City. To a spellbound audience, he declared that international attempts to monitor the fairness of national elections in June were as if "we were fighting the British government [itself] . . . they were united in a cause they knew was unjust. Whitism, racism—look at the way they stick together." Mugabe and the majority of his ruling party have largely maintained this same position over the past decade and a half, turning their backs on the rest of the world and choosing instead to build on a platform of pan-Africanism. In this context of forsaking Western judgments and standards, it may have been inevitable that animals would be placed in the line of fire.[19] With this shift, a different constellation of interests came into motion, one that privileged the deeply charged politics of land and race, eclipsing nature and its co-conspirators in the process.

WILDLIFE-BASED LAND REFORM

Despite the initial lack of action on the part of the government, growing concerns gradually led to stronger measures against wildlife poaching and slaughter. In October 2003, DNPWLM director-general Morris Mutsambiwa declared a ban on all hunting activities in Mlilo.[20] The directive was issued as a result of the large-scale plunder of the region's wildlife, including lions and a population of three hundred elephants protected by a presidential decree in 1990. The new residents responded angrily to the ban, with many of the influential politicians who had taken over the valley questioning whose "side" the

DNPWLM was on: according to their logic, resettled farmers were not empowering themselves arbitrarily to carry out sport hunting, but were utilizing the same statutory instrument that white farmers had benefited from for years. The DNPWLM, however, refused to reverse its decision, citing evidence that many of the new owners were using fake hunting quotas in their operations.

The hunting ban in Mlilo was lifted in August 2007, but environment and tourism minister Francis Nhema announced once again the state's intention to withdraw the safari-operating permits of conservancy and game ranch owners who failed to protect their wildlife and maintain the lands allocated to them.[21] "Though we promote the incorporation of indigenous people in the wildlife farming sector," Nhema declared, "we do not condone reports of massive poaching on a number of our conservancies. We need to be honest and to be professional as well[;] otherwise in two years time there will be no resources to talk about."[22] Mlilo, he noted, had deteriorated to the extent that animals were fleeing the conservancy into the neighboring national park in search of water. Ironically, in contrast to white farmers' narratives in chapter 4, the situation for wildlife had been completely reversed: prior to the invasions, when land in Mlilo was maintained in far better condition than the national park, the conservancy often served as a refuge for Hwange animals during times of drought. Now, it was the national park that had become a safe haven for conservancy animals.

Given the ongoing loss of wildlife, the state came to acknowledge that as long as people were allowed to resettle in conservancy areas, poaching would continue to be a problem. This precipitated the creation of a new wildlife-based land reform policy, tailored specifically for regions with low agricultural productivity. Under this policy, conservancy properties would all be acquired and owned by the state, and conservancies themselves would be administered as business corporations with individual shareholdings. People who had moved into areas where settlement was not permitted would be removed, and each acquired property would be assessed in terms of its value. Following the original logic of wildlife production, the subdivision of conservancy lands into smaller lots would be forbidden because this would restrict the movement of animals and hinder the growth of wildlife populations. Land that had already been subdivided would be merged once again, and residents would receive training in large-scale wildlife ranching.[23]

Another key set of reforms in this policy involved the official transition to "indigenization" for conservancies. This reflected a larger transformation in Zimbabwe's national economy in which new indigenization laws required that all businesses shift to a composition of at least 51 percent indigenous ownership. The wildlife-based land reform policy proposed three indigenization models for conservancies: current farmers teaming up with the DNPWLM and neighboring communal areas, with all three parties contributing capital and deriving benefits; current farmers working with neighboring communal areas only, with the DNPWLM fulfilling its customary regulatory and advisory role; and current farmers working with neighboring communal areas *and* private indigenous investors (Rukuni 2012). For the last option, indigenous investors would be chosen only if they were able to demonstrate interest and experience in wildlife conservation, business management expertise, and the ability to contribute capital assets to the venture. In all three of these options, once property values had been assessed, current operators would be required to divest their majority shareholding to cooperating partners, including local communities. Existing farmers would be encouraged to remain in operation *only* if they agreed to accept the terms of this indigenization policy (Rukuni 2012). The wildlife-based land reform program attempted to bring order to the chaotic state of private conservancies, where resettled small-scale farmers mixed with elite politicians, along with a handful of white farmers struggling to remain on their properties. The confusion and lack of transparency surrounding different actors in this setting created an environment where poaching and often corrupt commercial hunting practices continued to flourish. Despite its grand ambitions, none of the principles outlined in the wildlife-based reform policy were implemented in practice.

ANIMALS DON'T SEE IN COLOR

A decade and a half after the land invasions first began, the fast-track land reform program remains fiercely contested and controversial. The dominant image of the program that circulates in the global imagination is that of failure and economic collapse, fueled by political cronyism and corruption at the highest levels. According to this interpretation, both property rights and human rights were cast aside, and white commercial farmers and farmworkers were violently displaced in pursuit of land redistribution that was fundamentally unjust. Not coincidentally, this was also the version most often espoused by white farmers. At the same time, however, for the great majority of people in Zimbabwe, the fast-track land reform program represented the final embodiment of empowerment following the country's independence. Part of the difficulty in assessing the actual impacts of the land reform program comes from the lack of visibility of people's lives as well as institutions involved at the ground level. While there is no question that land reform dramatically transformed rural society in Zimbabwe, scholars have pointed to several factors that continue to produce negative perceptions of the program. Prosper Matondi (2012), for instance, highlights the timing of the land reforms. Zimbabwe was already falling into a downward economic spiral when the land reforms began; the "fastness" of the fast-track program instilled a sense of urgency but failed to allow for changes when mistakes were made; and finally, individual districts and provinces diverged widely in their capacities to implement the program.

While it is widely acknowledged that a particular group of black elites benefited disproportionately from the fast-track land reform program, many observers have pointed out that the majority of those involved in land reform profited. A number of scholars, moreover, have challenged what they call the "myths" of the land reform program, including the assertion that land reform has been a complete failure; that investment in new resettlement areas has been nonexistent; and that the rural economy has collapsed altogether (Scoones et al. 2010). Instead, based on their field data from Masvingo Province, Ian Scoones et al. suggest that people diversified their livelihoods according to the individual connections, ambitions, and resources at their disposal once they had established themselves on their new farms. Thus, the new resettlement land signified different things for different people. For some, it was the first time they had access to productive land as a source of primary livelihood. For others, these new holdings became a source of private accumulation or security for the future and for their children (Scoones et al. 2010). The wide range of these meanings and practices in turn made assessing the relative success of land reform extremely difficult.

Moreover, Matondi (2012) calls attention to the important irony that the very same qualities of the fast-track land reform program that were perceived negatively by the outside—including chaos, violence, underutilized land, food insecurity, and a pariah state, along with very specific racial dynamics—recalled a historical image that most people failed to recognize in political terms. The rhetoric adopted by the Commercial Farmers Union (CFU) is a familiar one by this point, mapping the very same logic that farmers articulated in wildlife production onto commercial agriculture. Time and again, Matondi suggests, white farmers emphasized their own high productivity while "caricaturing black agriculture as economically unviable and environmentally destructive. . . . the effect was to re-create the dualism of 'them' (black farmers) mismanaging the land, with 'we' (white farmers) being better in modern agricultural practices" (2012:7).

On the other hand, in the lower productivity agricultural areas, contests over wildlife remain more heated than ever. Tourism plunged in the first decade of the twenty-first century because of the country's deteriorating sociopolitical conditions, but in recent years the hunting safari industry has started to regain its previous momentum. Wildlife conservancies themselves have changed markedly, and individual properties are primarily owned and operated by influential politicians, including cabinet ministers and other senior officials from the ruling party. While establishing the identities of top politicians operating in conservancies is difficult because their direct involvement in the business is often disguised, the list of individuals with stakes in Mlilo now includes Joseph Made, minister of agriculture; Kembo Mohadi, minister of home affairs; Simon Khaya-Moyo, current chairman of ZANU-PF; Dumiso Dabengwa, president of the revived ZAPU; and Obert Mpofu, former provincial governor of Matabeleland North and now minister of mines.[24] Profits from wildlife on a national scale have gradually climbed back up to 50 percent of pre-2000 revenues, but many have expressed concern over controversial practices such as high hunting quotas, poaching, and poor wildlife management on private lands.[25]

In 2012, the Save Valley Conservancy, which headlined newspapers as the first place where animal massacres were reported over a decade earlier, became the site of controversy once again. As the largest private wildlife sanctuary in the country, the Save is also the most lucrative, generating incomes of up to $US30 million per year through commercial hunting. In July, safari operators discovered that they suddenly had been denied hunting permits even though many of their clients had already reserved specific trophy animals for upcoming hunts. The government issued the twenty-five permits instead to "indigenous farmers" who also received twenty-five-year land leases at the same time, under the rationale of indigenization. Not surprisingly, the beneficiaries of these permits were all top figures within ZANU-PF, such as the governor of the province, Titus Maluleke, and the minister of education, Stan Mudenge. With greater political and financial resources than in smaller-scale conservancies like Mlilo, members of the consortium mobilized in protest against the state's decision. They accused Mugabe loyalists of using black empowerment as a "cover for greed," noting that two-thirds of its wildlife ranch operators were already black Zimbabweans.[26] The conservancy employed over eight hundred workers, they argued, and channeled a portion of its earnings into a community trust established for five neighboring rural districts, thus supporting thousands of villagers. In their eyes, the hunting and land concessions awarded to these politicians posed a serious threat to the region's ecosystem.

Turning to the media to raise support, the consortium purchased advertising space in several Sunday newspapers and issued official statements. Refuting the claim that the Save was white-dominated, the consortium charged Mugabe with using color as a "racial tool" to "collapse world-renowned conservation efforts for short-term gain."[27] Under the slogan "Animals Don't See in Color" the group appealed, "We as humans can help stop using color as a racial tool to destroy the very people who are working for our common good."[28] Once again, this echoes the moral argument offered by Mlilo farmers before the invasions: nature, environment, and animals are neutral and apolitical, and those who steward nature should be seen as transcending politics as well. For the Save consortium, the timing worked out perfectly: together with Zambia, Zimbabwe was on the eve of co-hosting the United Nations World Trade Organization (UNWTO) general assembly. Once news of the political scandal in the Save Valley spread, Germany, France, Japan, and South Korea threatened not to participate in events on the Zimbabwean side unless the controversy was resolved.[29]

In a surprising turn of events, this time Mugabe himself reprimanded the senior officials and army generals who had won concessions in the Save, chiding them for acting out of greed and noting that all of the individuals in question already had multiple farms in other parts of the country.[30] He ordered that they move out immediately and announced that existing wildlife conservancies would be turned into national parks to stop the rush for lucrative safaris once and for all. The ZANU-PF politburo followed up by issuing a directive for the twenty-five individuals to vacate their lands and hand management over to the DNPWLM. Interestingly, however, several high-ranking officers from the security forces chose to defy the directive and forcibly took control of a ranch in Mwenezi.[31] Thus, equated with quick profits and material gain, wildlife has remained a highly coveted and contested resource, inciting challenges to Mugabe's authority even by members of his own political party.

RETURN TO WILDLIFE

When the UNWTO annual meeting finally took place in August 2013, the Zimbabwe minister of tourism, Walter Mzembi, pronounced that the gathering represented a "global endorsement" of Zimbabwe as a tourist destination.[32] While human rights organizations criticized the United Nations for allowing itself to be used as a propaganda tool, behind the scenes, over three hundred animals from the Save Valley Conservancy were transported 600 km across the country to stock Zambezi National Park, where the conference was taking place. The new migrants included 151 wildebeest, 100 impala, 60 zebras, 25 eland, and 10 giraffes. Conservation organizations noted the irony of this astronomical expense, especially given that the DNPWLM had not been able to pay its own staff wages for the previous three months. Nonetheless, these animals were brought in to create the spectacle of a lush, wildlife-rich Zimbabwe for the benefit of the global audience gathered for the conference. Clearly, the visibility of wildlife was still important.

So, while the government initially turned a blind eye to the animal killings set in motion by the land invasions, it has slowly restored wildlife to national agendas. There is no denying that wildlife remains one of the most valuable currencies—in both symbolic and material terms—that Zimbabwe has at its disposal today. As the battle over conservancies continues, the commercial hunting industry is seen as a source of near-mythical monetary gain. In the spotlight of international gatherings, public displays of wildlife are staged to assuage concerns about the nation's environmental conservation efforts. Individual animals conveniently serve as tools of diplomacy: Zimbabwe routinely trades animals with foreign countries, as in the example of four baby elephants from Hwange National Park that were sold to zoos in China in 2012.[33] After the alienation of many of the world's most powerful countries in the 2000s, the safekeeping and care of wildlife appear to be one way to begin regaining international goodwill.

Over the past fifteen years, Mlilo's physical and social landscapes have been transformed irreversibly. The white farmers that I spent time with during my fieldwork have long since disappeared and moved on to other countries, from Botswana and Tanzania to Scotland and Australia. Many have started new hunting and safari ventures in these places, drawing on expertise accumulated over decades and hoping for more stable political conditions this time around. Mlilo itself was swept into a new crisis in 2013, when the government awarded a special presidential grant to China Africa Sunlight Energy, a firm of joint investors from China and Zimbabwe, to begin prospecting for coal bed methane gas in a section of the valley bordering the national park.[34] Despite concerns voiced over the environmental impacts and chemical pollution this would create for the valley's water sources, construction of the mine and its residential complex began in July 2014.

During this same period, Zimbabwe signed a formal treaty with Angola, Botswana, Namibia, and Zambia to establish a transfrontier "peace park" encompassing an area of 440,000 km^2 that would include Mlilo and Hwange National Park.[35] Named the Kavango Zambezi Transfrontier Conservation Area (Kaza TFCA), the park incorporates national parks, game reserves, forest reserves, conservancies, and communal areas. The founding of Kaza TFCA, the world's largest conservation area, has been hailed as the most important development within the last century from a conservation perspective.[36] It is difficult to imagine how these two developments, seemingly at odds with each other, will affect the fate of the region's wildlife.

CECIL THE LION

More recently, in July 2015, an incident in Mlilo involving the death of a celebrity animal captured the world's attention and brought tensions between conservation and commercial hunting to the forefront. With his striking black mane, Cecil the lion had been the star attraction of his home in Hwange National Park. His movements had been closely monitored since 2008 by a team of scientists from the Wildlife Conservation Research Unit at the University of Oxford, and details of his biographical history were well known. With his tolerance for allowing vehicles and people to come within close range, Cecil was beloved among tourists, safari guides, and researchers alike. These encounters came to an abrupt end, however, when Walter Palmer, a dentist from Minnesota, shot and killed Cecil in an area of Mlilo just outside the national park. Palmer and the professional hunter who served as his local guide had purportedly tied a dead animal to the back of a vehicle and crossed the boundary into Mlilo to lure Cecil out of the national park's sanctuary.[37] Cecil was shot with a compound bow and escaped, but Palmer tracked him and killed him with a rifle forty hours later. He claimed Cecil's head as a trophy, and left the rest of the animal's body to decompose in the sun.

As news of Cecil's death broke, Walter Palmer's life took an immediate and irreversible turn: he became the target of death threats, internet shaming, and protests organized outside his dental practice in Bloomington, Minnesota. Cecil, on the other hand, became a global symbol of animal martyrdom overnight, inspiring memes such as "I am Cecil" and "#CatLivesMatter."[38] Zimbabwe's minister of environment, Oppah Muchinguri, demanded Palmer's immediate extradition from the United States so that he could stand trial for his crime.[39] American celebrities lobbied for the revocation of Palmer's US citizenship, along with the seizure of his home, dental practice, and all monetary assets. Calling for even more radical action, the People for the Ethical Treatment of Animals (PETA) released a public statement that Palmer should "be extradited, charged, and, preferably, hanged."[40]

As the details emerged, it was revealed that Walter Palmer had paid US$54,000 to add a lion to his already extensive trophy collection, which included a grizzly bear, a rhinoceros, a leopard, and another lion. He reportedly had no idea that the animal he eventually killed in Zimbabwe had been protected. Nevertheless, by leaving Cecil's carcass to decompose in the sun, Palmer was seen as guilty of a startling degree of disregard for the beloved lion. Moreover, not only was Cecil's death painfully prolonged, but he was also deliberately lured away from the national park and into private lands, turning him into fair game. The fact that he had been an important research animal for the team of Oxford zoologists raised his moral standing further. These combined factors turned Cecil into a cause célèbre. Spanning social media and late night talk shows, the outpouring of grief and sympathy for Cecil reached an unprecedented scale.

The explosive responses to Cecil's death soon compelled over forty airlines worldwide—including Delta Airlines, United Airlines, and American Airlines—to revise their company policies and prohibit the transportation of hunting trophies on their flights. Cecil's death also provided the final push for the US Fish and Wildlife Service to place lions under the legislative protection of the Endangered Species List, an act that would make bringing lion trophies into the country significantly more difficult.[41] While the proposal to have lions in eastern and southern Africa officially designated as a threatened species had been on the table for five years, the killing of Cecil was widely regarded to have been the defining moment that made this legislation possible. The United States was not alone, moreover; France and the UK have taken similar measures to ban the import of lion trophies into their countries. Conservationists have seen these developments as remarkable successes that were actuated by the Cecil "movement."

At the same time, these debates over trophy hunting have resulted in the emergence of another set of voices, in reaction *against* mourning for Cecil the lion. Zimbabweans were bemused to see their country receiving global media coverage for the first time in years—despite its continuing political violence and economic turmoil—simply because of one lion's death. Cecil was unknown to most Zimbabweans because he was a celebrity at Hwange National Park, where entrance fees are affordable only for foreign visitors. Thus, the hash tag "#ZimbabweanLivesMatter" emerged as a critique of what Zimbabweans saw as misplaced concern over the welfare of African animals, as opposed to African people. In an op-ed piece in the *New York Times*, Goodwell Nzou, a graduate student at Wake Forest University, observed, "In my village in Zimbabwe, surrounded by wildlife conservation areas, no lion has ever been beloved, or granted an affectionate nickname. They are objects of terror."[42] Wildlife clearly remains charged as a site of powerful emotion and deep ambivalence.

Aside from such important differences in meaning and experience in relation to lions, another element to consider in this story is the lion's name itself. Cecil was named after Cecil Rhodes, who led the British South Africa Company's expedition across the Transvaal and founded the territory of Rhodesia. The lion's death occurred during the same year that the #RhodesMustFall student protest movement swept across universities in South Africa.[43] This illuminates the larger context of just how powerfully the name "Cecil" evokes negative associations. Steeped in elitism, Cecil's name in fact served as a constant reminder of the association between nature, colonial power, privilege, and injustice. This illustrates, moreover, that despite attempts to nationalize wildlife through the indigenization program, animals have yet to change significantly in their figuration. Lions, once used to symbolize and consolidate white power, continue to be coded "white" and are seen as divisive and exclusionary. While the ties between nature and whiteness in Mlilo were no longer as sharply defined once white farmers had been ousted, these links would prove difficult to disentangle.

NATURE AND WHITENESS REVISITED

This work demonstrates how nature served as an essential vehicle and platform for constructions of whiteness in Mlilo. White farmers routinely called upon the environment to naturalize and legitimize their claims to belonging. Metaphors from nature were used to sanitize racial worldviews, as in the example of Marie's use of the wildebeest and the zebra to explain the logic of racial segregation. Nature played a pivotal role in the valley's transformations from cattle ranching to wildlife ranching, as farmers shifted from a form of intimate landscape knowledge that allowed for the efficient extermination of wildlife to one that ensured its conservation. Through the reinvention of their identities, moreover, farmers articulated their new role as environmentalists working in the interests of the nation-state to lessen the stigma of visible whiteness. Conservation thus served as a depoliticizing tool, displacing moral critiques of farmers' disproportionate privilege and turning access to land into a matter of technocratic expertise (Brosius 1999). Because of their pervasiveness in the physical landscape, animals figured centrally in people's "imaginative repertoires" (Brownlow 2000), and both wild species and domesticated animals were annexed in the making of racial hierarchies and symbolic power. And finally, because of wildlife's deep, historical meanings inextricably bound with white privilege, animals became the target of violent massacres in the country's conservancies during the land occupations. Thus, connections between nature and whiteness were forged through multiple sites of practice, lending one another discursive and material power within farmers' worlds.

Time and again, in diverse contexts, we see the workings of this alliance between nature and whiteness. Exploring the politics of science in colonial Africa, for example, Nancy Jacobs (2006) focuses on instances of collaboration between white Euro-American ornithologists and the African individuals who served as their research assistants. Questioning how these collaborations were shaped by understandings of racial difference, Jacobs looks closely at one of the most respected ornithologists in the early twentieth century, Reginald Ernest Moreau, whose success was dependent on the extensive knowledge of his main research assistant, Salimu Asmani. While Moreau acknowleged Asmani's contributions, his reports always entailed a "deskilling" of the position of the research assistant and the disaggregation of his findings from indigenous expertise. For Moreau, Jacobs explains, "race indicated the ability to know something worthwhile about birds" (2006:594). Accordingly, a report produced by Asmani, even though it was he who had noticed the unfamiliar call and mastered the song of a new species, was "lacking, not because the bird was rare and only briefly seen, but because the observer was African" (2006:591).

Similar racial politics permeate Donna Haraway's account of Carl Akeley's scientific expeditions in central Africa, in which Akeley's entourage is imagined to be "inaudible, invisible, except for comic relief and anecdotes about native life" (1989:48). The rules of behavior during these expeditions were designed to reinforce racial distinction and hierarchy at every turn. A black "boy" could not shoot without orders unless his master was down at the mercy of an animal (1989:53). Moreover, the behavior of the "boys" when confronted by a ferocious elephant was automatically interpreted as cowardice and served to enhance the majesterial "confrontation between white manhood and the noble beast" (1989:48).

Such dynamics resonate, in turn, with Anand Pandian's (2001) discussion of the imperial hunt in the later decades of the British Raj, in which the spectacle of terror embodied by the man-eating tiger constructed colonial subjects as passive and feminized spectators. In these narratives, the native villagers were depicted as utterly powerless in the face of a tiger's aggression, and could be rescued only by the intervention of the masculine white hunter. One of the most renowned tiger-slayers, Jim Corbett, figures in these stories "less as a representative of a formal administrative apparatus and more as a personal embodiment of capable sovereignty" (2001:88). Thus, the symbolic power won through the successful, spectacular hunt was hard to overestimate.

Currently, a different form of spectacular feat is enacted through the realm of extreme adventure sports. Just as in the encounter between man-eating tiger and white hunter, nature in this context continues to be a material and discursive site through which meanings of race are produced and naturalized (Braun 2003). As Bruce Braun suggests, the image of the white adventurer "individualizes the encounter with nature, envelops it within a discourse of courage and conquest, and sutures an anxious middle-class masculinity" (2003:181). Strikingly, within these representational economies of adventure, only white identities are sanctioned; the figure of the black or Latina adventurer has "no proper place" (2003:178). Braun identifies a recurrent theme within popular representations in which the journey into nature is constitutive of whiteness itself. Nature, in other words, serves as a "purification machine," or "a place where people *became white*" (2003:197, emphasis added).

The ties between nature and whiteness are enduring and resilient. Whether through the act of collecting knowledge or enacting conquest, risking death or performing love and appreciation, nature continues to be a critical site for the production of racial meaning and ideology. Braun's concept of "citationality" is useful in this context: he suggests that adventure enthusiasts find these practices deeply meaningful because they cite events from the past over and over again. Given the sedimentation of discourses of adventure, extreme adventure sports today are understood to be "the same as, or continuous with, acts of European exploration set in the past" (2003:189). The nature/whiteness dyad held meaning in Mlilo because of a similar citationality: the claims that farmers made in relation to nature were legible because of their repetition in countless other contexts. These claims were articulated explicitly, but they made sense only because of the deep, underlying, unspoken associations between whiteness and nature. As we have seen throughout this work, the effect of this was to aid, abet, and disguise the symbolic and material workings of power for white farmers in Zimbabwe. By naturalizing privilege through nature, they promoted the idea that given their achievements and expert knowledge, these lands were rightfully theirs, and they were meant to be there all along.

What happens, then, when people are cast from the environment on which their identities and livelihoods depend? Those in Mlilo who moved to other countries notably gravitated toward settings where similar engagements with nature were possible. Jon van den Akker and his sons, for example, moved to other parts of the continent to begin new safari ventures, which were always carefully framed within narratives of their previous success with wildlife conservation in Zimbabwe. Some moved to the pastoral countryside in the UK to reconnect with their "roots" and long-lost relatives; still others chose Australia for jobs in the tourism industry, marketing their own firsthand knowledge of southern Africa to package trips for Australian tourists. This raises the question of whether farmers chose these paths because they felt these were the only skill sets at their disposal, or whether the alignment between nature and whiteness was a comfortable and familiar one that people actively sought out in their new lives.

Amanda Hammar's work (2010) offers insight into the experiences of former large-scale commercial farmers in eastern Zimbabwe who moved across the border into Mozambique after losing their properties. As these farmers attempted to establish new farming endeavors with paprika and tobacco, their inclination was to implement agricultural techniques and organizational structures designed to reproduce familiar elements of their old lives, although often without success. For white former Rhodesians who emigrated to South Africa, on the other hand, Uusihakala (2008) finds the conception of self and homeland to be nearly synonomous with the romanticization of landscape and wilderness. She suggests that people turned toward the "bush as a moral guide" (2008:90), and every ex-Rhodesian she encountered professed a love for the outdoors. Thus, for white Rhodesian identity, the articulation of ties to nature remains just as potent after exile.

At the same time, some individuals chose to stay in the country despite the dramatic occupations that began in 2000. David Hughes (2010) identifies three colonial models that farmers resurrected in order to remain on their farms: they became conservationists, missionaries, or native commissioners. Re-creating themselves as advocates of the environment, the Bible, and black farmers, respectively, people learned to "play the game," some more successfully than others (2010:118). Perhaps most importantly, however, Hughes unflinchingly highlights the parallels between white privilege in southern Africa and places like North America. He exhorts his readers to consider what whites elsewhere have long taken for granted by virtue of their skin color: how racial privilege is won through environmental escapism.

The story in Zimbabwe thus transcends time and place in its implications. Whiteness, when paired with nature, erases the traces of its own fashioning. Nature, in turn, is heightened in value through its ties to whiteness. Upward social mobility, class distinction, education, and modernity: each of these is performed by enacting particular forms of engagement with nature. Outdoor summer camps, birdfeeders, planetariums, and IMAX nature documentaries all have an ideological dimension that underlies the cultivation of knowledge and caretaking of the environment. Similarly, viewing animals on safari, pet-keeping, and advocating for animal rights reveal one's enlightenment and ascendancy in relation to the natural world. On the other side of the coin, nature rises in estimation the more deeply sedimented its connection to whiteness becomes; it is idealized, romanticized, and imagined in increasingly pure and moral terms. Thus, nature and whiteness reproduce each other in meaning and power; they lend each other authority while rendering the process itself invisible.

Whiteness in Mlilo, then, reveals an essential aspect of the nature of whiteness. Articulations of identity in Mlilo emerged from long and deep ways of seeing and engaging with the environment. These dynamics are certainly specific to Mlilo, given the intimacy with landscape, the proximity of animals, and the recent reenchantment of wildlife. At the same time, they reflect much larger constellations of meaning that bundle together whiteness, nature conquest, and particular forms of environmental consciousness. These connections are clearly magnified in Mlilo, but they work only because they fit into an existing field of power, or what might be called a "white slot" that comes with its own set of hierarchical assumptions.[44] Even when economic privilege is forcibly removed, the links between nature and whiteness endure, as white farmers continue to call upon the environment to creatively configure the world and their places within it.

NOTES

FOREWORD

1   Donald Moore, Jake Kosek, and Anand Pandian, introduction to *Race, Nature, and the Politics of Difference*, ed. Donald Moore, Jake Kosek, and Anand Pandian (Durham, NC: Duke University Press, 2003), 31.

1. THE LEOPARD'S BLACK AND WHITE SPOTS

1   De Waal 1990:6. Robert Mugabe became president of Zimbabwe in 1987, when the position of prime minister was abolished.
2   See Godwin and Hancock 1993.
3   While many of these groups were led by well-known ex-combatants, the majority of "war vets" were in fact too young to have participated in the liberation war. The term was used to lend the land invasions a veneer of the celebrated moral standing ascribed to those who had fought for liberation.
4   This period has been called the "Third Chimurenga," translated as the "Third Uprising." The First Chimurenga occurred in 1896 in an armed uprising against the British South Africa Company; the Second Chimurenga refers to the war for independence, which took place between 1965 and 1980.
5   See Sullivan 2006; Frankenberg 2001, 1999, 1993; P. McIntosh 1989. Frankenberg complicates the idea of a universalizing unmarked whiteness in her 2001 work, referring to it as a mirage.
6   Under the GPA Robert Mugabe remained president, while MDC leader Morgan Tsvangirai assumed the position of prime minister. This power-sharing agreement lasted only a few years, however, and Mugabe's defeat of Tsvangirai in the disputed 2013 presidential election effectively ended the GPA.
7   "Boer" is a term used to refer to people of Afrikaner descent. Afrikaners are the majority group among white populations in contemporary South Africa; originally they were Dutch-speaking settlers who occupied the Eastern Cape beginning in the eighteenth century. "Boer" translates as "farmer" and often carries a negative connotation. The lyrics for the song "Dubula Ibhunu" include the following lines: "Cowards are scared. / Shoot, shoot, shoot them with a gun. / Shoot the Boer. / Shoot, shoot, shoot them with a gun."

8   See for example Comaroff and Comaroff 2009; Li 2000; Tsing 1999; Conklin 1997.

9   One useful framework for understanding this ontological distinction comes from Tim Ingold (2000), who distinguishes between the terms *globe* versus *sphere* to explain the assumptions that underlie our relationship with the environment.

10 Since its inception, Campfire has been heavily critiqued for unevenness in revenue distribution, ponderous administrative structures, and susceptibility to political influence. See for example Dzingirai 2003; Alexander and McGregor 2003, 2000; Murombedzi 2001; Sibanda 2001; Murphree and Metcalfe 1997; Madzudzo 1996; Child 1995; Nabane 1994.

11 Paired in contrast with "communal areas," "commercial areas" designate privately owned properties of land typically used for agricultural production or ranching.

12 Jon and Marie's three sons were married and had two children each. Their houses were dispersed throughout the property; the farthest one was thirty minutes' drive from Jon and Marie's house, which was always referred to as the "main house." Jon and Marie also had two daughters; one lived in the United States and the other lived on the family property with her husband, who was a professional hunter, and her two children.

13 The valley had church services one Sunday every other month, when a Dutch Reformed Church minister based in Bulawayo made the three-hour round-trip after finishing with the service for his own congregation. Mlilo had no church of its own; instead, the service was alternately hosted by different members of the community in their own homes. Because social gatherings were rare, the occasions were quite festive and attracted many residents of the valley, regardless of religious faith.

14 The Department of National Parks and Wild Life Management later changed its name to the Zimbabwe Parks and Wildlife Management Authority (ZimParks).

15 The colonial government designed and constructed veterinary grids to curtail the wanderings of errant cattle while continuing to allow automobile and pedestrian traffic. A typical grid consisted of a depression in the road, bridged by slim metal rods that made it impossible for a cow to cross with its narrow hooves. Its primary purpose was to prevent the transfer of bovine foot-and-mouth disease between cattle-ranching areas, as well as between cattle and wildlife.

16 Vleis—or seasonal shallow wetlands—are favorite congregation spots for animals due to their rich soils and flora. The detailed workings of their ecological systems in dryland contexts remain a mystery; however, vleis have received recognition as "key resources" critical to the sustainability of dryland agro-pastoral regimes (Scoones and Cousins 1993).

17 After the postcolonial government passed the Land Acquisition Act in 1992 (Moyo 2000), white commercial farms were designated for resettlement on the basis of low productivity. Game ranches, with their vast expanses of seemingly unoccupied land, were especially susceptible to designation under this system.

18 For further discussion of Africa as an unspoiled paradise representing the antithesis of Europe, see Neumann 1998, 1995; Adams and McShane 1992; MacKenzie 1988; Anderson and Grove 1987.

19 The representation of Africa as a paradise has always been an ambivalent one, existing simultaneously with the image of the continent as a forbidding wasteland.

20 Basic shared terminology such as "loading," "aiming," and "shooting" reveals the common underpinnings of hunting and photographic practices.

21 Many lodges and camps provided "sighting lists" with the names of local species, which guests could check off during the course of the day as they came across new animals. The parallels between this recreational activity and the historical fixation with conquering the natural world through hunting and scientific taxidermy are noteworthy.

22 The majority of hunting was done with rifles, but some individuals opted for compound bow hunting.

23 A client's wish list of species—usually no more than four animals per hunt—was negotiated with the safari outfit prior to his or her arrival in Zimbabwe. This step was essential because the Department of National Parks and Wild Life Management issued different hunting quotas to each property every year. For the most popular companies, yearly quotas were often sold out well in advance of the beginning of the hunting season.

24 Theodore Roosevelt, a renowned sport hunter himself, once declared in reference to this celebrated figure, "Mr. Selous is the last of the big game hunters of Southern Africa, the last of the mighty hunters whose experience lay in the greatest hunting ground which this world has seen since civilized man has appeared herein" (May 23, 1907).

25 Workers and their families lived in whitewashed compounds that stood within walking distance of the main homestead but were tucked far away enough to remain out of the sight.

26 House workers could be men as well as women; for example, there were more male cooks because men had better access to training when it came to preparing Western dishes.

27 *Baas* is the Afrikaans word for "boss." The term was used as a title of address by workers in households of both English and Afrikaner descent.

28 Although everyone agreed on the necessity of maintaining anti-poaching squads, the fact that communication between employers and employees was relatively infrequent often left farmers in the dark when it came to knowing the actual activities and movements of patrols. One rancher discovered, for example, that a worker who was widely acknowledged to be his right-hand man had been operating a lucrative black market in bushmeat—wildlife taken illegally from the rancher's property—for many months, with the cooperation of his anti-poaching squad.

29 This lifestyle, specifically coined the "Rhodesian way of life," was one in which settlers had an absolute sense of entitlement to domestic workers (Godwin and Hancock 1993:8–9). This in turn proved pivotal in the creation of a white Rhodesian identity, with the colonial government reinforcing the idea that nowhere else in the world could people so easily afford domestic help. Such ideas formed key elements in the campaign not only to convince people to immigrate to Southern

Rhodesia but also to persuade whites who were already there to remain. As in other colonial contexts, therefore, moving to Rhodesia signified upward social mobility.

30 As one might expect, tensions existed between the old-timers and the newcomers, who found it very difficult to gain acceptance among the long-established families. Specific examples of such tensions are presented in later chapters.

31 Typical positions included wildlife guides who took visitors out on game drives, secretaries and accountants for the more affluent wildlife producers, auto mechanics who maintained the game drive vehicles, photographers and videographers for hunting safaris, bush camp managers, and advertising staff.

32 In the years leading up to the land invasions, the tourism industry revolving around wildlife expanded to become the second highest income-generating business in the country, surpassed only by tobacco exports. More significantly, wildlife enterprises became the top source of foreign exchange, a form of currency considered far more desirable than local currency because of its stable value. Not surprisingly, political uncertainties in Zimbabwe since the land invasions have caused a collapse in tourism revenues, which have suffered a 90 percent decrease compared with the 1990s.

33 For young men who grew up in the bush, skills required by the wildlife industry— tracking, hunting, knowledge of local flora and fauna, and equipment maintenance and repair—came naturally, and as a result, they regarded the family business as providing opportunities just as promising as any other business sector in the country. Daughters more commonly left their homes when they married or chose to pursue alternative careers, although there are some exceptions. Given the generally conservative attitudes, as well as the Afrikaner cultural tradition through which only sons are entitled to inherit property—although the majority of families in Mlilo were of British descent, rather than Afrikaner—women tended to face a much more difficult time than their brothers if they chose to remain on the farms where they spent their childhoods.

34 For other influential works within this field, see Gallagher and Twine 2012; Mohanram 2007; Wray 2006; López 2005; Rasmussen et al. 2001; Frankenberg 1999; Hartigan 1999; Hale 1998; Kinchloe et al. 1998; Cooper and Stoler 1997; Delgado and Stefancic 1997; Dyer 1997; Fine et al. 1997; Hill 1997; McClintock 1995; Wellman 1993; Ware 1992; Blee 1991; Crapanzano 1985.

35 Both Alexandra Fuller and Peter Godwin have been influential in creating a new space for ex–white southern African voices in the literary world. See, for example, Fuller's *Don't Let's Go to the Dogs Tonight* (2001) and *Cocktail Hour under the Tree of Forgetfulness* (2011), as well as Godwin's *Mukiwa: A White Boy in Africa* (1996) and *When a Crocodile Eats the Sun* (2007). Other examples of recent memoirs by white southern Africans include Douglas Rogers's *Last Resort: A Memoir of Mischief and Mayhem on a Family Farm in Africa* (2009), Robyn Scott's *Twenty Chickens for a Saddle: The Story of an African Childhood* (2009), Lauren St. John's *Rainbow's End: A Memoir of Childhood, War, and an African Farm* (2008), and Wendy Kann's *Casting with a Fragile Thread: A Story of Sisters and Africa* (2006).

2. A SHORT SETTLER HISTORY

1   Various versions of Mzilikazi's name appear in earlier texts, including "Moseleka-tse" and "Mziligazi."

2   "Amandebele" is the Ndebele term for the people as a group; however, for the sake of uniformity with existing literature on the subject, I use the more common reference of "Ndebele."

3   Examples of Moffat's influence included the mitigation of punishments when he was present during trials of suspected criminals and a relaxation of the prohibitions against marriage for adult men serving in the military (Wallis 1976).

4   Interestingly, Friedrich Posselt, who served as a native commissioner in various districts of Southern Rhodesia from 1908 to 1941, ends his book by appealing to the chivalry of his own people "to record their tribute to the valour and ability of a great Bantu sovereign, by honouring his name with a worthy memorial" that would mark his royal tomb (1935:192).

5   Gold was discovered in both Mashonaland and Matabeleland during the 1860s; the "goldfields" were celebrated through the sensational accounts by Henry Hartley and Carl Mauch: "The rocks sparkle with gold; gold peeps out from every hillside; in the bed of every stream the sand is clothed with it" (quoted in Palmer 1977:22).

6   MacKenzie (1988) lists the many legendary hunters, including F. C. Selous, who traveled through this region only after obtaining permission from Mzilikazi and Lobengula. Lobengula in particular was interested in ensuring that his own men continued to have exclusive access to the best hunting areas.

7   These descriptions resonate with classic narratives of ethnic opposition in Africa that posit the subjugation of a peaceful agricultural majority by a fierce pastoral minority. See Malkki 1995 and Mamdani 2001 for a discussion of "mythico-histories" and colonial policies that lie at the heart of contemporary tensions between the Hutu and Tutsi in Burundi and Rwanda.

8   Julian Cobbing (1976) presents a strong case against the emphasis on militarization and centralization within the Ndebele state; he argues that such characterizations, along with descriptions of the supposedly rigid caste system—*zansi, enhla,* and *holi*—continue to reflect the biases of nineteenth-century European observers, who were predisposed to discover "feudal" social relations in Africa.

9   Other scholars in fact contest the existence of clear-cut Shona and Ndebele distinctions from the nineteenth century, instead maintaining that the opposition emerged much more recently, in large part through aggressive ethnic-based recruitment by nationalist movements during the liberation war (Werbner 1991).

10   Interestingly, the higher recognition assigned to the Ndebele by whites remains just as strong today. White Zimbabweans continue to refer to the Shona—often jokingly, but with conviction—as "snake-eyed Shona" or "shifty Shona." In contrast, they stoutly insist that the Ndebele are noble and proud, and will never steal.

11   Much to their frustration, for example, many missionaries were prevented by the Ndebele state from entering Shona regions to conduct evangelical work (Summers 1994).

12 Ranger quotes Rhodes, who wrote in a letter to his associate: "I saw at once the danger of our position if a series of articles appeared in the papers from a man of Selous['s] position claiming that Mashonaland was independent of Lobengula . . . I gave him personally £2,000 out of my own private fund . . . I consider I did the right thing with Selous" (1967b:274–275).

13 The "First Rand" refers to the main gold reef on the Witwatersrand, discovered in 1886; this discovery precipitated the immediate genesis of colonial Rhodesia (Phimister 1988). Rhodes feared that the Witwatersrand would upset the balance of British supremacy in South Africa by placing economic power in the hands of the Afrikaners. He proposed finding a "Second Rand" farther north that would secure Britain's position in the Cape Colony.

14 For all of their mining efforts, prospectors found only 779 ounces of gold in 1892.

15 A smallpox epidemic ravaged the army at the same time, further diminishing its ranks.

16 By 1901, there were 11,100 Europeans in Southern Rhodesia, in contrast to 850 in Northern Rhodesia and 314 in Nyasaland (Palmer 1977).

17 Since the publication of Ranger's influential book *Revolt in Southern Rhodesia* (1967a), accounts of these uprisings have undergone considerable revision. Beach (1986), for example, disputes the degree of collaboration between the Ndebele and Shona rebellions, as well as the intentionality of political resistance by religious leaders like Kaguvi and Nehanda. Evidence has also emerged revealing that many Shona dynasties—especially in the south—allied themselves with the British because they feared victory by the Ndebele even more than continued misrule under the colonial government.

18 In addition, most of the colony's armed forces had already been sent south to the Transvaal to take part in the Jameson Raid, an invasion orchestrated by Rhodes and his henchman, Leander Starr Jameson, to overthrow the Kruger government.

19 The different ways in which the two risings ended is revealing: Rhodes reached a peace agreement with Ndebele leaders, who were recognized as equals, while the Shona were hunted down and killed inside caves through the use of dynamite (Ranger 1967a).

20 The Orange Free State was an independent Boer sovereign republic in southern Africa during the second half of the nineteenth century, and later a British colony and a province of the Union of South Africa.

21 Tensions between British and Afrikaner settlers were exacerbated by the Second Anglo-Boer War, which began in South Africa in 1899. Many British Rhodesians left their occupations and volunteered their services to the military during this period.

22 Among its many objectives, the committee was charged with setting up training farms for new settlers, experimenting with tobacco crops, and creating a land bank that provided low-interest loans to farmers.

23 From "Women's Life," in *The Imperial Colonist*, August 1902:72, cited in Kennedy 1987:36.

24 By 1908, only 2 percent of the total immigrant population had come from Britain, suggesting that this campaign was largely a failure (Kennedy 1987).

25 In reality, few Africans could accumulate enough capital to purchase freehold farms—by 1925, only fourteen farms were owned by Africans—but European farmers feared that this would soon change (Palmer 1977).

26 The popular demand for segregation was inspired by the segregationist framework that had been established in the Natal Province of South Africa. The Southern Rhodesian government later adopted this model in creating their own system of segregation.

27 Relations between church and state were in fact quite strained during this period; when the emerging black elite began forming political associations, the government blamed missionaries, charging that they had focused too much on cultivating intellect among Africans, to the exclusion of more "practical" skills. West argues, however, that the "stereotypical mission-educated African, a racial leveler who shirked manual labor while surreptitiously poring over political treatises and plotting to bring about social equality between black and white," existed only in the imaginations of settlers and officials (2002:39). In actuality, many missionaries shared the settlers' racist views and treated Africans in cruel and demeaning ways.

28 The African Reserves, which would later come to be known as Tribal Trust Lands, were created in the 1890s in Matabeleland and in the early 1900s in Mashonaland. Originally the reserves were intended to allow supervision of Africans to prevent any further uprisings, but this goal was eclipsed by the more pressing need to generate an inexpensive African labor force for the development of the colony (Riddell 1978).

29 Most of these Native Purchase Areas lay in the desolate low-lying regions close to the country's borders, and in some cases were infested with tsetse fly, rendering them useless as agricultural properties (Phimister 1988).

30 See Worby (2000) for an illustration of the twinning of political exigencies with promises of black prosperity and moral uplift in the context of development in Gokwe and Sanyati.

31 In order to subsidize the export of European-produced cattle and beef, the Cattle Levy Act of 1931 charged a heavy tax for African cattle owners who slaughtered more than five head of cattle for local consumption. The Natives Registration Act, passed in 1936, prevented African producers from selling produce, chickens, eggs, and beer in the European areas of Salisbury (Schmidt 1992).

32 The government justified the lower prices for grain produced by Africans, as opposed to Europeans, by arguing that the hours of labor invested by African farmers' families cost nothing, while their European counterparts had to pay wages to all of their workers (Schmidt 1992).

33 Under this system, sometimes referred to as "Socialism-for-the-Whites," the state set prices on most commercial crops and guaranteed their purchase when they were marketed (Herbst 1990:22).

34 ZAPU and ZANU were originally one nationalist movement under the leadership of Joshua Nkomo, but differences in approach led to a split when Nkomo's

opponents broke away in 1963 and formed ZANU. The division in nationalist camps later came to reflect ethnic oppositions among blacks, with ZAPU based in Matabeleland, and ZANU in Mashonaland.

35 As White (2003) demonstrates, both Kenneth Kaunda of Zambia and Samora Machel of Mozambique were intimately involved in shaping the liberation war in Rhodesia. Other countries were involved as well, including China, the Soviet Union, and the United States.

36 As noted in an earlier section of this chapter, liberation discourses invoked the Chimurenga uprisings of 1896–97 and an ongoing tradition of spiritual resistance against colonial oppression. See Bhebe and Ranger 1995a, 1995b; Kriger 1992; and Lan 1985 for a discussion of the complex relationships between villagers, religious leaders, and liberation soldiers during the war.

37 By 1980, approximately two hundred thousand white Rhodesians, representing two-thirds of the total population, had fled the country to find new homes abroad.

38 In the context of the immediate inconveniences posed by global sanctions, the government urged its citizens to unite behind its efforts, sacrifice luxuries to which they were accustomed, and maintain their defiance to the rest of the world. Rumors of successful resistance to sanctions by individual "heroes" romanticized Rhodesian sanction-busting and bolstered national pride (Godwin and Hancock 1993).

39 See Ian Smith, *The Great Betrayal: The Memoirs of Ian Douglas Smith* (1997), a book found on almost every white Zimbabwean family's bookshelf.

40 For example, the *African Times*, which had a black readership of 2 million in 1975, continued to "portray a Black world in the image preferred by White Rhodesia: it was happy, loyal, and acquiescent, needing only to be reminded of its good fortunes in being governed by civilized men" (Godwin and Hancock 1993:146).

41 Godwin and Hancock (1993) present the song's lyrics: "We're Rhodesians, and we'll fight through thick and thin, we'll keep our land a free land, stop the enemy coming in. We'll keep them north of the Zambezi till that river's running dry. And this mighty land will prosper, for Rhodesians never die."

42 Other terms of reference designed to dehumanize liberation war fighters were "vermin," "sub-humans," "Neanderthals," and "animals." Adding further context, Alexandra Fuller explains that only black Rhodesians called the liberation war "Chimurenga." "The whites called it 'the Troubles,' 'This Bloody Nonsense.' And sometimes the 'war.' A war instigated by 'uppity blacks,' 'cheeky kaffirs,' 'bolshy *muntus*,' 'restless natives,' 'the houts'" (2001:26).

43 One might speculate that continued belief in their own moral correctness functions as a defense for white Zimbabweans in the diaspora, who find themselves exposed to less naive interpretations of race relations and histories in southern Africa.

44 In March 1997, however, the Catholic Commission for Justice and Peace in Zimbabwe (CCJPZ) succeeded in compiling an extraordinarily comprehensive report on the disturbances in the region, based on interviews of persons with firsthand experience of the atrocities and careful corroboration of sources.

3. BLACK BABOONS AND WHITE RUBBISH TREES

1   Wildebeest and zebra are commonly found grazing together in their natural environment, which biologists believe increases both species' ability to sense danger and protect themselves from predators. Upon hearing this story, some people have asked the question of whether part of the value of the metaphor came from the implicit understanding that one of these species is typically considered much more beautiful than the other. This is certainly possible, although Marie made no reference to differences in appearance. The primary usefulness of this comparison for her lay in the fact that zebra and wildebeest maintain social distance even while occupying the same physical space.

2   Since the study of whiteness emerged as a unified field of inquiry in the late 1990s (see Delgado and Stefancic 1997; Fine et al. 1997; Frankenberg 1999; M. Hill 1997; Kinchloe et al. 1998), many scholars have critiqued the term *whiteness* itself, arguing that its use runs the risk of recentering, rather than decentering, whiteness as a monolithic, undifferentiated category frozen in time. No alternative terms have successfully taken its place, however, perhaps reflecting the tyranny that these social categories continue to exercise over us. Instead, scholars have made the shift to using the term *"critical* whiteness studies" (see Rasmussen et al. 2001).

3   By 1999, over two-thirds of the white population had left the country, leaving fewer than one hundred thousand behind. Since the land invasions began in 2000, tens of thousands of others have left Zimbabwe to resettle in South Africa, Zambia, and Mozambique, as well as countries overseas.

4   This process includes not only the hemorrhaging of the white Zimbabwean population but also the disappearance of long-standing cultural icons such as Meikles department store in Bulawayo. The dining room on the top floor was considered *the* place to lunch for farmers' wives who had come into town for the day to do their shopping. Complete with waiters in crisp white uniforms, this space evoked memories of colonial grandeur. At the same time, markers of the past have a tendency to reappear at unexpected moments. In the late 1990s, the Zimbabwean government, which had run out of funds to print new stationery, began using old letterhead from the Rhodesian government as a temporary solution. This sudden collapsing between the past and present was unsettling for many people.

5   Crapanzano's portrayal of residents in a small vineyard community near Cape Town as comfortable, self-absorbed racists was fiercely contested by white South African scholars as well as white audiences more broadly. Nancy Scheper-Hughes, another well-known American anthropologist, conducted research in the same community more than a decade later, in a different political context, when the country was making the transition to democratic rule. Schepher-Hughes suggests that critics saw Crapanzano's depictions as biased and unfair, "projecting an image of white South African racists to ease the guilt of American whites" (2007:184).

6   In her work on contemporary white Kenyans, Janet McIntosh terms this insistence on denial "structural oblivion," a state that includes the refusal to acknowledge

reasons for resentment by less privileged groups, as well as a lack of recognition for how white ideologies continue to uphold their own elite positions (2016:10).

7   I witnessed this reaction firsthand among several tourists from the Netherlands, who questioned with thinly veiled contempt why farmers of Afrikaner descent insisted on calling themselves "European" when they had no similarities whatsoever to "actual Europeans."

8   This self-representation by urban whites regarding their acceptance of racial integration proved inconsistent with many actions and sentiments that surfaced during unguarded moments. In my experience, rural whites were often much more comfortable being around blacks—although this comfort was not necessarily synonymous with tolerance or respect—because black Zimbabweans constituted a more integral part of their everyday lives.

9   The "war vet" in this situation was one of the newly arrived occupants on Bezedenhuit's farm. He and a number of other land invaders crowded around Bezedenhuit's truck as he tried to drive past and refused to budge from in front of the truck.

10 This, of course, was too simple an interpretation; some people have observed that black Zimbabwean women involved in marriages to white farmers are often the most abused, both physically and emotionally. White men who marry black women are therefore not necessarily exonerated from charges of racism.

11 "Fighting for gay rights in Zimbabwe," *BBC News Online*, October 23, 1999.

12 Here, Rob is referring to the drafting of a new constitution that was later rejected by a national vote in the referendum elections in February 2000. During 1999, numerous constitutional assembly meetings were held across the country to gather input from citizens about how the constitution should be changed. One of the key revisions in the new draft was to assign the government greater powers to redistribute land.

13 Blair Rutherford (2001) presents similar examples of Hurungwe farmer "pioneer stories" in which farmers first forge into a landscape of "wildness" and then, through hard work, unfailing perseverance, and the endurance of countless discomforts, succeed in converting the wilderness into agriculturally productive land.

14 The term *nanny* is often used by white Zimbabweans to refer to all black women, regardless of occupation. It usually has a negative connotation; for example, people referred to Grace Mugabe, Robert Mugabe's second wife, as "just another nanny."

15 It's important to note that such cross-racial bonding would never have been permissible between men and women, with or without the fiction of friendship.

16 The sister of an influential political figure in the neighboring communal area, Cathy was on good terms with Charlie and occasionally stopped by his house for tea.

17 One farmer who was known to be a "terrible tyrant" in his relationship with the people of the communal area bordering his property was said to round up any cattle he found on his land and fine each person Z$100 before he would return the animals. He was also known to kill warthogs, poison the meat, and then leave it at

the boundary fence between his property and the communal area in order to kill dogs commonly used for hunting and poaching. At one point, deciding that they had had enough, hundreds of people in the communal area coordinated to bring their livestock onto the farmer's property at the same time so that it would be impossible for him to fine them all, but would instead be forced to let them graze for free.

18 The British colonists privileged the Ndebele, but the latter are an ethnic minority constituting 11 percent of the country's population, as opposed to 85 percent who are Shona. Following independence, political power shifted to the Shona because of their demographic dominance. Their historical treatment at the hands of the Ndebele is often cited in contemporary debates about nationhood to explain essentialized differences and tensions between the two groups.

19 While the specific charges of conspiracy are fascinating in terms of what they reveal about state paranoia and its attitudes toward both white and black farmers in this region, I refrain from outlining them here in order to protect the identities of my informants.

20 White Zimbabweans tap into black critiques of the state wherever possible. For example, most people have an exhaustive knowledge of contemporary politics and are able to cite black political figures who express disillusionment toward the government. Another surprising example was a book called *Out of America* (1997), which was a favorite among many people. Written by an African American writer named Keith Richburg, this work presents a very pessimistic view of contemporary problems in Africa, going so far as to express gratitude that slavery took the author's ancestors away from the continent to a better life in America. Not surprisingly, this book caused a huge controversy within the African American community, but in the white Zimbabwean context, it was received as an important critique of all that was wrong with Africa.

21 Somewhat predictably, this tends to occur among younger people rather than older generations, but there were certainly exceptions to this pattern. Differences seemed to emerge out of ethnicity as well, with individuals of Afrikaans descent expressing more willingness to use the label of "white African," whereas many people with a British background continued to place importance on the "European" part of their identities. This difference most likely relates to the different histories and experiences of the two groups within Africa.

22 Primary schools in the area are often located 4 or 5 km from the main road, and students might have to walk for an hour or so before finding a ride or catching a bus to Bulawayo or Hwange.

23 In Ndebele, *shupha* means "to bother or harass." The term is one of many words that white farmers have incorporated into their everyday language.

4. REINSTATING NATURE, REINVENTING MORALITY

1 *Paw-paw* is the term commonly used for papaya in Zimbabwe.

2 This is perhaps the best-known debate in agrarian economics, beginning with Garrett Hardin's famous essay, "The Tragedy of the Commons" (1968).

3 The primary fear lay in the possible transfer from wildlife to cattle of foot-and-mouth disease, also known as "hoof-and-mouth," a bovine disease which has recently resurfaced in European cattle industries. The Rhodesian government also supported wildlife eradication as a method of controlling the tsetse fly, which kills cattle and causes human sleeping sickness. Similarly, animals recognized as major carriers of rabies, including dogs, were systematically exterminated (Mutwira 1989).

4 Animals identified as the exclusive province of white settlers often became targets of symbolic violence in resistance against the government. This theme resurfaces in postcolonial contexts, as we shall see in later chapters.

5 As noted in chapter 2, Tribal Trust Lands, or TTLs, constituted the colonial classification for areas designated for black populations. After independence, these lands became known as "communal areas."

6 By law, every animal had to walk through dip tanks containing chemicals that killed disease-bearing ticks once a week. This controlled the outbreak of sicknesses such as red water, theileriosis, heartwater, and gall sickness.

7 The Wildlife Producers Association was founded in 1985, with headquarters based in Harare.

8 These steps coincided with the gradual process of selling cattle on the beef market without rebuilding the herd, as Jon had done each year in the past.

9 From 1975 to 1985, as part of its infrastructural support for the emerging interest in wildlife on private properties, the government began offering national parks animals for sale with the objective of restocking depleted commercial areas. Professional "animal capture" units were also formed to minimize trauma in the translocation of animals. Between 1985 and 1992, these capture units translocated over fifteen thousand animals to different parts of the country (WPA 1992).

10 In 1997, a white rhino at a "live game sale" in South Africa fetched a price of over US$14,000 (Child 1998).

11 This physical transformation took place through the tearing down of fences that originally demarcated boundary lines between individual properties.

12 As testimony to this wealth, Jon had the largest big-screen television I had ever seen. It stood chest-high and dominated one whole wall of his living room. He explained proudly that it had been a gift from his children, and it was one of only three televisions of its kind in the whole country.

13 An important index of this recognition was the fact that donor agencies insisted on the active participation of wildlife producers—referred to as "stakeholders"—before releasing aid packages to national parks. Wildlife producers interpreted this inclusion as an attempt to ensure the proper monitoring of donor aid by people with strong expertise in conservation, unlike many national parks staff.

14 Given economic instabilities in Zimbabwe, it proved much more lucrative to work as a wildlife guide and earn foreign income—some freelance professional guides charged their employers over US$100 per day, a veritable fortune in Zimbabwean terms—than to work as a business or computer consultant, for example.

15 The wealthier families of Mlilo were finally able to afford the installation of

electricity, paying for the construction of power lines themselves, but less well-off households continued to rely on generators and paraffin for their power.

16 In the opening vignette of this chapter, Jon Van den Akker's observation that young people no longer want to be doctors or lawyers, but aspire instead to become professional hunters to make "big money" implicitly critiques what he considers to be the misguided motivations of people entering the industry.

17 For an analysis of the role of private wildlife conservancies in southern Africa, see Murphree and Metcalfe 1997.

18 Established in the late 1980s, the Save Valley Conservancy (SVC) in the lowveld region of eastern Zimbabwe constitutes the country's largest and best-known conservancy. An amalgamation of twenty-four properties, the Save spans 3,387 km^2 and is the largest private wildlife reserve in Africa (Wolmer et al. 2003). The Mlilo Conservancy constitution is almost an exact replica of the one adopted by the SVC.

19 At its inception, one idea that came under intense scrutiny was the possibility of inviting a neighboring communal area involved with the Communal Areas Management Programme for Indigenous Resources (Campfire), a program enabling communities to participate in wildlife utilization, to become a member of the conservancy. The impetus for including a communal area in the creation of the conservancy was to increase the valley's eligibility for external funding. Although ultimately the proposal was not passed because some members thought it would be "too complicated" to incorporate a communal area, the serious consideration given to this proposal—which would have been unthinkable in the past—illustrates the degree to which farmers were beginning to concede certain principles and recognize the need to work within changing structures.

20 There were notable exceptions to the average size of wildlife ranching properties in the country; for example, in Matabeleland South, a single wildlife producer could own up to a million acres before the land occupations.

21 The purchase and transfer of these animals require complicated negotiations and coordination at every stage. Although every effort is made to minimize physical and emotional trauma to the animals, a few always die during the stress of capture and transit, or from exhaustion and failure of adjustment after they reach their destinations. The purchasing farmer must absorb these costs, as well as the considerable expense of quarantining the animals in holding pens for several months before they are released into their new environments.

22 Duffy (1997), among other scholars, characterizes the problem of the mobile nature of wildlife by conceptualizing animals as a "fugitive resource." The term has also been applied to aquatic animals such as fish, as well as water itself.

23 These principles are drawn from a management strategy report prepared by a conservancy consultant. The title and author of the document are intentionally concealed here in order to avoid invalidating the use of pseudonyms throughout this work.

24 These numbers included 71 eland, 56 buffalo, 89 zebra, and 83 wildebeest. Because Heron hoped to build up these herds, he deliberately refrained from hunting any

of these species on his property for a period of a few years. He was aware, however, that all of the animals he had painstakingly translocated were vulnerable once they crossed the boundary into his neighbors' lands. This created the impetus to secure his investments by erecting a game fence around the perimeter of his entire property.

25 Although the second principle in the constitution allowed for the excision of any properties whose owners did not comply with conservancy policy, in reality this was a difficult measure to enforce because the property in question might be located right in the middle of the valley, where it bordered several other properties.

26 Safe and ethical hunting practices dictate that a wounded animal—especially buffaloes, which are known to be the most dangerous—should be tracked until a fatal shot is delivered.

27 Harriet Ritvo argues that the maintenance and display of captive "exotic" animals offered an "especially vivid rhetorical means of re-enacting and extending the work of empire" (1987:205). For further discussion of the history of captive animal exhibits and their political utility, see Davies 2000; K. Anderson 1998; Haraway 1989.

28 Culling is an elaborate operation, often involving the use of helicopters, labor forces of hundreds of men to process the carcasses, days of planning to isolate an appropriate herd, and complicated coordination to ensure that none of the animals escape. Many infant elephants were captured and flown to zoos in Europe and the United States.

29 Critics of course expressed the concern that this partial relaxation could have serious negative ramifications for elephant populations in other parts of the continent. Because it is difficult to monitor illegal versus legal ivory, people feared that poaching would increase dramatically in areas where elephants were still endangered.

30 These sales were restricted to already existing stocks of ivory.

31 Other possibilities have been explored more recently, such as the implantation of contraceptive drugs in sexually mature female elephants. Actually implementing this proposal, however, would require further experimentation as well as planning.

32 This type of "foot-dragging" on the part of the state is in some ways reminiscent of the "weapons of the weak" deployed by peasants in Malaysia (Scott 1987). This introduces the question of whether states might also have their own repertories of everyday resistance, particularly against politically and economically powerful groups within the citizenry.

33 Marie confirmed this news, which she had also read in the newspaper that morning. She added an interesting side note to the story, however, when she explained that the Japanese had originally intended to donate the money to the Gwanda district, but the councilors there had snubbed the Japanese representatives. In the politics of development, Japan has consistently fallen below Western countries in prestige, even though Japan was at one point the biggest donor in Zimbabwe.

34 Lions Club International is a charitable organization with 1.4 million members in 193 countries, and is well known throughout the world for its efforts to alleviate blindness caused by eye cataracts. Many farmers in Mlilo have belonged to the local chapter of the club for decades, and coordinate at least one event a year to raise money for its charities.

35 Here, "pumps" refer to the electric pumps that draw water up from underground aquifers. These aquifers never dry out, and thus, in theory, a well-managed national park should be able to supply water to resident wildlife even in times of drought. The engines for these pumps require constant maintenance, and making the rounds of three or four pumps located on one's property can often consume an entire morning or afternoon.

5. THE USES OF ANIMALS

1 In tourism lingo, a "chalet" refers to a guest room that stands as an independent structure. Most small-scale safari lodges and bush camps have chalet-style accommodations, which are usually tented camps or thatch-roofed rondavels designed to invoke "traditional" architecture.

2 "Problem Animals" constitute a legal category that identifies individual animals reported as causing havoc within village communities. Problem Animal Control (PAC), a subdivision of the DNPWLM, has the authority to relocate or exterminate such animals.

3 For this insight, I would like to thank Carole Crumley, who was a discussant for the panel "Reading History in the Landscape" at the 2002 American Anthropological Association annual meeting in New Orleans.

4 For a discussion of the role of laughter in mediating relations between state and civil society, see Mbembe 1992; Bayart 1993.

5 Although focusing on plants rather than animals, Comaroff and Comaroff (2000) describe a national debate in South Africa in which exotic species of flora were condemned as environmentally destructive and highly undesirable, while indigenous plant species were praised and celebrated. The Comaroffs suggest that this masked a more insidious xenophobic discourse that targeted black migrant workers from neighboring countries.

6 During the same period, in contrast, the British executed four hundred dachshunds, which were thought to be "too German." German shepherds, having been deemed too useful as police dogs, escaped a similar fate; their breed name was changed to "Alsatian" (Swart 2002).

7 See Candea 2010; Hayward 2010; Kosek 2010; Helmreich 2009; Kirksey and Helmreich 2010; Lowe 2010; Parreñas 2012.

8 The concept of the "uses" of animals comes from Hugh Raffles's work (2003) on the scientific expeditions of Henry Walter Bates in the Amazon. The title of this chapter is inspired by Raffles's chapter, "The Uses of Butterflies."

9 The story of the man-eating lions of Tsavo, which was popularized by the 1996 film *The Ghost and the Darkness*, is based on real events in Kenya in 1898. During

the construction of a railway bridge over the Tsavo River, two large male lions systematically killed and ate forty railway workers, bringing construction to a halt. The lions were eventually shot and killed, but have been immortalized by the speculations they raised about the intelligence and intentionality of lions. Their bodies are on display at the Field Museum in Chicago today.

10 The government offered a reward of up to £2 for every pair of lion ears brought in by a settler (much like the bounty system on the American frontier).

11 One family, for example, tallied their losses to lions at 127 head of cattle for a single year.

12 I am indebted to an anonymous reviewer for drawing my attention to the significance of language in the names given to these lions.

13 Adopted from Ndebele, *shupha* means "to bother." (This word is used frequently by white farmers. For example, parents often admonish their children to stop *shupha*-ing them.)

14 Once the land invasions began, the Van den Akker farm was the last in the valley to be occupied. Jon maintained that this was because some still believed that the property was protected by lions.

15 Although not addressed in this chapter, Jon also had three domesticated elephants that accompanied the family to the agricultural show as well.

16 In recent decades, a blurring of boundaries has occurred in national conservation debates, conflating the fate of animals once labeled "varmints" with the fate of Native Americans, who were subject to similar campaigns of extermination and eviction. Alec Brownlow (2000) suggests that as a result, restoration projects today appear to be driven more by guilt and shame over historical injustices inflicted upon Native Americans, rather than scientific and ecological arguments. For similar discussions on the contested imagery and redefinition of whales and dolphins, see Einarsson 1993; Davis 1997; Erikson 1999.

17 Birds seem to be the most popular animals for use as national symbols, perhaps because bird species vary tremendously from region to region, allowing nations to claim distinctive animals found only within their borders. Countries often have more than one national symbol, however, and the most prevalent one in Zimbabwe is "Great Zimbabwe," an architectural structure that is widely recognized to be the most significant archaeological site in sub-Saharan Africa. Another interesting example of "animal as nation" takes the form of national canine breeds. The Rhodesian Ridgeback, also known as the "lion dog," gained tremendous popularity in the first half the twentieth century, paralleling the rise of white settler nationalism and statehood (Schoonakker 2003).

18 "Lalapha okungekho qhude kuyasa" (Pelling 1977).

19 *Sunday Mail Magazine*, January 17, 1999.

20 Interestingly, while there was no stigma attached before 1914 to a country that did not have national parks, the absence of parks was considered shameful after 1919 (Carruthers 1989), pointing to a significant shift in global perceptions toward the importance of national parks.

21 The more traditional paradigm of preservationism espouses non-interventionist

models of conservation, while sustainable utilization engages in nondestructive levels of resource use, and channels derivative profits back into conservation efforts. In the specific case of elephants, animals in overpopulated regions are culled, their tusks and skins sold, and the generated income absorbed back into the financial budgets of the originating national parks, village communities, or individual households. Although widely accepted as one of the most pragmatic approaches to conservation today, the paradigm aroused violent opposition for many years because it ran directly counter to ideas about nature's grandeur and sanctity.

22 See Dzingirai 2003; Alexander and McGregor 2003, 2000; Murombedzi 2001; Sibanda 2001; Murphree and Metcalfe 1997; Child 1995; Nabane 1994.

23 James S. Shikwati, "Ivory and eco-imperialists," *Washington Post*, November 10, 2002; Emily Wax, "Ivory ban has high cost for rural Africans: Resurgent elephants trample harvests," *Washington Post Foreign Service*, November 10, 2002.

24 This partial lifting of the ivory ban resulted in the sale of approximately 110,000 pounds of raw ivory to Japan over the course of two years. The subsequent US$5 million profit was then redirected toward elephant conservation efforts in Zimbabwe, Botswana, and Namibia. At a CITES conference held in November 2002, these same three countries, joined by South Africa and Zambia, proposed another one-time sale, to be followed by annual trade under the governance of strict quotas.

25 Godfrey Marawanyika, "Zim plans to sell wild animals to Nigeria," *Zimbabwe Independent*, February 9, 2001.

26 Forward Maisokwadzo, "$3 billion park project hangs in balance," *Zimbabwe Independent*, January 12, 2001.

27 In revenue, tourism ranked second only to the tobacco industry; however, the tourism industry had additional cachet as the highest-ranking source of *foreign exchange* revenue, which has been in perpetual shortage in the national economy during the past few years. These revenue figures have dropped dramatically since the beginning of the land invasions in 2000, with the collapse of the industry overall.

28 The state, of course, is not a monolithic entity; different actors and branches within the state often have competing visions and objectives.

29 Pit bulls, for example, have come to be associated with very distinctive meanings (see Weaver 2012).

30 Among the outside dogs, the ones trained for tracking and hunting enjoyed the most prestige, but they also tended to have the shortest lives because of the many risks in their line of work. One couple, for example, who imported two dozen hunting hounds from Britain to start a business that specialized in leopard hunts, found that by the end of two years, only five of their dogs remained alive.

31 While much thicker in consistency, *sadza* is similar to grits in American cuisine. *Sadza* constitutes the main staple food for black Zimbabweans; many white farmers often served *sadza* at their tables as well.

32 Historically, these dogs were called "kaffir dogs."

33 Swart (2008) offers an interesting analysis of how Africanis, a mixed breed similar to the dogs found in the communal lands in Zimbabwe, has gained popularity in South Africa in recent years. She argues that Western purebreds have taken second place as the Africanis comes to represent the "true" indigenous African dog, in close dialogue with new articulations of nationalism.

34 This idea is quite common, not only in Zimbabwe but also in countries such as Kenya, Tanzania, and the United States.

6. WILDLIFE CONTESTED

1 For a more detailed account of this crisis as it was unfolding, see Worby and Suzuki 2001.

2 The land reform program, in which these land invasions played a central role, has been called the Third Chimurenga, or the third "revolutionary struggle." The liberation war is known as the Second Chimurenga.

3 Many observed that the majority of the individuals occupying white farms throughout the country were in fact too young to have participated in the liberation war. It was widely believed that the label of "war vets" was mobilized in this context to lend moral legitimacy to the invasions.

4 "Armed poachers wreak havoc in Mat North," *Zimbabwe Independent*, January 5, 2001; "Land invasions put game in danger," *Sunday Times*, November 26, 2000; "Zim's wildlife falls prey to politics," *Mail and Guardian*, November 3, 2000.

5 Endangered species in this area include black rhinos and white rhinos, wild dogs, Liechtenstein's hartebeest, aardwolves, and pangolins. The Save also supported the most successful rhino-breeding program in Africa, boasting a 10 percent yearly growth rate (Du Toit 1999).

6 *Mail and Guardian*, November 3, 2000.

7 "Invasions could cost Zimbabwe $1b in grants," *Zimbabwe Independent*, December 8, 2000. The figure of Z$1 billion was a substantial amount before inflation began to rise at an astronomical rate in the early 2000s.

8 *Zimbabwe Independent*, January 12, 2001. The Gaza-Kruger-Gonarezhou Transfrontier Park was proposed by Zimbabwe in partnership with Mozambique and South Africa as the continent's first transnational park, where tourists could travel freely across national borders, initiating new experiments in regional governance. On December 9, 2002, the heads of state of South Africa, Zimbabwe, and Mozambique signed a treaty establishing the park, which was renamed the Great Limpopo Transfrontier Park.

9 *Mail and Guardian*, November 3, 2000 (emphasis added).

10 This represented a devastating loss for many endangered species because their populations were often strongest in private game conservancies. Seventy percent of the country's black rhinos, for example, were found on commercial lands prior to these events.

11 "It's 'fair game' in conservancies," *Zimbabwe Standard*, May 10, 2002.

12 *Zimbabwe Standard*, May 10, 2002. Ian Smith served as prime minister of Rhode-

sia when the country declared independence from Britain in 1965 and remained prime minister for the next fourteen years.

13 "Poachers wiping out wild animals in Zimbabwe: The start of Mugabe's land-invasion plan has spelled the end for protected species," *Globe and Mail*, May 21, 2002.

14 "Report slams resettlement in conservancies," *Zimbabwe Independent*, October 29, 2002.

15 While this view became the dominant interpretation of the fast-track land reform program among white farmers as well as the global media, some have challenged the idea that land reform in Zimbabwe was a failure. This issue will be revisited later in this chapter.

16 "We can't put a policeman behind every animal," *Financial Times*, August 2, 2003.

17 Although countries such as Great Britain and the United States had openly condemned the political crisis in Zimbabwe by this point, the delicate complexity of the situation made a more direct course of action—or indeed even the appropriateness of one—difficult to determine.

18 The concept of *le pratique sauvage* (Elder et al. 1998) provides a useful framework for understanding these dynamics, particularly in relation to how valuations of animal-based practices determine hierarchies between the "civilized" and the "primitive."

19 In reality, the government remains more dependent than ever upon foreign donor funds because of the rapidly disintegrating economy. The state's defiant stance was interpreted as a political maneuver to deflect attention away from the more deeply embedded problems that plague the country.

20 "Chefs protest hunting ban," *Zimbabwe Independent*, October 23, 2003.

21 "Curb poaching or lose permit—Nhema," *Herald*, August 20, 2007.

22 *Herald*, August 20, 2007.

23 "Government approves wildlife land-based policy," *Herald*, October 12, 2006.

24 "Ministers strike it rich in conservancies," *Financial Gazette*, October 8, 2011. This list, originally communicated through a classified US cable, names top-ranking politicians with stakes in hunting on private lands. These individuals were of particular interest to the American government because they fell in the category of Specially Designated Nationals and were subject to sanctions by the United States.

25 *Financial Gazette*, October 8, 2011.

26 Associated Press, "Wildlife group: Politicians threaten animal haven," August 24, 2012.

27 Associated Press, "Zimbabwe conservationists: Wildlife threatened," August 26, 2012.

28 Associated Press, August 26, 2012.

29 "Wildlife conservancies must comply with indigenisation laws," *Herald*, July 17, 2012.

30 "Mugabe blasts army generals," *Zimbabwe Independent*, September 21, 2012.

31 "Politburo directives ignored by security chiefs," *SW Radio Africa*, May 28, 2014. The three individuals were a brigadier-general, a police assistant commissioner, and an army captain.

32 "Mugabe buses in wildlife for UN Summit 'propaganda.'" *Telegraph Online*, August 28, 2014.

33 This caused controversy as China was accused of stealing African wildlife, especially when one of the baby elephants died soon after arriving in the country. See "Victory for animal welfare: Zimbabwe releases baby elephants," *Africa Geographic*, January 22, 2013. At the beginning of 2015, the announcement that Zimbabwe was set to ship eighty-seven baby elephants from Hwange National Park to China, Thailand, France, and the United Arab Emirates created yet another controversy, this time much greater in scale. The baby elephants were valued at $40,000 to $60,000 each, and the fact that their final destinations were unclear—whether zoos, wildlife parks, or wealthy individual buyers—generated further criticism. Zimbabwe has adopted the position that the country is facing an elephant overpopulation problem, and the decision to export baby elephants is more humane than reducing populations through culling.

34 "Chinese mining activities spark uproar," *Standard*, May 23, 2013.

35 "Huge new peace park must deliver benefits," *Cape Argus*, August 23, 2011.

36 *Cape Argus*, August 23, 2011.

37 "American hunter killed Cecil, beloved lion who was lured out of his sanctuary," *New York Times*, July 28, 2015.

38 "Killer of Cecil the lion finds out that he is a target now, of internet vigilantism," *New York Times*, July 29, 2015.

39 "Cecil the lion: Zimbabwe asks U.S. to extradite dentist," *CNN World*, August 3, 2015.

40 "PETA calls for Walter Palmer to be 'hanged' for killing Cecil the lion," *Washington Post*, July 30, 2015.

41 "After Cecil furor, U.S. aims to protect lions through Endangered Species Act," *New York Times*, December 20, 2015.

42 Goodwell Nzou, "In Zimbabwe, we don't cry for lions," *New York Times*, August 4, 2015.

43 The Rhodes Must Fall movement began in March 2015, when students protested a statue of Cecil Rhodes on the campus of the University of Cape Town. This developed into a larger movement to decolonize university educational systems in South Africa, resulting in protests at several other institutions across the country and in the UK.

44 Similar to the "savage slot" or "indigenous slot" (see Trouillot 1991; Li 2000), the "white slot" is articulated with distinctive markers and associations.

BIBLIOGRAPHY

Achebe, Chinua. 1975. "An image of Africa: Racism in Conrad's *Heart of Darkness*." Lecture presented at the University of Massachusetts, Amherst, February 18, 1975.

Adams, Jonathan, and Thomas McShane. 1992. *The Myth of Wild Africa: Conservation without Illusion*. New York: Norton.

Agamben, Giorgio. 2004. *The Open: Man and Animal*. Stanford: Stanford University Press.

Alexander, Jocelyn. 1991. "The unsettled land: The politics of land redistribution in Matabeleland, 1980–1990." *Journal of Southern African Studies* 17(4): 582–610.

Alexander, Jocelyn, and JoAnn McGregor. 2003. "'Our sons didn't die for animals': Attitudes to wildlife and the politics of development; Campfire in Nkayi and Lupane districts." In *The Historical Dimensions of Democracy and Human Rights in Zimbabwe*. Vol. 2, *Nationalism, Democracy, and Human Rights*, edited by Terence Ranger, 162–183. Harare: University of Zimbabwe Publications.

———. 2000. "Wildlife and politics: Campfire in Zimbabwe." *Development and Change* 31(3): 605–627.

———. 1996. "Democracy, development and political conflict: Rural institutions in Matabeleland North after Independence." Paper presented at the International Conference on the Historical Dimensions of Democracy and Human Rights, Zimbabwe, September 1996.

Alexander, Jocelyn, JoAnn McGregor, and Terence Ranger. 2000a. "Ethnicity and the politics of conflict: The case of Matabeleland." In *War, Hunger, and Displacement: The Origins of Humanitarian Emergencies*, edited by E. Wayne Nafziger, 305–332. Oxford: Oxford University Press.

———. 2000b. *Violence and Memory: One Hundred Years in the "Dark Forests" of Matabeleland*. Oxford: James Currey.

Anderson, Benedict. 1991. *Imagined Communities: Reflections on the Origin and Spread of Nationalism*. New York: Verso.

Anderson, David, and Richard Grove, eds. 1987. *Conservation in Africa: People, Policies and Practice*. Cambridge: Cambridge University Press.

Anderson, Kay. 1998. "Animals, science, and spectacle in the city." In *Animal Geographies: Place, Politics, and Identity in the Nature-Culture Borderlands*, edited by Jennifer Wolch and Jody Emel, 27–50. London: Verso.

Appadurai, Arjun. 1996. *Modernity at Large: Cultural Dimensions of Globalization.* Minneapolis: University of Minnesota Press.

———. 1986. "Introduction: Commodities and the politics of value." In *The Social Life of Things: Commodities in Cultural Perspective,* edited by Arjun Appadurai, 3–63. Cambridge: Cambridge University Press.

Arluke, Arnold, and Boria Sax. 1995. "The Nazi treatment of animals and people." In *Reinventing Biology: Respect for Life and the Creation of Knowledge,* edited by Lynda Birke and Ruth Hubbard, 228–260. Bloomington: Indiana University Press.

Atwood, Margaret. 1998. "Animal victims." In *The Wild Animal Story,* edited by Ralph H. Lutts, 215–224. Philadelphia: Temple University Press.

Bain, Read. 1928. "The culture of canines." *Sociology and Social Research* (July-August): 545–556.

Baker, Steve. 2001. *Picturing the Beast: Animals, Identity, and Representation.* Champaign: University of Illinois Press.

Bakhtin, Mikhail. 1981. *The Dialogic Imagination: Four Essays.* Translated by Caryl Emerson and Michael Holquist. Austin: University of Texas Press.

Bayart, Jean-Francois. 1993. *The State in Africa: The Politics of the Belly.* London: Longman.

Beach, David N. 1994. *The Shona and Their Neighbors.* Oxford: Blackwell.

———. 1986. *War and Politics in Zimbabwe, 1840–1900.* Gweru, Zimbabwe: Mambo Press.

———. 1984. *Zimbabwe before 1900.* Gweru, Zimbabwe: Mambo Press.

———. 1980. *The Shona and Zimbabwe, 900–1850.* Gweru, Zimbabwe: Mambo Press.

Beinart, William, and Peter Coates. 1995. *Environment and History: The Taming of Nature in the USA and South Africa.* London: Routledge.

Berger, John. 1991 [1980]. *About Looking.* New York: Vintage International.

Bhabha, Homi. 2004 [1994]. *The Location of Culture.* London: Routledge.

Bhebe, Ngwabi. 1977. *Lobengula of Zimbabwe.* London: Heinemann.

Bhebe, Ngwabi, and Terence Ranger. 1995a. *Society in Zimbabwe's Liberation War,* vol. 2. Harare: University of Zimbabwe Publications.

———. 1995b. *Soldiers in Zimbabwe's Liberation War,* vol. 1. Harare: University of Zimbabwe Publications.

Bilger, Burkhard. 2001. "A shot in the ark." *New Yorker,* March: 74–83.

Blee, Kathleen. 1991. *Women of the Klan: Racism and Gender in the 1920s.* Berkeley: University of California Press.

Bond, Ivan. 2001. "Campfire and the incentives for insitutional change." In *African Wildlife and Livelihoods: The Promise and Performance of Community Conservation,* edited by David Hulme and Marshall Murphree, 227–243. Oxford: James Currey.

Borland, Katherine. 1996. "'The India Bonita of Monimbó': The politics of ethnic identity in the New Nicaragua." In *Beauty Queens on the Global Stage: Gender, Contests, and Power,* edited by Colleen Ballerino Cohen, Richard Wilk, and Beverly Stoeltje, 75–88. New York: Routledge.

Braun, Bruce. 2003. "On the raggedy edge of risk: Articulations of race and nature after biology." In *Race, Nature, and the Politics of Difference,* edited by Donald

Moore, Jake Kosek, and Anand Pandian, 175–203. Durham, NC: Duke University Press.

Brosius, Peter. 1999. "Green dots, pink hearts: Displacing politics from the Malaysian rainforest." *American Anthropologist* 101(1): 36–57.

Brownlow, Alec. 2000. "A wolf in the garden: Ideology and change in the Adirondack landscape." In *Animal Spaces, Beastly Places: New Geographies of Human-Animal Relations*, edited by Chris Philo and Chris Wilbert, 141–158. London: Routledge.

Bruner, Edward. 2001. "The Maasai and the Lion King: Authenticity, nationalism, and globalization in African tourism." *American Ethnologist* 28(4): 881–908.

Buckle, Catherine. 2014. *Innocent Victims: Rescuing the Stranded Animals of Zimbabwe's Farm Invasions*. Ludlow, UK: Merlin Unwin.

———. 2001. *African Tears: The Zimbabwe Land Invasions*. Johannesburg: Covos Day Books.

Bulmer, Ralph. 1967. "Why is the cassowary not a bird?" *Man* 2(1): 5–25.

Candea, Matei. 2010. "'I fell in love with Carlos the meerkat': Engagement and detachment in human-animal relations." *American Ethnologist* 37(2): 241–258.

Carruthers, Jane. 1989. "Creating a national park, 1910 to 1926." *Journal of Southern African Studies* 15(2): 188–216.

Cartmill, Matt. 1993. *A View to a Death in the Morning: Hunting and Nature through History*. Cambridge, MA: Harvard University Press.

Castree, Noel, and Bruce Braun. 1998. "The construction of nature and the nature of construction: Analytical and political tools for building survivable futures." In *Remaking Reality: Nature at the Millennium*, edited by Bruce Braun and Noel Castree, 46–53. London: Routledge.

Catholic Commission for Justice and Peace in Zimbabwe (CCJPZ). 1997. *Breaking the Silence, Building True Peace: Report on the 1980s Disturbances in Matabeleland and the Midlands*. Harare: Legal Resources Foundation.

Child, Graham. 1998. "The wildlife industry in South Africa in 1997 and what this implies for Zimbabwe." Working paper. Harare: WISDOM Institute.

———. 1995. *Wildlife and People: The Zimbabwean Success: How the Conflict between Animals and People Became Progress for Both*. Harare: Wisdom Foundation.

Clifford, James. 1988. *The Predicament of Culture: Twentieth-Century Ethnography, Literature, and Art*. Cambridge, MA: Harvard University Press.

———. 1986. "Introduction: Partial truths." In *Writing Culture: The Poetics and Politics of Ethnography*, edited by James Clifford and George Marcus, 1–26. Berkeley: University of California Press.

Cobbing, Julian. 1976. "The Ndebele under the Khumalos, 1820–96." PhD diss., University of Lancaster.

———. 1974. "The evolution of Ndebele amabutho." *Journal of African History* 15: 607–631.

Coetzee, J. M. 1982. *Waiting for the Barbarians*. New York: Penguin.

Cohen, Colleen Ballerino, Richard Wilk, and Beverly Stoeltje, eds. 1996. *Beauty Queens on the Global Stage: Gender, Contest, and Power*. New York: Routledge.

Comaroff, Jean, and John L. Comaroff. 2009. *Ethnicity Inc.* Chicago: University of Chicago Press.

——. 2000. "Naturing the nation: Aliens, apocalypse, and the postcolonial state." *HAGAR International Social Science Review* 1(1): 7–40.

——. 1991. "'How beasts lost their legs': Cattle in Tswana economy and society." In *Herders, Warriors, and Traders: Pastoralism in Africa*, edited by John G. Galaty and Pierre Bonte, 33–61. Boulder, CO: Westview Press.

——. 1990. "Goodly beasts and beastly goods: Cattle and commodities in a South African context." *American Ethnologist* 17(2): 195–216.

Conklin, Beth A. 1997. "Body paint, feathers, and VCRs: Aesthetics and authenticity in Amazonian activism." *American Ethnologist* 24(4): 711–737.

Cooper, Frederick, and Ann Stoler, eds. 1997. *Tensions of Empire: Colonial Cultures in a Bourgeois World*. Berkeley: University of California Press.

Cousins, Ben. 1992. "A conceptual framework for the analysis of communal grazing regimes." In *Institutional Dynamics in Communal Grazing Regimes in Southern Africa*, edited by Ben Cousins, 13–38. Harare: Centre for Applied Social Sciences.

Crapanzano, Vincent. 1985. *Waiting: The Whites of South Africa*. New York: Random House.

Crosby, Alfred. 1986. *Ecological Imperialism: The Biological Expansion of Europe, 900–1900*. Cambridge: Cambridge University Press.

D'Anglure, Bernard Saladin. 1994. "Nanook, super-male: The polar bear in the imaginary space and social time of the Inuit of the Canadian Arctic." In *Signifying Animals: Human Meaning in the Natural World*, edited by Roy Willis, 178–195. London: Routledge.

Darnton, Robert. 1985. *The Great Cat Massacre and Other Episodes in French Cultural History*. New York: Vintage.

Daston, Lorraine, and Katharine Park. 2001. *Wonders and the Order of Nature, 1150–1750*. New York: Zone Books.

Davies, Gail. 2000. "Virtual animals in electronic zoos: The changing geographies of animal capture and display." In *Animal Spaces, Beastly Places: New Geographies of Human-Animal Relations*, edited by Chris Philo and Chris Wilbert, 243–267. London: Routledge.

Davis, Susan. 1997. *Spectacular Nature: Corporate Culure and the Sea World Experience*. Berkeley: University of California Press.

Delgado, Richard, and Jean Stefancic, eds. 1997. *Critical White Studies: Looking behind the Mirror*. Philadelphia: Temple University Press.

Derrida, Jacques. 2008. *The Animal That Therefore I Am*. New York: Fordham University Press.

Desmond, Jane. 1999. *Staging Tourism: Bodies on Display from Waikiki to Sea World*. Chicago: University of Chicago Press.

De Waal, Victor. 1990. *The Politics of Reconciliation: Zimbabwe's First Decade*. Trenton: Africa World Press.

Douglas, Mary. 1975. *Implicit Meanings: Essays in Anthropology*. London: Routledge.

——. 1966. *Purity and Danger: An Analysis of the Concepts of Pollution and Taboo.* London: Routledge.

Dubow, Jessica. 2009. *Settling the Self: Colonial Space, Colonial Identity and the South African Landscape.* Saarbrücken: VDM Verlag.

Duffy, Rosaleen. 2000. *Killing for Conservation: Wildlife Policy in Zimbabwe.* Bloomington: Indiana University Press.

——. 1997. "The environmental challenge to the nation-state: Superparks and national parks policy in Zimbabwe." *Journal of Southern African Studies* 23(3): 441–451.

Du Toit, Raoul. 1999. "Case study of policies that support sustainable development in Africa: The Save Valley Conservancy, Zimbabwe." Copenhagen: Scandinavian Seminar College Africa Project Paper No. 10.

Dyer, Richard. 1997. *White.* New York: Routledge.

Dzimba, John. 1998. *South Africa's Destabilization of Zimbabwe, 1980–89.* London: Macmillan.

Dzingirai, Vupenyu. 2003. "Campfire is not for Ndebele migrants: The impact of excluding outsiders from Campfire in the Zambezi Valley, Zimbabwe." *Journal of Southern African Studies* 29(2): 445–459.

——. 1995. "Take back your Campfire: A study of local level perceptions to electric fencing in the framework of Binga's Campfire programme." Harare: University of Zimbabwe Centre for Applied Social Sciences Occasional Paper Series.

Einarsson, Neils. 1993. "All animals are equal but some are cetaceans: Conservation and culture conflict." In *Environmentalism: The View from Anthropology*, edited by Kay Milton, 73–84. London: Routledge.

Elder, Glen, Jennifer Wolch, and Jody Emel. 1998. "*Le pratique sauvage*: Race, place, and the human-animal divide." In *Animal Geographies: Place, Politics, and Identity in the Nature-Culture Borderlands*, edited by Jennifer Wolch and Jody Emel, 72–90. London: Verso.

Emel, Jody. 1998. "Are you man enough, big and bad enough? Wolf eradication in the US." In *Animal Geographies: Place, Politics, and Identity in the Nature-Culture Borderlands*, edited by Jennifer Wolch and Jody Emel, 91–116. London: Verso.

Emel, Jody, and Jennifer Wolch. 1998. "Witnessing the animal moment." In *Animal Geographies: Place, Politics, and Identity in the Nature-Culture Borderlands*, edited by Jennifer Wolch and Jody Emel, 1–24. London: Verso.

Erikson, Patricia Pierce. 1999. "A-whaling we will go: Encounters of knowledge and memory at the Makah Cultural Research Center." *Cultural Anthropology* 14(4): 556–583.

Evans-Pritchard, E. E. 1969 [1940]. *The Nuer: A Description of the Modes of Livelihood and Political Institutions of a Nilotic People.* Oxford: Oxford University Press.

Environmental Consultants Ltd. 1992. *Wildlife: Relic of the Past, or Resource of the Future?* Harare: Zimbabwe Trust.

Ferguson, James. 1994. *The Anti-Politics Machine: "Development," Depoliticization, and Bureaucratic Power in Lesotho.* Cambridge: Cambridge University Press.

Fine, Michelle, Lois Weis, Linda Powell, and L. Mun Wong, eds. 1997. *Off White: Readings on Race, Power, and Society.* New York: Routledge.

Foster, Jeremy. 2008. *Washed with Sun: Landscape and the Making of White South Africa.* Pittsburgh: University of Pittsburgh Press.

Frankenberg, Ruth. 2001. "The mirage of unmarked whiteness." In *The Making and Unmaking of Whiteness,* edited by Birgit Brander Rasmussen, Eric Klinenberg, Irene J. Nexica, and Matt Wray, 72–96. Durham, NC: Duke University Press.

———. 1999 [1997]. "Local whitenesses, localizing whiteness." In *Displacing Whiteness: Essays in Social and Cultural Criticism,* edited by Ruth Frankenberg, 1–33. Durham, NC: Duke University Press.

———. 1993. *White Women, Race Matters: The Social Construction of Whiteness.* Minneapolis: University of Minnesota Press.

Fuentes, Agustin. 2010. "Naturalcultural encounters in Bali: Monkeys, temples, tourists, and ethnoprimatology." *Cultural Anthropology* 25(4): 600–624.

Fuller, Alexandra. 2011. *Cocktail Hour under the Tree of Forgetfulness.* New York: Penguin.

———. 2001. *Don't Let's Go to the Dogs Tonight: An African Childhood.* New York: Random House.

Galaty, John. 1989. "Cattle and cognition: Aspects of Maasai practical reasoning." In *The Walking Larder: Patterns of Domestication, Pastoralism, and Predation,* edited by Juliet Clutton-Brock, 215–230. London: Unwin Hyman.

Gallagher, Charles A., and France Winddance Twine, eds. 2012. *Retheorizing Race and Whiteness in the 21st Century: Changes and Challenges.* New York: Routledge.

Geertz, Clifford. 1973. *The Interpretation of Cultures.* New York: Basic Books.

Glickman, Stephen. 1995. "The spotted hyena from Aristotle to the Lion King: Reputation is everything." In *Humans and Other Animals,* edited by Arien Mack, 87–123. Columbus: Ohio State University Press.

Godwin, Peter. 2007. *When a Crocodile Eats the Sun: A Memoir of Africa.* New York: Little, Brown.

———. 1996. *Mukiwa: A White Boy in Africa.* New York: Harper Perennial.

Godwin, Peter, and Ian Hancock. 1993. *Rhodesians Never Die: The Impact of War and Political Change on White Rhodesia, c. 1970–1980.* New York: Oxford University Press.

Goldstein, Donna. 2003. *Laughter out of Place: Race, Class, Violence, and Sexuality in a Rio Shantytown.* Berkeley: University of California Press.

Goodale, Jane. 1995. *To Sing with Pigs Is Human: The Concept of Person in Papua New Guinea.* Seattle: University of Washington Press.

Goodwin, June, and Ben Schiff. 1995. *Heart of Whiteness: Afrikaners Face Black Rule in the New South Africa.* New York: Scribner.

Gordimer, Nadine. 1972. *The Conservationist.* New York: McGraw-Hill.

Government of Southern Rhodesia. 1923. *A Report of the Committee of Enquiry in Respect of the Cattle Industry of Southern Rhodesia.* Salisbury, Rhodesia: Government Printer.

Greenhouse, Carol. 2002. "Introduction: Altered states, altered lives." In *Ethnogra-*

phy in *Unstable Places: Everyday Lives in Contexts of Dramatic Political Change*, edited by Carol Greenhouse, Elizabeth Mertz, and Kay Warren, 1–34. Durham, NC: Duke University Press.

Grundy, Trevor, and Bernard Miller. 1979. *The Farmer at War*. Salisbury, Rhodesia: Modern Farming Publications.

Guggenheim, Scott. 1994. "Cock or bull: Cockfighting, social structure, and political commentary in the Philippines." In *The Cockfight: A Casebook*, edited by Alan Dundes, 133–173. Madison: University of Wisconsin Press.

Gullo, Andrea, Unna Lassiter, and Jennifer Wolch. 1998. "The cougar's tale." In *Animal Geographies: Place, Politics, and Identity in the Nature-Culture Borderlands*, edited by Jennifer Wolch and Jody Emel, 139–161. London: Verso.

Hale, Grace Elizabeth. 1998. *Making Whiteness: The Culture of Segregation in the South, 1890–1940*. New York: Vintage Books.

Hall, Stuart. 1988. "The toad in the garden: Thatcherism among the theorists." In *Marxism and the Interpretation of Culture*, edited by Cary Nelson and Lawrence Grossberg, 35–57. Urbana: University of Illinois Press.

Hammar, Amanda. 2010. "Ambivalent mobilities: Zimbabwean commercial farmers in Mozambique." *Journal of Southern African Studies* 36(2): 395–416.

Hanlon, Joseph, Jeanette Manjengwa, and Teresa Smart. 2013. *Zimbabwe Takes Back Its Land*. Boulder, CO: Kumarian Press.

Haraway, Donna. 2008. *When Species Meet*. Minneapolis: University of Minnesota Press.

———. 1991. *Simians, Cyborgs, and Women: The Reinvention of Nature*. New York: Routledge.

———. 1989. *Primate Visions: Gender, Race, and Nature in the Making of Modern Science*. New York: Routledge.

Hardin, Garrett. 1968. "The tragedy of the commons." *Science* 162: 1243–1248.

Harding, Susan. 2000. *The Book of Jerry Falwell: Fundamentalist Language and Politics*. Princeton, NJ: Princeton University Press.

———. 1991. "Representing fundamentalism: The problem of the repugnant cultural Other." *Social Research* 58(2): 373–393.

———. 1987. "Convicted by the Holy Spirit: The rhetoric of fundamental Baptist conversion." *American Ethnologist* 14(1): 167–181.

Harris, Marvin. 1989 [1974]. *Cows, Pigs, Wars, and Witches: The Riddles of Culture*. New York: Vintage Books.

Hartigan, John. 1999. *Racial Situations: Class Predicaments of Whiteness in Detroit*. Princeton, NJ: Princeton University Press.

Hay, Douglas. 1975. *Albion's Fatal Tree: Crime and Society in Eighteenth-Century England*. New York: Pantheon Books.

Hayward, Eva. 2010. "Fingeryeyes: Impressions of cup corals." *Cultural Anthropology* 25(4): 577–599.

Helmreich, Stefan. 2009. *Alien Ocean: Anthropological Voyages in Microbial Seas*. Berkeley: University of California Press.

Herbst, Jeffrey. 1990. *State Politics in Zimbabwe*. Berkeley: University of Calfornia Press.

Herskovitz, Melville. 1926. "The cattle complex of East Africa." *American Anthropologist* 28: 230–272.

Hill, Jane. 1995. "The voices of Don Gabriel: Responsibility and self in a modern Mexican narrative." In *The Dialogic Emergence of Culture*, edited by Dennis Tedlock and Bruce Mannheim, 97–147. Urbana: University of Illinois Press.

Hill, Mike, ed. 1997. *Whiteness: A Critical Reader*. New York: New York University Press.

Hodder-Williams, Richard. 1983. *Conflict in Zimbabwe: The Matabeleland Problem*. London: Institute for the Study of Conflict.

Hole, Hugh Marshall. 1995 [1932]. *The Passing of the Black Kings*. Bulawayo, Zimbabwe: Books of Zimbabwe.

Howell, Philip. 2000. "Flush and the *banditti*: Dog-stealing in Victorian London." In *Animal Spaces, Beastly Places: New Geographies of Human-Animal Relations*, edited by Chris Philo and Chris Wilbert, 35–55. London: Routledge.

Howell, Signe. 1996. "Nature in culture or culture in nature? Chewong ideas of 'humans' and other species." In *Nature and Society: Anthropological Perspectives*, edited by Philippe Descola and Gisli Palsson, 127–144. London: Routledge.

Hughes, David. 2010. *Whiteness in Zimbabwe: Race, Landscape, and the Problem of Belonging*. New York: Palgrave Macmillan.

———. 2006. "Hydrology of hope: Farm dams, conservation, and whiteness in Zimbabwe." *American Ethnologist* 33(2): 269–287.

———. 2001. "Rezoned for business: How eco-tourism unlocked black farmland in eastern Zimbabwe." In "The New Agrarian Politics in Zimbabwe," edited by Eric Worby. Special issue, *Journal of Agrarian Change* 1(4): 575–599.

———. 1999. "Refugees and squatters: Immigration and the politics of territory on the Zimbabwe-Mozambique Border." *Journal of Southern African Studies* 25(4): 533–552.

Ingold, Tim. 2000. *The Perception of the Environment: Essays on Livelihood, Dwelling and Skill*. New York: Routledge.

Jacobs, Nancy. 2006. "The intimate politics of ornithology in colonial Africa." *Comparative Studies in Society and History* 48(3): 564–603.

Jacobs, Sean. 2009. *Reflections on Mahmood Mamdani's "Lessons of Zimbabwe."* Concerned Africa Scholars Bulletin No. 82. http://concernedafricascholars.org/bulletin/issue82/jacobs/.

James, Wendy. 1994. "Antelope as self-image among the Uduk." In *Signifying Animals: Human Meaning in the Natural World*, edited by Roy Willis, 196–203. London: Routledge.

Jansen, Doris, Ian Bond, and Brian Child. 1992. "Cattle, wildlife, both or neither: A summary of survey results for commercial ranches in Zimbabwe." Harare: Multispecies Animal Production Systems Project and Department of National Parks and Wildlife Management Project Paper No. 30.

Jones, Neville. 1953. *Rhodesian Genesis: The Story of the Early Days of Southern Rho-*

desia Compiled from the Reminiscences of Some of the Pioneers. Glasgow: Robert MacLehose.

Kann, Wendy. 2006. *Casting with a Fragile Thread: A Story of Sisters and Africa.* New York: Picador.

Katz, Cindi. 1998. "Whose nature, whose culture? Private productions of space and the 'preservation' of nature." In *Remaking Reality: Nature at the Millennium*, edited by Bruce Braun and Noel Castree, 43–63. London: Routledge.

Kelsky, Karen. 2001. *Women on the Verge: Japanese Women, Western Dreams.* Durham, NC: Duke University Press.

Kennedy, Dane. 1987. *Islands of White: Settler Society and Culture in Kenya and Southern Rhodesia, 1890–1939.* Durham, NC: Duke University Press.

Kete, Kathleen. 1994. *The Beast in the Boudoir: Petkeeping in Nineteenth-Century Paris.* Berkeley: University of California Press.

Kinchloe, Joe, Shirley Steinberg, Nelson Rodriguez, and Ronald Chennault, eds. 1998. *White Reign: Deploying Whiteness in America.* New York: St. Martin's Press.

Kirksey, S. Eben, and Stefan Helmreich. 2010. "The emergence of multispecies ethnography." *Cultural Anthropology* 25(4): 545–576.

Kohn, Eduardo. 2013. *How Forests Think: Toward an Anthropology beyond the Human.* Berkeley: University of California Press.

———. 2007. "How dogs dream: Amazonian natures and the politics of transspecies engagement." *American Ethnologist* 34(1): 3–24.

Kosek, Jake. 2010. "Ecologies of empire: On the new uses of the honeybee." *Cultural Anthropology* 25(4): 650–678.

Kriger, Norma. 1992. *Zimbabwe's Guerrilla War: Peasant Voices.* Cambridge: Cambridge University Press.

———. 1991. "The politics of creating national heroes: The search for political legitimacy and national identity." In *Soldiers in Zimbabwe's Liberation War*, edited by Ngwabi Bhebe and Terence Ranger, 139–162. Harare: University of Zimbabwe Publications.

Krog, Antjie. 2000. *Country of My Skull: Guilt, Sorrow, and the Limits of Forgiveness in the New South Africa.* New York: Broadway Books.

Lan, David. 1985. *Guns and Rain: Guerrillas and Spirit Mediums in Zimbabwe.* Berkeley: University of California Press.

Latour, Bruno. 1987. *Science in Action: How to Follow Scientists and Engineers through Society.* Cambridge, MA: Harvard University Press.

Leach, Edmund. 1989 (1974). *Claude Lévi-Strauss.* Chicago: University of Chicago Press.

———. 1964. "Anthropological aspects of language: Animal categories and verbal abuse." In *New Directions in the Study of Language*, edited by Eric H. Lenneberg, 23–63. Cambridge, MA: MIT Press.

Lessing, Doris. 2000 (1950). *The Grass Is Singing.* New York: Harper Perennial.

Lévi-Strauss, Claude. 1963a. *Structural Anthropology.* Translated by Claire Jacobson and Brooke Grundfest Schoepf. New York: Basic Books.

———. 1963b. *Totemism.* Translated by Rodney Needham. Boston: Beacon Press.

Li, Tania. 2000. "Articulating indigenous identity in Indonesia: Resource politics and the tribal slot." *Comparative Studies in Society and History* 42(1): 149–179.

Lienhardt, Godfrey. 1961. *Divinity and Experience: The Religion of the Dinka.* Oxford: Clarendon Press.

López, Alfred J., ed. 2005. *Postcolonial Whiteness: A Critical Reader on Race and Empire.* Albany: State University of New York Press.

Lorimer, Jamie. 2015. *Wildlife in the Anthropocene: Conservation after Nature.* Minneapolis: University of Minnesota Press.

Lowe, Celia. 2010. "Viral clouds: Becoming H5N1 in Indonesia." *Cultural Anthropology* 25(4): 625–649.

MacBruce, James. 1992. "Domestic and regional security." In *Zimbabwe in Transition,* edited by Simon Baynham, 211–213. Stockholm: Almqvist and Wiskell International.

MacKenzie, John. 1988. *The Empire of Nature: Hunting, Conservation, and British Imperialism.* Manchester, UK: Manchester University Press.

Madzudzo, Elias. 1996. "Producer communities in a community based wildlife management programme: A case study of Bulilimamangwe and Tsholotsho districts." Harare: University of Zimbabwe Centre for Applied Social Sciences Occasional Paper Series.

Malamud, Randy. 2003. "How people and animals coexist." *Chronicle Review,* January 24, 2003.

Malkki, Liisa. 1995. *Purity and Exile: Violence, Memory, and National Cosmology among Hutu Refugees in Tanzania.* Chicago: University of Chicago Press.

Mallon, Florence. 1995. *Peasant and Nation: The Making of Postcolonial Mexico and Peru.* Berkeley: University of California Press.

Mamdani, Mahmood. 2001. *When Victims Become Killers: Colonialism, Nativism, and the Genocide in Rwanda.* Princeton, NJ: Princeton University Press.

Matondi, Prosper Bvumiranayi. 2012. *Zimbabwe's Fast Track Land Reform.* London: Zed Books.

Mbembe, Achille. 2001. *On the Postcolony.* Berkeley: University of California Press.

———. 1992. "The banality of power and the aesthetics of vulgarity in the post-colony." *Public Culture* 4(2): 1–30.

McClintock, Anne. 1995. *Imperial Leather: Race, Gender and Sexuality in the Colonial Contest.* New York: Routledge.

———. 1994. "The angel of progress: Pitfalls of the term 'post-colonialism.'" In *Colonial Discourse and Post-Colonial Theory: A Reader,* edited by Patrick Williams and Laura Chrisman, 291–304. New York: Columbia University Press.

McCulloch, Jock. 2000. *Black Peril, White Virtue: Sexual Crime in Southern Rhodesia, 1902–1935.* Bloomington: Indiana University Press.

McIntosh, Janet. 2016. *Unsettled: Denial and Belonging among White Kenyans.* Berkeley: University of California Press.

McIntosh, Peggy. 1989. "White privilege and male privilege: A personal account of coming to see correspondences through work in Women's Studies." Wellesley: Wellesley College Center for Research on Women Working Paper No. 189.

Meredith, Martin. 2002. *Our Votes, Our Guns: Robert Mugabe and the Tragedy of Zimbabwe.* New York: Perseus Books.

Minahen, Charles. 1997. "Humanimals and anihumans in Gary Larson's gallery of the absurd." In *Animal Acts: Configuring the Human in Western History,* edited by Jennifer Ham and Matthew Senior, 231–251. New York: Routledge.

Moffat, Robert. 1976 [1945]. *The Matabele Journals of Robert Moffat, 1829–1860,* vols. 1 and 2. Salisbury: National Archives of Rhodesia.

Mohanram, Radhika. 2007. *Imperial White: Race, Diaspora, and the British Empire.* Minneapolis: University of Minneosota Press.

Moore, Donald. 1998. "Subaltern struggles and the politics of place: Remapping resistance in Zimbabwe's Eastern Highlands." *Cultural Anthropology* 13(3): 344–381.

Moore, Donald, Anand Pandian, and Jake Kosek. 2003. "The cultural politics of race and nature: Terrains of power and practice." In *Race, Nature, and the Politics of Difference,* edited by Donald Moore, Jake Kosek, and Anand Pandian, 1–70. Durham, NC: Duke University Press.

Moreton-Robinson, Aileen, Maryrose Casey, and Fiona Nicoll, eds. 2008. *Transnational Whiteness Matters.* Lanham, MD: Lexington Books.

Morgan, Lewis Henry. 1985 [1878]. *Ancient Society.* Tucson: University of Arizona Press.

Moyo, Sam. 2000. "The political economy of land acquisition and redistribution in Zimbabwe, 1990–1999." *Journal of Southern African Studies* 26(1): 5–28.

Mullin, Molly. 1999. "Mirrors and windows: Sociocultural studies of human-animal relationships." *Annual Review of Anthropology* 28: 201–224.

Murombedzi, James. 2001. "Committees, rights, costs and benefits: Natural resource stewardship and community benefits in Zimbabwe's Campfire programme." In *African Wildlife and Livelihoods: The Promise and Performance of Community Conservation,* edited by David Hulme and Marshall Murphree, 280–297. Oxford: James Currey.

Murphree, Marshall, and Simon Metcalfe. 1997. "Conservancy policy and the Campfire programme in Zimbabwe." Harare: University of Zimbabwe Centre for Applied Social Sciences Technical Paper Series, 1/97.

Murray, D. J. 1970. *The Governmental System in Southern Rhodesia.* London: Oxford University Press.

Mutwira, Roben. 1989. "Southern Rhodesian wildlife policy (1890–1953): A question of condoning game slaughter?" *Journal of Southern African Studies* 15(2): 250–262.

Nabane, Nontokozo. 1994. "A gender sensitive analysis of a community based wildlife utilization initiative in Zimbabwe's Zambezi Valley." Harare: University of Zimbabwe Centre for Applied Social Sciences Occasional Paper Series.

Naipaul, V. S. 1979. *A Bend in the River.* New York: Vintage Books.

Nájera-Ramírez, Olga. 1996. "The racialization of a debate: The *charreada* as tradition or torture." *American Anthropologist* 98(3): 505–511.

Neumann, Roderick. 1998. *Imposing Wilderness: Struggles over Livelihood and Nature Preservation in Africa.* Berkeley: University of California Press.

————. 1995. "Ways of seeing Africa: Colonial recasting of African society and landscape in Serengeti National Park." *Ecumene* 2(2): 149–169.

Ohnuki-Tierney, Emiko. 1990. "The monkey as self in Japanese culture." In *Culture through Time: Anthropological Approaches*, edited by Emiko Ohnuki-Tierney, 128–153. Stanford: Stanford University Press.

Olson, Mancur. 1971. *The Logic of Collective Action: Public Goods and the Theory of Groups*. Cambridge, MA: Harvard University Press.

Ortner, Sherry. 1999. *Life and Death on Mt. Everest: Sherpas and Himalayan Mountaineering*. Princeton, NJ: Princeton University Press.

Ostrom, Elinor. 1990. *Governing the Commons: The Evolution of Institutions for Collective Action*. Cambridge: Cambridge University Press.

Palmer, Robin. 1977. *Land and Racial Domination in Rhodesia*. Berkeley: University of California Press.

Pandian, Anand. 2001. "Predatory care: The imperial hunt in Mughal and British India." *Journal of Historical Sociology* 14(1): 79–107.

Parreñas, Rheana. 2012. "Producing affect: Transnational volunteerism in a Malaysian orangutan rehabilitation center." *American Ethnologist* 39(4): 673–687.

Peet, Richard, and Michael Watts. 1996. "Liberation ecology: Development, sustainability, and environment in an age of market triumphalism." In *Liberation Ecologies: Environment, Development, and Social Movements*, edited by Richard Peet and Michael Watts, 1–45. New York: Routledge.

Pelling, J. N. 1977. *Ndebele Proverbs and Other Sayings*. Gweru, Zimbabwe: Mambo Press.

Perry, Pamela. 2003. *Shades of White: White Kids and Racial Identities in High School*. Durham, NC: Duke University Press.

Peters, Pauline. 1994. *Dividing the Commons: Politics, Policy, and Culture in Botswana*. Charlottesville: University of Virginia Press.

Philo, Chris, and Chris Wilbert. 2000. "Animal spaces, beastly places: An introduction." In *Animal Spaces, Beastly Places: New Geographies of Human-Animal Relations*, edited by Chris Philo and Chris Wilbert, 1–34. London: Routledge.

Phimister, Ian. 1988. *An Economic and Social History of Zimbabwe, 1890–1948: Capital Accumulation and Class Struggle*. London: Longman.

Pilossof, Rory. 2012. *The Unbearable Whiteness of Being: Farmers' Voices from Zimbabwe*. Harare: Weaver Press.

Posel, Deborah. 1999. "Whiteness and power in the South African civil service: Paradoxes of the apartheid state." *Journal of Southern African Studies* 25(1): 99–119.

Posselt, Friedrich W. T. 1935. *Fact and Fiction: A Short Account of the Natives of Southern Rhodesia*. Bulawayo, Zimbabwe: Mardon Printers.

Raffles, Hugh. 2010. *Insectopedia*. New York: Pantheon Books.

————. 2002. *In Amazonia: A Natural History*. Princeton, NJ: Princeton University Press.

Ranger, Terence. 1967a. *Revolt in Southern Rhodesia, 1896–7: A Study in African Resistance*. Evanston: Northwestern University Press.

———. 1967b. "The rewriting of African history during the scramble: The Matabele dominance in Mashonaland." *African Social Research* 4: 271–282.

Rappaport, Roy. 1984 [1967]. *Pigs for the Ancestors: Ritual in the Ecology of a New Guinea People*. New Haven, CT: Yale University Press.

Rasmussen, Birgit Brander, Eric Klinenberg, Irene J. Nexica, and Matt Wray, eds. 2001. *The Making and Unmaking of Whiteness*. Durham, NC: Duke University Press.

Richburg, Keith B. 1997. *Out of America: A Black Man Confronts Africa*. New York: Harper Collins.

Riddell, Roger. 1978. *The Land Problem in Rhodesia: Alternatives for the Future*. Gwelo, Zimbabwe: Mambo Press.

Ritvo, Harriet. 1997. *The Platypus and the Mermaid and Other Figments of the Classifying Imagination*. Cambridge, MA: Harvard University Press.

———. 1987. *The Animal Estate: The English and Other Creatures in the Victorian Age*. Cambridge, MA: Harvard University Press.

Roediger, David. 1999. *The Wages of Whiteness: Race and the Making of the American Working Class*. New York: Verso.

Rogers, Douglas. 2009. *Last Resort: A Memoir of Mischief and Mayhem on a Family Farm in Africa*. New York: Three Rivers Press.

Rothfels, Nigel. 2008. *Savages and Beasts: The Birth of the Modern Zoo*. Baltimore: Johns Hopkins University Press.

Rukuni, Mandivamba. 2012. "Re-framing the wildlife based land reform programmes." *Sokwanele*, October 3, 2012.

Runge, C. Ford. 1986. "Common property and collective action in economic development." *World Development* 14(5): 623–635.

Rutherford, Blair. 2001. *Working on the Margins: Black Workers, White Farmers in Postcolonial Zimbabwe*. Harare: Weaver Press.

Ryan, James. 2000. "'Hunting with the camera': Photography, wildlife, and colonialism in Africa." In *Animal Spaces, Beastly Places: New Geographies of Human-Animal Relations*, edited by Chris Philo and Chris Wilbert, 203–221. New York: Routledge.

Salisbury, Joyce. 1997. "Human beasts and bestial humans in the Middle Ages." In *Animal Acts: Configuring the Human in Western History*, edited by Jennifer Ham and Matthew Senior, 9–21. New York: Routledge.

Saunders, Nicholas. 1994. "Tezcatlipoca: Jaguar metaphors and the Aztec mirror of nature." In *Signifying Animals: Human Meaning in the Natural World*, edited by Roy Willis, 159–177. London: Routledge.

Scheper-Hughes, Nancy. 2007. "Violence and the politics of remorse: Lessons from South Africa." In *Subjectivities: Ethnographic Investigations*, edited by Joao Biehl and Byron Good, 179–233. Berkeley: University of California Press.

Schmidt, Elizabeth. 1992. *Peasants, Traders, and Wives: Shona Women in the History of Zimbabwe, 1870–1939*. Portsmouth, NH: Heinemann.

Schoonakker, Bonny. 2003. "Creatures of their times." *Sunday Times*, September 21.

Schroeder, Richard. 2012. *Africa after Apartheid: South Africa, Race, and Nation in Tanzania*. Bloomington: Indiana University Press.

Schwartz, Marion. 1997. *A History of Dogs in the Early Americas*. New Haven, CT: Yale University Press.

Scoones, Ian, and Ben Cousins. 1993. "A participatory model of agricultural research and extension: The case of *vleis*, trees and grazing schemes in the dry south of Zimbabwe." Harare: University of Zimbabwe Centre for Applied Social Sciences Natural Resource Management Occasional Paper Series.

Scoones, Ian, Nelson Marongwe, Blasio Mavedzenge, Jacob Mahenehene, Felix Murimbarimba, and Chrispen Sukume. 2010. *Zimbabwe's Land Reform: Myths and Realities*. Suffolk: James Currey.

Scott, James C. 1999. *Seeing like a State: How Certain Schemes to Improve the Human Condition Have Failed*. New Haven, CT: Yale University Press.

———. 1987. *Weapons of the Weak: Everyday Forms of Peasant Resistance*. New Haven, CT: Yale University Press.

Scott, Robyn. 2009. *Twenty Chickens for a Saddle: The Story of an African Childhood*. New York: Penguin.

Selous, Frederick Courteney. 1894. "Travel and adventure in southeast Africa." *Atlantic Monthly* 74(44): 558–559.

———. 1881. *A Hunter's Wanderings in Africa*. London: Richard Bentley.

Sharp, John. 2002. "'Non-racialism' and its discontents: A post-apartheid paradox." *International Social Science Journal* 50(156): 243–252.

Sibanda, Jackson. 2001. *Wildlife and Communities at the Crossroads: Is Zimbabwe's Campfire the Way Forward?* Harare: Sapes Books.

Smith, Ian. 1997. *The Great Betrayal: The Memoirs of Ian Douglas Smith*. London: Blake.

Steyn, Melissa. 2001. *"Whiteness Just Isn't What It Used to Be": White Identity in a Changing South Africa*. Albany: State University of New York Press.

St. John, Lauren. 2008. *Rainbow's End: A Memoir of Childhood, War, and an African Farm*. New York: Scribner.

Stoler, Ann. 2002. *Carnal Knowledge and Imperial Power: Race and the Intimate in Colonial Rule*. Berkeley: University of California Press.

———. 2000. *Race and the Education of Desire: Foucault's History of Sexuality and the Colonial Order of Things*. Durham, NC: Duke University Press.

Strathern, Andrew. 1971. *The Rope of Moka: Big Men and Ceremonial Exchange in Mount Hagen*. Cambridge: Cambridge University Press.

Sullivan, Shannon. 2006. *Revealing Whiteness: The Unconscious Habits of Racial Privilege*. Bloomington: Indiana University Press.

Summers, Carol. 1994. *From Civilization to Segregation: Social Ideals and Social Control in Southern Rhodesia, 1890–1934*. Athens: Ohio University Press.

Suzuki, Yuka. 2007. "Putting the lion out at night: Domestication and the taming of the wild in Zimbabwe." In *Where the Wild Things Are Now: Domestication Reconsidered*, edited by Molly Mullin and Rebecca Cassidy, 229–247. Oxford: Berg Press.

———. 2001a. "Drifting rhinos and fluid properties: The turn to wildlife production in Zimbabwe." *Journal of Agrarian Change* 1(4): 600–625.

———. 2001b. "Wildlife producers in the equation of crisis." In *Zimbabwe: The Politics of Crisis and the Crisis of Politics*, edited by Eric Worby and Yuka Suzuki, 60–64. New Haven, CT: Yale University Council on International and Area Studies Working Paper Series.

Swart, Sandra. 2008. "Dogs and dogma: A discussion of the socio-political construction of dog 'breeds' as a window onto social history." In *Canis Africanis: A Dog History of Southern Africa*, edited by Lance Van Sittert and Sandra Swart, 267–288. Leiden: Brill.

Taussig, Michael. 1992. *The Nervous System*. New York: Routledge.

Thomas, Keith. 1983. *Man and the Natural World: A History of the Modern Sensibility*. New York: Pantheon.

Trouillot, Michel-Rolph. 1991. "Anthropology and the savage slot." In *Recapturing Anthropology: Working in the Present*, edited by Richard Fox, 17–44. Santa Fe, NM: School of American Research.

Tsing, Anna. 2005. *Friction: An Ethnography of Global Connection*. Princeton, NJ: Princeton University Press.

———. 1999. "Becoming a tribal elder, and other green development fantasies." In *Transforming the Indonesian Uplands: Marginality, Power, and Production*, edited by Tania Murray Li, 159–202. Amsterdam: Harwood.

Tuan, Yi-fu. 1984. *Dominance and Affection: The Making of Pets*. New Haven, CT: Yale University Press.

Tylor, Edward Burnett. 1958 [1874]. *Primitive Culture*. New York: Harper.

Uusihakala, Katja. 2008. *Memory Meanders: Place, Home and Commemoration in an ex-Rhodesian Diaspora Community*. Helsinki: University of Helsinki Press.

Valeri, Valerio. 2000. *The Forest of Taboos: Morality, Hunting, and Identity among the Huaulu of the Moluccas*. Madison: University of Wisconsin Press.

Vialles, Noelie. 1994. *Animal to Edible*. Translated by J. A. Underwood. Cambridge: Cambridge University Press.

Von Blanckenburg, Peter. 1994. *Large Commercial Farmers and Land Reform in Africa: The Case of Zimbabwe*. Aldershot: Avebury.

Wallis, J. P. R. 1976 (1945). "General introduction." In *The Matabele Journals of Robert Moffat, 1829–1860*, vol. 1. Salisbury: National Archives of Rhodesia.

Ware, Vron. 1992. *Beyond the Pale: White Women, Racism, and History*. New York: Verso.

Weaver, Harlan. 2012. "The 'forever home': Race and place in pit bull rescue." Paper presented at the annual meeting for the American Anthropological Association, San Francisco. November 18, 2012.

Weiss, Ruth. 1994. *Zimbabwe and the New Elite*. London: I. B. Tauris.

Wellman, David. 1993. *Portraits of White Racism*. Cambridge: Cambridge University Press.

Werbner, Richard. 1998. *Memory and the Postcolony: African Anthropology and the Critique of Power*. London: Zed Books.

———. 1995. "Human rights and moral knowledge: Arguments of accountability in Zimbabwe." In *Shifting Contexts: Transformations in Anthropological Knowledge*, edited by Marilyn Strathern, 99–116. New York: Routledge.

———. 1991. *Tears of the Dead: The Social Biography of an African Family*. London: Edinburgh University Press.

West, Michael. 2002. *The Rise of an African Middle Class: Colonial Zimbabwe, 1898–1965*. Bloomington: Indiana University Press.

White, David Gordon. 1991. *Myths of the Dog-Man*. Chicago: University of Chicago Press.

White, Luise. 2015. *Unpopular Sovereignty: Rhodesian Independence and African Decolonization*. Chicago: University of Chicago Press.

———. 2003. *The Assassination of Herbert Chitepo: Texts and Politics in Zimbabwe*. Bloomington: Indiana University Press.

———. 2001. "Race, regiment, and counter-insurgency: An exploration in military history and ideas about nationality in Rhodesia." New Haven, CT: Yale University Program in Agrarian Studies Colloquium Series, October 12, 2001.

Wildlife Producers Association (WPA) of Zimbabwe. 1998. "Policy for wildlife on alienated land." Harare: Wildlife Producers Association.

———. 1997. "Commercial wildlife production in Zimbabwe." Harare: Wildlife Producers Association.

———. 1992. "Conservation with utilisation." Harare: ZTA Publications and Modern Farming Publications.

Wilson, Kathleen. 2003. *The Island Race: Englishness, Empire, and Gender in the Eighteenth Century*. New York: Routledge.

Wise, Steven. 2000. *Rattling the Cage: Toward Legal Rights for Animals*. Cambridge, MA: Perseus.

Wolf, Eric. 1982. *Europe and the People without History*. Berkeley: University of California Press.

Wolmer, William, Joseph Chaumba, and Ian Scoones. 2003. "Wildlife management and land reform in southeastern Zimbabwe: A compatible pairing or a contradiction in terms?" *Sustainable Livelihoods in Southern Africa: Institutions, Governance and Policy Processes*. Sussex: University of Sussex Institute of Development Studies, Research Paper No. 1.

Worby, Eric. 2010. "Address unknown: The temporality of displacement and the ethics of disconnection among Zimbabwean immigrants in Johannesburg." *Journal of Southern African Studies* 36(2): 417–431.

———. 2003. "Tyranny, parody, and ethnic polarity: Ritual engagements with the state in northwestern Zimbabwe." In *The Culture of Power in Southern Africa: Essays on State Formation and the Political Imagination*, edited by Clifton Crais, 183–206. Portsmouth, NH: Heinemann.

———. 2001a. "Introduction: The politics of crisis." In *Zimbabwe: The Politics of Crisis and the Crisis of Politics*, edited by Eric Worby and Yuka Suzuki. New Haven, CT: Yale Center for International and Area Studies Working Paper Series.

———. 2001b. "A redivided land? New agrarian conflicts and questions in Zimbabwe." In "The New Agrarian Politics in Zimbabwe," edited by Eric Worby. Special issue, *Journal of Agrarian Change* 1(4): 475–509.

———. 2000. "'Discipline without oppression': Sequence, timing and marginality in

Southern Rhodesia's post-war development regime." *Journal of African History* 41: 101–125.

———. 1997. "Eleven guilty men from Goredema: Parallel justice and the moralities of local administration in northwestern Zimbabwe." *Anthropologica* 39(1–2): 71–77.

———. 1994. "Maps, names, and ethnic games: The epistemology and iconography of colonial power in northwestern Zimbabwe." *Journal of Southern African Studies* 20(3): 371–392.

Worby, Eric, and Yuka Suzuki, eds. 2001. *Zimbabwe: The Politics of Crisis and the Crisis of Politics.* New Haven, CT: Yale University Council on International and Area Studies Working Paper Series.

Wray, Matt. 2006. *Not Quite White: White Trash and the Boundaries of Whiteness.* Durham, NC: Duke University Press.

INDEX

Page references in italics refer to illustrations

animals (*cont.*)
    practices concerning, 108; as royal
        symbols, 108; spectacles of domina-
        tion, 109; strategic manipulation of,
        115; surplus, 97, 125; symbolic violence
        against, 141, 168n4; translocation of,
        97–100, 168n9; uses of, 110, 171n8; as
        vermin, 113; victimization of, 140–43.
        See also wildlife
anthropology, engagement with world, 24
anti-poaching squads, 18, 259n28
Asmani, Salimu, 153
Australia, whiteness in, 20

baboons, as metaphor for Africans,
        54–55, 73
Bakhtin, Mikhail, 52
Bates, Henry Walter, 9, 171n8
BBC Special Award for Outstanding
        Work in Animal Welfare, 142
Beach, David N., 162n17
bears: hunting quotas for, 128; predatory,
        127
Beinart, William, 124
Berger, John: "Why Look at Animals?,"
        107
Bezuidenhout, Philip, 53, 166n9
birds, as national symbols, 172n17
Blee, Kathleen, 20
Braun, Bruce, 154
Brazil, racial hierarchy of, 53–54
British South Africa Company (BSAC), 29;
        agrarian settlements under, 32; con-
        quest of Matabeleland, 31; Land Settle-
        ment Committee, 32, 162n22; and
        Ndebele sovereignty, 30; royal charter
        of, 30, 33; uprising against, 157n4
Brownlow, Alec, 172n16
Bulawayo, BSAC occupation of, 31
Burton, Richard, 16
bushmeat, black market for, 139, 159n28

Cape Town, racism in, 165n5
captive animal exhibits, 96, 170n27

Catholic Commission for Justice and
        Peace in Zimbabwe (CCJPZ), 163n44
cats: feral, 127; gendered identity of,
        132–33
cattle-dipping, compulsory, 84, 168n6
Cattle Levy Act (Southern Rhodesia), 34
cattle ranching: cooperation in, 83; in
        droughts, 89; economic crisis in,
        81–82, 84; environmental suitability
        for, 82; government consolidation of,
        82; incentives for, 82; large-scale, 81;
        during liberation war, 84; in Mlilo,
        81–85; predators in, 83–84; refrigera-
        tion techniques for, 82; self-contained,
        91; as state initiative, 81; transition to
        wildlife ranching, 9, 24, 84–95
Cecil the Lion: moral standing of, 151;
        name of, 152; research on, 150; shoot-
        ing of, 150–52; symbolism of, 150
Central African Federation, 35
chaos, narratives of, 48–51
children, white: bonds with black
        Zimbabweans, 64–65; experience of
        race, 70–71; interracial boundaries of,
        63–65; in land invasions, 19
Chimurenga uprisings: and black nation-
        alism, 32; First, 157n4; in liberation
        discourse, 163n36; Second, 36, 157n4,
        174n2; Third, 157n4, 174n2
China, sale of animals to, 149, 176n33
China Africa Sunlight Energy (firm),
        prospecting in Zimbabwe, 149
citizenship: politics of, vii; race-based,
        141; white southern African, 20–21;
        white Zimbabwean farmers', 4–5;
        Zimbabwean versus Rhodesian, 117
civil servants, Rhodesian: land grants
        to, 82
Coates, Peter, 124
Cobbing, Julian, 161n8
cockerel, Zimbabwean symbolism of,
        121–22
Cold Storage Company, beef refrigeration
        by, 82

colonialism, British: dissemination of
modernity, 117; favored peoples under,
29; justification of, 31; patriarchal, 68;
self-deprecation following, 56; spiritual resistance to, 163n36; surveillance under, 63
colonization, hydrology in, 21. *See also*
water
Comaroff, Jean and John L., 171n5
commercial crops, state price regulations
for, 163nn32–33
Commercial Farmers Union (CFU), 13,
19, 105; on land reform, 146; Mlilo
chapter of, 87, 96; negotiations with
War Veterans Association, 142
commercial farms, white: occupation of,
4, 105, 136; resettlement of, 158n17. *See
also* cattle ranching; farmers, white
Zimbabwean
Communal Areas Management Programme for Indigenous Resources
(Campfire), 10–11, 12, 125, 169n19;
critiques of, 158n10; problem animal
measures, 129–30
Community-Based Natural Resource
Management (CBNRM), 10–11
conservation: as depoliticizing tool, 152;
donor agencies for, 168n13; failures
in Zimbabwe, 101; global paradigm
of, 123; in Indonesia, 8; sustainable
utilization in, 124–25, 128, 173n21;
Zimbabwean strategy for, 86, 143. *See
also* environmentalism
constitutional referendum, Zimbabwean
(1999), rejection of, 136, 166n12
Convention on International Trade in
Endangered Species (CITES), 97, 125,
173n24
Corbett, Jim, 154
cougars, in suburban areas, 127
Crapanzano, Vincent, 23, 50, 165n5; on
self-description, 48–49
Crockett, Davy, 54
culture: Afrikaners', 133; false conscious-

ness in, 50
culture, African: natural environment in,
122–23
culture, Zimbabwean: traditional, 12;
white farmers', 24, 54

Dabengwa, Dumiso, 147
dachshunds, British execution of, 171n6
Derrida, Jacques: on human-animal
boundaries, 109–10
Detroit: "hillbillies" of, 52; racial identity
in, 47
diaspora, white Zimbabwean, 37,
164nn37,43
difference: animals in construction of,
134; ideological constructions of, 101;
urban/rural, 52–54, 166n8
difference, racial: as interpretive grid,
75; projection onto Others, 55–56;
in research, 153; as social marker, 71;
wildlife in construction of, 134, 135
dissidents: control of, 43; dehumanization
of, 37, 163n42; in Matabeleland, 41–42
dogs: Afrikaners', 133; Africanis, 174n33;
in communal land, 133; conception of
race, 133, 174n34; hazards for, 131–32;
inside/outside, 131–32, 173n30; "kaffir,"
173n32; kidnapping of, 130–31; resembling lions, 111; social categories of,
131. *See also* African hunting dog
domestic workers, Zimbabweans, 18,
159nn26,29
Dubow, Jessica, 21
"Dubula Ibhunu" (Shoot the Boer, song),
7, 157n7
Duffy, Rosaleen, 169n22
dugong, symbolism of, 120
Dutch Indies, whiteness in, 20
Dutch Reformed Church (Bulawayo),
158n13

ecotourism, global, 79
education, Zimbabwean: environmental,
103; integrated, 64

elephants: agency of, 128–29; contraception for, 170n31; culling of herd, 97, 170n28, 173n20, 176n33; damage to crops, 127, 128–29; domesticated, 172n15; as endangered species, 97; environmental impact of, 97; global sovereignty over, 97; social groups of, 98; state control of, 96–100; as state property, 99; translocation of, 97–100; in Zimbabwean imaginary, 96

Emel, Jody, 118

endangered species: African hunting dog, 118; elephants as, 97; massacre of, 174nn5,10

environment: in constitution of whiteness, 13; globe versus sphere in, 158n10

environmentalism: farmers' brokerage of, 24; in identity politics, 102; legitimizing function of, 103–4; naturalization of, 79; Western, 102. *See also* conservation

ethnography: multispecies, viii, 110; narrators' integrity in, 48; neutrality in, 23–24; and political controversy, 24

exceptionalism, Rhodesian, 52

farmers, African: land pressures on, vii–viii

farmers, black Zimbabwean: critique of whites, 56; dualism with white farmers, 146; relations with white Zimbabweans, 69, 137, 166n8

farmers, white Rhodesian: in Great Depression, 34, 61; "hillbilly" stereotype of, 52, 90; living standards of, 35; self-descriptions of, 48–52

farmers, white Zimbabwean, *81*; acceptance of indigenization policy, 145; and anti-poaching squads, 159n28; articulation of identity, 103; brokerage of environmentalism, 24; citizenship rights of, 4–5; colonial models of, 154; community service of, 71, 76;

conceptualization of nature, 89–90; conceptualization of pet ownership, 132; conservation efforts of, 101; conspiracy charges against, 69–70, 167n19; cultural production by, 24, 54; discrediting of state agendas, 107; drought management measures, 101; emigration of, 154; entitlement among, 16; eviction of, 14, 152; fining of workers, 68–69; hostility toward neighbors, 72, 165n17; hunting by, 78–79; idealization of past, 24; identity as wildlife producers, 80; imaginary of state, 100; index of morality, 71; Lions Club membership, 171n34; loss of legitimacy, 70; marriage prospects of, 46; moralizing position of, 101–104; in Mozambique, 154; multiple modes of discourse, 24, 60; multiple worldviews of, 77; nature/whiteness dyad of, 154; Ndebele word use, 167n23; as Other, 102; patriarchalism of, 67–69, 166n17; perception of inequalities, 23; performance of stories, 56; pets of, 130–35; on politics of crisis, 100–101; popular assumptions concerning, 5; power over employees, 68–69; on professional hunters, 113; professional hunter training, 88; in racially charged incidents, 53, 166n9; racism of, 22, 23–24, 58; reinvention of, 80, 117, 118, 152; relations with black farmers, 69, 137, 166n8; reputations of, 71–72; scientific authority of, 102; transition to wildlife ranching, 89–90; treason charges against, 121; use of nature, 44; use of nostalgia, 44; violence against, 4; and war veterans, 14, 106–7, 142; worldview of animals, 110; worldviews of, 22–23, 24. *See also* narratives, white farmers'

fences: as archetypes of division, 95; removal of, 168n11; in wildlife ranching, 92–95, 170n24

Fifth Brigade: terror regime of, 42; "tribalist" violence by, 43; violence against whites, 69

foot-and-mouth disease, prevention of, 168n3

friendship, cross-racial, 66–67; hierarchy in, 67; male, 166n15; in nondomestic space, 67; as transgressive, 76

Fuller, Alexandra, 20, 160n35, 164n42

Gaza-Kruger-Gonarezhou Transfrontier Park, 126, 174n8; withdrawal of funding for, 139

German shepherds, 109; British use of, 171n6

Germany, response to land invasions, 139

The Ghost and the Darkness (film), 171n9

giraffes, delivery problems with, 100

Global Political Agreement (GPA), 7; end of, 157n6

Godwin, Peter, 20, 51, 160n35

Gokwe, black prosperity in, 163n30

gold: British prospecting for, 28, 30, 162n14; discovery of, 161n5, 162n13; of Witwatersrand, 162n13

Goldstein, Donna, 53–54

Goodwin, June: *Heart of Whiteness*, 20

Great Depression, in Southern Rhodesia, 34, 61

Great Limpopo Transfrontier Park, 174n8

"Great White Hunters," 29; mythology of, 17

"Great Zimbabwe" (architectural structure), 172n17

Green Bombers (paramilitary youth group), 140

guerrilla movements: demobilization for, 40; as terrorism, 37; ZAPU, 40

Hammar, Amanda, 154

Harare *Sunday Mail Magazine*, on Miss Wildlife pageant, 122

Haraway, Donna, 110, 113, 153

Hardin, Garrett: "Tragedy of the Commons," 95, 167n2

Harding, Susan, 22

Harrison, Meryl, 142

Hartigan, John, 47

Hartley, Henry, 161n5

hierarchies, racial: animals in, 153; Brazilian, 53–54; in cross-racial friendships, 67; role of language in, 63; in scientific expeditions, 153

hierarchies, social: animals in, 104, 114, 131

Hitler, Adolf: canine companions of, 109

Hughes, David McDermott, 21, 23, 154

human-animal relationships, viii, 108; boundaries in, 109–10, 127, 128

hunters, white, 17, 29, 86, 161n6; authenticity of, 113; master narratives of, 109; Zimbabwean farmers, 78–79

"Hunters for the Hungry" organization, 17

hunting: class power differentials in, 108; DNPWLM ban on, 143–44; ethical, 170n26; imperial performance of, 108, 153–54; as index of masculinity, 112; in Nazi ideology, 109; power relations in, 108; of predatory lions, 112; profitability of, 149; quotas, 101; spectacular displays of, 109; symbolic power in, 154; by white Zimbabwean farmers, 78–79; of zebra, 78–79. *See also* safaris, hunting

Hunzvi, Chenjerai, 142

Hutu-Tutsi conflict, 161n7

Hwange Colliery, bankruptcy of, 58

Hwange National Park (Zimbabwe), 10; Cecil the Lion's residence in, 150; drought in, 144; elephants from, 96, 97; environmental pressures on, 99; foreign tourists to, 86; "game drives" in, 16; gas prospecting near, 149; Management Plan, 101; sale of animals from, 149, 176n33; translocation of elephants from, 98–100; wildlife farmers' input for, 90; wildlife ranching animals from, 92

Hwange Town agricultural show, lions at, 115–16

identity: indigenous, 103; politics of, 107
identity, cultural: landscape in, 21; symbolic capital of, 102
identity, Rhodesian: collective, 36–37; environmental policies in, 83
identity, Zimbabwean: African, 39; racial, 7; transitions in, 70–71; white farmers', 80, 103; wildlife in, 126
independence, Zimbabwean, 3; empowerment following, 145; landscape following, viii; post-independence racial formations of, 5–6; whiteness following, 7
indigenization laws, Zimbabwean, 144–45
Indonesia, environmental conservation in, 8
Ingold, Tim, 158n9
Intensive Conservation Association (ICA), 13
International Monetary Fund (IMF): aid to Mozambique, 58; pressure on Mugabe, 143
intimacy, interracial, 63–64; as site of transgression, 76
ivory: illegal versus legal, 170n29; from Ndebele nation, 28; sale of, 97, 124, 170n29, 173n24

Jacobs, Nancy, 153
jaguars, in Aztec society, 111
Jameson Raid (Transvaal), 162n18
Japan: aid to Zimbabwe, 100, 170n33; sale of ivory to, 125, 173n24

Kaguvi (religious leader), 162n17
Kaunda, Kenneth, 163n35
Kavango Zambezi Transfrontier Conservation Area (Kaza TFCA), 150
Kenyans, white: structural oblivion of, 165n6
Khaya-Moyo, Simon, 147

killer whales, renaming of, 118
Kohn, Eduardo, 110
Kriger, Norma, 39
Kruger National Park (South Africa), 124

Lancaster House Agreement (1979), 36
Land Acquisition Act (Zimbabwe, 1992), 158n17
Land Apportionment Act (Southern Rhodesia, 1930), 34
land invasions, viii; animal massacres during, 138; of arid areas, 136, 138, 140; beginning (2000), 173n27; cost of, 139, 174n7; following constitutional referendum defeat, 136; impasse in, 7; legitimizing attempts for, 138; markers of, 136; Mlilo during, 14, 136–37; Mugabe and, 24; political uncertainty following, 160n32; reform measures for, 143–45; war veterans', 4, 14, 44, 105–6, 136, 157n3; of white commercial farms, 4, 105, 136; women and children in, 19; ZANU-PF's role in, 4
land reform: benefit for black elites, 146; controversies surrounding, 145; delegitimization of, 107; effect on tourism, 147; lack of transparency in, 145; myths of, 146; positive evaluations of, 146, 175n15; state arguments for, 137; timing of, 146; transformation of rural Zimbabwean society, 146; wildlife-based, 143–45. *See also* Chimurenga, Third
landscape, Zimbabwean: following independence, viii
landscapes: in cultural identity, 21; racialized, 114
land use, paradigm shifts in, 85
laughter, in state-society relations, 171n4
leopard proverb, Ndebele, 2, 3, 120
leopards, in Zimbabwean symbolism, 122
Lessing, Doris: *The Grass Is Singing*, 63
Lévi-Strauss, Claude, 108, 110
Li, Tania, 103

liberation war, Rhodesia, 36, 38, 39, 164n35; captive animals in, 116; cattle ranching during, 84

Lindu (indigenous people), articulation of identity, 103

lions: at agricultural shows, 115–16; bounties on, 172n10; Chinese dogs resembling, 111; domestication of, 113–16, 134–35; imagery of, 111; killing of, 116–17; man-eating, 171n9; opportunistic scavenging by, 111; predatory, 112; in Roman gladiatorial arena, 111; semi-domesticated, 115; symbolization of white power, 152; taxidermic specimens of, 112–13; in Western imaginary, 111

Lions Club International, 171n34; St. Luke's Hospital of, 100

lion trophies, ban on, 151

Livingstone, David, 16

Lobengula (Ndebele ruler), 28–29; concession to British, 30; death of, 31; Mashonaland independence from, 162n12; and white hunters, 161n6

Lwane (domesticated lion), 114

Mabhena, Welshman (governor of Matabeleland North), 72–75; code-switching by, 74; hostility toward, 74, 75; racial insults by, 73–75

Machel, Samora, 163n35

MacKenzie, John, 161n6

Made, Joseph, 147

Malawi, independence of, 35

Malaysia, "weapons of the weak" in, 170n32

Malema, Julius, 7

Maluleke, Titus, 147–48

marriage, interracial, 45–47, 166n10

Martin, Martinus Jacobus, 32

Mashonaland: British casualties in, 31; gold in, 30, 161n5; independence from Lobengula, 162n12; Pioneer column in, 30; ZANLA in, 40

Matabeleland (western Zimbabwe): African Reserves of, 163n28; colonial brutality in, 27; dissidents in, 41–42; European invasion of, 31; European travelers to, 28, 29; genocide allegations in, 40; gold in, 161n5; independence of, 30; Ndebele immigrants to, 28; terror in, 39–40; white settlers of, 27; ZAPU in, 39; ZIPRA in, 40, 41

Matabeleland North, governor of, 72–75. See also Mlilo

Matondi, Prosper, 146

Mauch, Carl, 161n5

Maviyane-Davies, Chaz: leopard proverb image, 2; cockerel proverb image, 121

McIntosh, Janet, 165n6

meaning: attached to pit bulls, 173n29; pets in construction of, 130; racial, 154; of wildlife, 117, 124, 126

megafauna, charismatic, 89, 97, 119

Mfula (communal area): animal predators in, 128; district councilor of, 12–13; governor's visit to, 72–75; involvement with Campfire, 12

Mfula health clinic, 73; farmers' help with, 72, 73

miscegenation, nature metaphors for, 46–47

missionaries: murder of, 41; to Ndebele, 28, 29; to Shona, 161n11; support for segregation, 34; in Zambia, 77

Miss Wildlife beauty pageant, 122–23, 126

Mlilo (pseudonymous community, Matabeleland North): appeal to nation-state, 104; arid soil of, 136, 138; authenticity of setting, 17; black families of, 18, 159nn25–26; boundaries of, 72; cattle ranching in, 81–85; children of, 64–65; church services at, 158n13; community tensions in, 91, 92–95; decline of wildlife in, 85; demise of, 27; electrification of, 168n15; ethnographic research in, 10–14; family relation-

60–62, 76, 112; interpretation of, 50; moral force of, 50, 76; Mugabe in, 56–57, 58, 59; origin stories in, 60–61; patriarchalism in, 67–69; politicians in, 56–57; post-colonial decline in, 56–63, 76; self-description in, 48–52; sites of compromise in, 60; validation of white perspective, 71

nationalism, Zimbabwean: Ndebele-Shona distinction in, 161n9

national parks: global perceptions of, 172n20; symbolism of, 124; transfrontier, 126, 139, 149–50, 174n8

national parks, Zimbabwean: disrepair of, 100–101; sale of animals, 168n9; water management in, 101, 171n35

nation-states, animal-based practices of, 108

Native Americans: injustices toward, 172n16; spirituality of, 118

Natives Registration Act (Southern Rhodesia), 35

nature: as adversary, 112; ascendancy in relation to, 154; control of, 101; farmers' conceptualization of, 89–90; in political discourse, 123–24; as purification machine, 154; role in contesting power, 120; whiteness and, 8–9, 24, 152–56; "white slot" in, 156, 176n44

nature metaphors: black Zimbabweans', 55; cultural assumptions in, 75–76; for segregation, 46–47, 152; white Zimbabweans', 46–47, 54–56, 76, 152, 165n1

Nazis, animal protection practices of, 109

Ndebele language: animal names in, 114; white farmers' knowledge of, 167n23

Ndebele nation: boundaries of, 29; colonial encounter with, 27–31; European bias concerning, 161n8; missionaries to, 28, 29; Rhodes's war with, 30–31; white hunters in, 29; wildlife resources of, 28

Ndebele people: agreement with Rhodes, 162n19; attack against British, 31–32;

British preference for, 28–29, 167n18; cockerel proverb of, 121, 121–22; distinction from Shona, 161nn9–10; intermarriage with Shona, 38; minority status of, 27, 167n18; relationship with Shona, 29, 40, 43, 70, 162n17; reputation for honesty, 70; smallpox among, 162n15; Super ZAPU murder of, 41; white admiration for, 27; white representations of, 28–29

Nehanda (religious leader), 162n17

Neumann, Roderick, 140–41

New Jersey Fish and Game Council, bear-hunting quota of, 128

Nhema, Francis, 144

Nigeria, import of wildlife, 126

Nkomo, Joshua: agreement with Mugabe, 42–43; discrediting of, 41; dismissal of, 43; nationalist leadership of, 163n34

North America, white privilege in, 154

Nyasaland, 35

Nzou, Goodwell, 152

Orange Free State, 32, 60, 162n20

ornithologists, white: African research assistants of, 153

Ortner, Sherry, 52

Other: animal, 110; animal practices regarding, 108; cultural, 22–26; racial imaginaries of, 55–56; realities of, 52; white farmers as, 102

ozitshwala (dissidents), 42

Palmer, Robin, 29

Palmer, Walter: killing of Cecil the Lion, 150–51

Pandian, Anand, 153

Park, Mungo, 16

Parks and Wildlife Act (Zimbabwe, 1975), 85

pastoralists, African: land pressures on, vii–viii

patriarchalism, of white Zimbabwean farmers, 67–69

paw-paw trees, 79, 167n1
Pelling, J. N., 3
People for the Ethical Treatment of Animals (PETA), on Cecil the Lion, 150–51
Peters, Pauline, 95
pets: in construction of meaning, 130; farmers', 130–35; gendered construction of, 131, 132–33; kidnapping of, 130–31; social logics of, 110, 130–31
photography, wildlife, 16
Pioneer Column (South African settlers), 30, 37; trek northward, 32, 112
pit bulls, meanings attached to, 173n29
polar bears, in Inuit society, 111
politicians: ownership of conservancies, 147; use of baboon metaphor, 55, 73
Posselt, Friedrich, 161n4
power: animal iconographies of, 120; micro-environments of, 69; over farm employees, 68–69; reproduction of, 23; sharing of, 7, 43; symbolic, 63, 152, 154
power relations: animals in, 109; black-white, 68–69, 106; in hunting, 108; of whiteness, 19
le pratique sauvage, 175n18
preachers, fundamentalist, 22
preservationism, traditional paradigm of, 172n21
privilege, white: in Africa, 5–6; in North America, 154; through environmental escapism, 154
privilege, Zimbabwean: reproduction of, 23; structural oblivion in, 165n6
Problem Animal Control (PAC) teams, 129, 171n2

race: as absolute, 75; boundaries in, 46, 47, 63–65; children's experience of, 70–71; cultural assumptions about, 24; cultural politics of, vii; fluidity of, 6; role in wildlife industry, 13; stratification processes of, 20; white ethnosociologies of, 70

race relations, natural history of, viii
racial discourse: localized, 47; multiple modes of, 54, 76–77
racial formation: local, 47; post-independence, 5–6; symbolic distinctions in, 76; white Zimbabweans', 54
racial identity, discourse of whiteness in, 6
racial identity, white Zimbabwean, 8; environmental consciousness in, 9; everyday, 47; exoticization of, 51–52; reassertion of, 75; segregation in, 76; transgression of, 47
racism: among white Rhodesians, 163n27; and animal welfare, 108; inconsistency in, 24; objectivity concerning, 23; of white Zimbabwean farmers, 22, 54–55, 58; white Zimbabweans' perception of, 52
Raffles, Hugh, 110, 171n8
Raj, British: imperial hunt in, 153–54
Rand (gold): First, 162n13; Second, 30
Ranger, Terence, 162n12; Revolt in Southern Rhodesia, 162n17
reconciliation, Zimbabwean, 4, 38–39; reversal of, 6, 39–44, 59
Reichs-Tierschutzverein (Association for the Protection of Animals of the Reich), 109
research, racial politics of, 153
resistance, everyday, 170n32
rhinos, black: massacre of, 139, 174n10
rhinos, white: cost of, 8, 168n10
Rhodes, Cecil, 152; agreement with Afrikaners, 32; agreement with Ndebele, 162n19; bribe to Selous, 30, 162n12; removal of statue, 176n43; war with Ndebele, 30–31
Rhodesia: African hunting dogs in, 118; "Beautiful" myth, 48; church-state relations in, 163n27; colonial monuments of, 39; liberation war, 36, 38, 39, 164n35; reward for predators in, 111; sanctions against, 35, 36, 164n38;

Scoones, Ian, 146
segregation: ideological/cultural reasons for, 47; missionaries' support for, 34; nature metaphors for, 46–47, 152; in white identity, 76
self, and homeland, 154
self-representation, 48–51; discursive limits of, 112; false consciousness in, 50
Selous, Frederick Courteney, 17, 159n24, 161n6; in Matabeleland, 29; Rhodes's bribe to, 30, 162n12
settlers, white African: aspiration of, 5
settlers, white Zimbabwean: custodianship of land, viii; ethnography of, viii; as exotic Other, 10; in Mlilo, 82; post-colonial, 6; relations to land, vii–viii; stereotypes of, 5; stigma of history for, 5; symbolic power of, 63. *See also* farmers, white Zimbabwean; Rhodesians, white; Zimbabweans, white
Shaka (Zulu monarch), 27
Shamuyarira, Nathan, 38
Shona language, animal names in, 114
Shona people: attack against British, 31; distinction from Ndebele, 29, 161nn9–10; intermarriage with Ndebele, 38; majority status of, 27, 167n18; missionary access to, 161n11; relationship with Ndebele, 29, 40, 43, 70, 162n17
smallpox, among Ndebele, 162n15
Smith, Ian, 35, 140, 174n12
snow leopard, symbolism of, 120
society, Rhodesian: diversity in, 36
society, Zimbabwean: breakdown in, 142; effect of land reform on, 146
Society for the Prevention of Cruelty to Animals (SPCA), on domesticated lions, 115–16
South Africa: Afrikaner nationals in, 124; anti-apartheid struggle in, 7; cultural identity of, 21; destabilization policy

of, 41; educational protests in, 176n43; exotic flora of, 171n5; migration to Tanzania from, 21; Natal Province of, 163n26; nature in nationhood of, 124; transition to democracy, 165n5; whiteness transitions in, 65; white Rhodesians in, 154. *See also* Afrikaners
Specially Designated Nationals, Zimbabwean, 175n19
spirituality, Native American: wolves in, 118
Steyn, Melissa, 21, 65
Super ZAPU, Operation Drama of, 41. *See also* Zimbabwe African People's Union (ZAPU)
Swart, Sandra, 118, 131, 174n33

Tanzania, whiteness crisis in, 21
taxidermy, colonial, 16
Texas, wildlife industry in, 17
tourism industry, effect of automobiles on, 123
tourism industry, Zimbabwean, 13, 126, 148; conflict with nontourist enterprises, 126; effect of land reform on, 147; expertise in, 126; foreign exchange revenue from, 173n27. *See also* wildlife tourism, Zimbabwean
tourists, Japanese, 13
Tribal Trust Lands (Rhodesia), 35, 163n28, 168n5; cattle-dipping in, 84
trophy hunting: debates over, 151; fees for, 17, 125
Tsavo, lions of, 111, 171n9
tsetse fly, control of, 168n3
Tsvangirai, Morgan, 4; Mugabe's defeat of, 157n6

Unilateral Declaration of Independence (UDI), 35, 36, 85
United Nations World Trade Organization (UNTWO), 148
University of Zimbabwe, Centre for Applied Sciences, 10–11

wildlife tourism, Zimbabwean, 8, 113; accommodations for, 87, 88, 171n1; income-generating, 126; profitability of, 79; safaris in, 16–17. *See also* tourism industry, Zimbabwean

wildness: Christian view of, 83; in pioneer narratives, 166n13

Wolmer, William, 99

wolves, in Western imaginations, 118

wolves, North American: extermination of, 117; restoration to landscape, 118; as symbol of wildness, 119

women, black Zimbabwean: in interracial marriages, 166n10; as nannies, 166n14

women, European: immigration to Southern Rhodesia, 32–33

women, white Zimbabwean: deference to husbands, 45; in land invasions, 19; occupations of, 19, 160n33; on segregation, 64, 76

Worby, Eric, 31, 69

World Bank, pressure on Mugabe, 143

World Wide Fund for Nature, wildlife ranching survey, 88

xenophobia, and animal welfare, 108

Zambezi National Park, Save Valley Conservancy animals in, 149

Zambia, independence of, 35

zebra: hunting of, 78–79; in nature metaphors, 46, 76, 152, 165n1; Zimbabwean symbolism of, 120–21, 122

Zimbabwe: animal trade of, 149, 168n9, 176n33; black critiques of, 167n20; breakdown in civil society, 142; censorship of violence, 40; center-periphery tension in, 126; conservation strategy, 86; core/periphery relationships in, 90; economic instability in, 168n14; export of wildlife, 126; faunal resources of, 91; foreign aid to, 100, 170n33, 175n19; foreign economic influence in, 57, 60; generational con-

flicts in, 90; health services system, 38; inequality in, 6; Japanese aid to, 100, 170n33; landscapes of affect in, vii; linguistic misunderstanding in, 62–63; local moral economies of, 69; markers of past in, 165n4; microenvironments of power, 69; national symbols of, 39, 120–22; national unity for, 39; Natural Regions IV–V, 82; park disrepair in, 100–101; "peace park" treaty of, 149–50; political legitimacy in, 39; politics of nationhood, 43–44; power sharing in, 7; racial conflict in, 44; racial transformations in, 6; railways of, 58; reconciliation period of, 4, 6, 38–39; South African agents in, 41; sovereignty over resources, 126; state corruption in, 3, 107; state distrust of conservancies, 99; state perception of wildlife, 96; white emigration from, 59, 154, 163n37, 165nn3–4; wildlife management strategies, 86, 124–26

Zimbabwe African National Union (ZANU), 36; arrest of ZIPRA commanders, 41; conflict with ZAPU, 39, 40, 41, 163n34; ruling status of, 41; Unity Accord with ZAPU (1987), 43

Zimbabwe African National Union--Patriotic Front (ZANU-PF): anti-white campaign of, 53; defiance of Mugabe, 148, 175n31; hunting permit scandal, 147–48; immorality of, 69; paramilitary youth force of, 140; power-sharing agreement of, 7, 43; propaganda of, 73; role in land invasions, 4, 136; torture by, 70

Zimbabwe African People's Union (ZAPU), 36; conflict with ZANU, 39, 40, 41, 163n34; in Matabeleland, 39; Mugabe's campaign against, 42, 43; in South African destabilization campaign, 41; state violence against, 43; Unity Accord with ZANU (1987), 43. *See also* Super ZAPU

Zimbabwean National Society for the Prevention of Cruelty to Animals (ZNSPCA), 141; negotiations with War Veterans Association, 142

Zimbabweans: game-viewing opportunities of, 123

Zimbabweans, black: domestic workers, 18, 159nn26,29; elites, 39, 137, 146; environmental education for, 103; ethnic hierarchies among, 70; family *baas* of, 18, 159n27; hiring of land occupiers, 137; Ndebele-speaking, 55; linguistic failure among, 62–63; media depictions of, 163n40; nature metaphors of, 55; settlers' relationships to, vii; whites' affection for, 24; whites' terms for, 22; in wildlife industry, 18

Zimbabweans, white: of British descent, 160n33; on changing racial identity, 71; chaos narratives of, 48–51; citizenship rights of, 4–5; cross-racial friendships of, 66–67; displacement of, vii; emigration of, 59, 154, 163n37, 165nn3–4; engagement with world, 52; "false" consciousness of, 50; frugality of, 91; on land invasions, 44; levels of awareness, 50; loyalty to Rhodesia, 48; as *mukhiwa*, 55; nature metaphors, 46–47, 54–56, 76, 152, 165n1; office holders, 7, 10; perception of racism, 52; post-reconciliation, 6–7; preservation of worldviews, 49–51; on reconciliation, 38; Rhodesian-ness of, 38; self-defensiveness for, 163n43; self-presentation of, 53; on Shona people, 161n10; single, 19; tension with newcomers, 160n30; urban/rural differences, 52–54, 166n8; in Western scholarship, 22. *See also* farmers, white Zimbabwean; narratives, white farmers'; Rhodesians, white

Zimbabwe Broadcasting Corporation, 100

Zimbabwe Department of National Parks and Wild Life Management (DNPWLM), 87; on "adopt an elephant" program, 98–99; control of problem animals, 129; financial problems of, 149; hunting ban by, 143–44; hunting quotas of, 101; Problem Animal Control teams, 129, 171n2; on Save Valley conservancy, 139; war veterans' complaints to, 106; wildlife-based reforms, 145

Zimbabwe Ministry of Environment and Tourism, conflict with Mlilo Conservancy, 99, 100

Zimbabwe National Liberation Army (ZANLA), 40; Fifth Brigade members from, 42

Zimbabwe People's Revolutionary Army (ZIPRA), 59; arrests of members, 41, 42; defections from, 40–41

ZISCO (Zimbabwe Iron and Steel Company), 58

zoos, racialized depictions by, 109

CULTURE, PLACE, AND NATURE
Studies in Anthropology and Environment

The Kuhls of Kangra: Community-Managed Irrigation in the Western Himalaya, by Mark Baker

The Earth's Blanket: Traditional Teachings for Sustainable Living, by Nancy Turner

Property and Politics in Sabah, Malaysia: Native Struggles over Land Rights, by Amity A. Doolittle

Border Landscapes: The Politics of Akha Land Use in China and Thailand, by Janet C. Sturgeon

From Enslavement to Environmentalism: Politics on a Southern African Frontier, by David McDermott Hughes

Ecological Nationalisms: Nature, Livelihood, and Identities in South Asia, edited by Gunnel Cederlöf and K. Sivaramakrishnan

Tropics and the Traveling Gaze: India, Landscape, and Science, 1800–1856, by David Arnold

Being and Place among the Tlingit, by Thomas F. Thornton

Forest Guardians, Forest Destroyers: The Politics of Environmental Knowledge in Northern Thailand, by Tim Forsyth and Andrew Walker

Nature Protests: The End of Ecology in Slovakia, by Edward Snajdr

Wild Sardinia: Indigeneity and the Global Dreamtimes of Environmentalism, by Tracey Heatherington

Tahiti Beyond the Postcard: Power, Place, and Everyday Life, by Miriam Kahn

Forests of Identity: Society, Ethnicity, and Stereotypes in the Congo River Basin, by Stephanie Rupp

Enclosed: Conservation, Cattle, and Commerce among the Q'eqchi' Maya Lowlanders, by Liza Grandia

Puer Tea: Ancient Caravans and Urban Chic, by Jinghong Zhang

Andean Waterways: Resource Politics in Highland Peru, by Mattias Borg Rasmussen

Conjuring Property: Speculation and Environmental Futures in the Brazilian Amazon, by Jeremy M. Campbell

Forests Are Gold: Trees, People, and Environmental Rule in Vietnam, by Pamela D. McElwee

The Nature of Whiteness: Race, Animals, and Nation in Zimbabwe, by Yuka Suzuki

CPSIA information can be obtained
at www.ICGtesting.com
Printed in the USA
BVOW08s0328010317
477441BV00001B/2/P